MW00413061

Unmasking Psychological Symptoms

How Therapists Can Learn to Recognize the Psychological Presentation of Medical Disorders

Barbara Schildkrout

WILEY

John Wiley & Sons, Inc.

This book is printed on acid-free paper. ⊗

Copyright © 2011 by John Wiley & Sons, Inc. All rights reserved.

Published by John Wiley & Sons, Inc., Hoboken, New Jersey.
Published simultaneously in Canada.

No part of this publication may be reproduced, stored in a retrieval system, or transmitted in any form or by any means, electronic, mechanical, photocopying, recording, scanning, or otherwise, except as permitted under Section 107 or 108 of the 1976 United States Copyright Act, without either the prior written permission of the Publisher, or authorization through payment of the appropriate per-copy fee to the Copyright Clearance Center, Inc., 222 Rosewood Drive, Danvers, MA 01923, (978) 750-8400, fax (978) 646-8600, or on the Web at www. copyright.com. Requests to the Publisher for permission should be addressed to the Permissions Department, John Wiley & Sons, Inc., 111 River Street, Hoboken, NJ 07030, (201) 748-6011, fax (201) 748-6008.

Limit of Liability/Disclaimer of Warranty: While the publisher and author have used their best efforts in preparing this book, they make no representations or warranties with respect to the accuracy or completeness of the contents of this book and specifically disclaim any implied warranties of merchantability or fitness for a particular purpose. No warranty may be created or extended by sales representatives or written sales materials. The advice and strategies contained herein may not be suitable for your situation. You should consult with a professional where appropriate. Neither the publisher nor author shall be liable for any loss of profit or any other commercial damages, including but not limited to special, incidental, consequential, or other damages.

This publication is designed to provide accurate and authoritative information in regard to the subject matter covered. It is sold with the understanding that the publisher is not engaged in rendering professional services. If legal, accounting, medical, psychological or any other expert assistance is required, the services of a competent professional person should be sought.

The contents of this work are intended to further general scientific research, understanding, and discussion only and are not intended and should not be relied upon as recommending or promoting a specific method, diagnosis, or treatment by physicians for any particular patient. The publisher and the author make no representations or warranties with respect to the accuracy or completeness of the contents of this work and specifically disclaim all warranties, including without limitation any implied warranties of fitness for a particular purpose. In view of ongoing research, equipment modifications, changes in governmental regulations, and the constant flow of information relating to the use of medicines, equipment, and devices, the reader is urged to review and evaluate the information provided in the package insert or instructions for each medicine, equipment, or device for, among other things, any changes in the instructions or indication of usage and for added warnings and precautions. Readers should consult with a specialist where appropriate. The fact that an organization or Web site is referred to in this work as a citation and/or a potential source of further information does not mean that the author or the publisher endorses the information the organization or Web site may provide or recommendations it may make. Further, readers should be aware that Internet Web sites listed in this work may have changed or disappeared between when this work was written and when it is read. No warranty may be created or extended by any promotional statements for this work. Neither the publisher nor the author shall be liable for any damages arising herefrom.

Designations used by companies to distinguish their products are often claimed as trademarks. In all instances where John Wiley & Sons, Inc. is aware of a claim, the product names appear in initial capital or all capital letters. Readers, however, should contact the appropriate companies for more complete information regarding trademarks and registration.

For general information on our other products and services please contact our Customer Care Department within the U.S. at (800) 762-2974, outside the United States at (317) 572-3993 or fax (317) 572-4002.

Wiley also publishes its books in a variety of electronic formats. Some content that appears in print may not be available in electronic books. For more information about Wiley products, visit our Web site at www.wiley.com.

Library of Congress Cataloging-in-Publication Data

Schildkrout, Barbara.
   Unmasking psychological symptoms : how therapists can learn to recognize the psychological presentation of medical disorders / Barbara Schildkrout.
      p. ; cm.
   Includes bibliographical references and indexes.
   ISBNs 978-0-470-63907-8; 978-1-118-10616-7; 978-1-118-10615-0; 978-1-118-10614-3; 978-1-118-08359-8
1. Medicine, Psychosomatic. 2. Diagnosis, Differential. I. Title.
   [DNLM: 1. Psychophysiologic Disorders—etiology. 2. Psychophysiologic Disorders—psychology. 3. Diagnosis, Differential. 4. Somatoform Disorders—diagnosis. WM 90]
   RC49.S345 2011
   616.08—dc22

                                                                              2011010995

Printed in the United States of America

10 9 8 7 6 5 4 3 2 1

To Aaron Schildkrout and Emily Schildkrout Fine

"Education is not the filling of a pail but the lighting of a fire."
                    —Widely attributed to W.B. Yeats

"Science is a way to teach how something gets to be known, what is not known, to what extent things *are* known (for nothing is known absolutely), how to handle doubt and uncertainty, what the rules of evidence are, how to think about things so that judgments can be made, how to distinguish truth from fraud, and from show."
                    —Richard Feynman

Contents

Acknowledgments

Although writing is a solitary occupation, I have never been alone while working at my computer. A community of family, friends, and supporters has been precious and invaluable to me. Some have shared their clinical experiences. Others have been there as fellow writers. Some have promoted my work, been generous with their ideas, or thoughtfully wrestled with my questions. Some have simply continued to believe in the value of this project and to trust that I would actually finish it, even after years.

In addition, I have written in the company of clinicians and researchers whose work stretches back over decades. I would like to acknowledge my gratitude to these scientists, each fascinated by one thing or another, each following his or her own curiosity and advancing our collective understanding.

I am deeply grateful to my patients, who have been a source of inspiration. I know many may have felt vulnerable, terrified, crazy, defective, ashamed, or bad, but I have experienced each as courageous, determined, strong, and worthy. I feel immeasurably grateful for their trust, for the deep look at life they have given me, and for what they have taught me about illness, about surviving, and about transforming suffering into empathy, wisdom, and creativity. Clinicians may provide understanding, deep comfort, healing, or sometimes even a true cure. But one irony of being a therapist is that all the giving pales in comparison to what clinicians gain from their patients. This is the secret scaffolding that sustains the work of therapy.

In a long career, one's colleagues and friends are often one and the same. Thank you to my friends/colleagues George and Ellen Fishman, Gerald and Corinne Adler, Howard and Jeannette Corwin for their wise counsel and enthusiastic encouragement. George Fishman has been a true companion of intellect and spirit in grappling with the brain and mind. I am grateful to Gerald Adler for his wholehearted support of my work on this book over many years.

It is impossible to articulate the many ways in which Jeane Ungerleider and William Stone have helped to sustain me and this project—as talking-late-into-the-night consultants, readers, and generous and loving friends.

I wish to extend a special thanks to Dr. Carol Nadelson for her remarkable responsiveness and savvy advice, for her help with editing, and also for her friendship. Karen Greenberg's companionship in teaching and friendship has nurtured my growth. I immeasurably value her spirit and authenticity. Also I would like to thank my peer group for their years of camaraderie as fellow psychiatrists, and for their encouragement and help with editing: Miriam Freidin, Eileen Kahan, and Beverly St. Claire. I am grateful to Beverley Freedman, Ralph Freidin, Fred Kanter, Michael Marcus, Anne Stambler, and Judith Waligunda for sharing, along with others, their clinical perspectives. I also want to express appreciation to Lisa Sutton and Michael Miller for providing me with opportunities to present my work to others and to Eric First for his early help with library research.

I am extremely grateful to Albert Galaburda who graciously welcomed me into the clinical rounds of the Cognitive Neurology Unit at Beth Israel Deaconess Medical Center in Boston, providing an invaluable opportunity for me to learn from neurologists, psychologists, psychiatrists, and social workers working at the border of neurology and psychiatry. I also offer my thanks to other members of the Cognitive Neurology Unit who have been friends and supporters, including the neuropsychologists Sara Hoffschmidt and Bonnie Wong, and especially Margaret O'Connor; social worker, Lissa Kapust; and my psychiatrist colleagues Mark Thall and Laura Safar. Thank you also to Michael Alexander, Daniel Cohen, Alvaro Pascual-Leone, and Daniel Press who have taught and inspired me.

Some friends have been especially supportive as experienced writers in their own right. Thank you to Rhonda Cutler, Elizabeth Marcus, and Vicki Steifel. Meg Campbell, a dear and inspiring friend, has taught me the rejuvenating power of play and narrative transport. Chad Lindner generously offered his sound advice to me at a time when I needed it, along with help from my friends Lois Kanter and Lindsay Kanter. Standish and Nancy Hartman, my dear friends, have been compassionate and strong supporters through thick and thin.

I am deeply indebted to John Kerr, who saw the value in this project and encouraged me nearly from its inception. He read and edited early drafts and has been an astute advisor along the way.

I am immeasurably grateful to my editor Patricia Rossi, who recognized the importance of this book project and then shepherded it through to fruition. She has been ever available, responsive, helpful, and wise.

Thank you also to my family. First, thank you to my mother, Betty Bell, for believing in the value of education and for always being there. My father did not live to see this book published, but his inquisitive mind and zeal for problem solving were inspirational throughout my life. Mollie Schildkrout, who had a long career as a pediatrician and psychiatrist, has always been supportive; I am grateful for our many talks, exploring complex dilemmas in life and medicine. Thank you to my beloved son-in-law, Aaron Fine, who has been encouraging and caring throughout.

Motherhood is a powerful experience, and my children, Aaron Schildkrout and Emily Schildkrout Fine, have helped to shape who I am and how I see the world. Words cannot begin to express my gratitude to them for their unwavering enthusiasm for me as a writer since their early years. They also have helped with ideas, editing, computer problems, and the mechanics of referencing. I immeasurably value Emily's natural empathy, integrity in relationships, loyalty, and shared passion for writing and thinking about patients. Aaron's keen mind, clarity of thought, intense drive, fierce introspection, and deep companionship are precious to me. Most of all I am grateful to Aaron and Emily for being my best teachers and for becoming my dear friends.

Chapter 1

The Nature of the Problem

Introduction

More than 100 somatic disorders are capable of mimicking psychological conditions. This reality presents every therapist with an important clinical challenge—to unmask psychological signs and symptoms that are being caused by medical disorders. When you are seeing a patient who appears to have a psychological problem, how might you assess whether that individual could have an underlying, discrete medical condition that is actually causing or complicating the presentation? And how might such an evaluation be accomplished during an interview? This book addresses these questions.

In our work as therapists, we have learned to be attuned to the subtleties of our patients' emotional lives, but we are often ill prepared to detect clues that mark the presence of covert organic illness. Yet, an important part of our job is to unmask any physical condition a patient might have. This is a vital undertaking, because fully effective mental health treatment is only possible once contributing medical disorders have been accurately diagnosed.

This book facilitates an expansion of your observational and listening skills. Using clinical stories, it introduces a variety of medical disorders and shows how these conditions are often camouflaged in people's lives. Discussions are included on how to approach somatic complaints, which particular mental status findings point to organic dysfunction, and how to conduct a thorough assessment.

This book is about well-described somatic disorders that may not look like they are physical because they initially or primarily affect the individual's mental and behavioral life. Many widespread and familiar maladies can masquerade as mental disorders: thyroid disorders, diabetes, Alzheimer's disease and other dementias, sleep apnea and other sleep disorders, temporal lobe epilepsy, HIV, the long-term consequences of head trauma, Lyme disease, and the side effects of medications, to name only a few. These and other physical conditions are common in patients who are seen by mental health practitioners; these medical conditions are also often the very source of the presenting clinical picture.

The goal of this book is to help clinicians learn to identify when there is evidence for an underlying organic condition so as to be able to effectively refer patients for a medical workup. It is crucial for mental health practitioners to initiate a medical consultation when signs, symptoms, and patterns of behavior have led to a concern that a patient might have an underlying medical disorder. A therapist may not know exactly what somatic condition a patient has, but it is possible to learn how to identify the evidence that some condition is likely to exist. Identifying the evidence will facilitate a medical evaluation that is targeted for the patient's particular symptom constellation and maximize the likelihood of unmasking any covert illness.

Unfortunately, there are no simple questionnaires, no "acid tests" that signal with certainty that a patient has an underlying physical condition. Making a diagnostic assessment is both a science and an art. As with being an accomplished therapist, the task is personally challenging and thoroughly engaging. It involves utilizing not only a body of information but also a library of experience. It calls for reasoned thinking as well as creativity and seasoned intuition. It requires using one's interpersonal and observational skills and maintaining one's clinical curiosity. While these skills are integral to being an excellent clinician and healer in any field, they are central to the sometimes lifesaving work of making a diagnostic assessment.

Learning skills that will help you to unmask psychological symptoms is a vitally important undertaking. Here is what Drs. Barbara L. Yates and Lorrin M. Koran concluded after thoroughly reviewing the modern research studies on the topic of their chapter, "Epidemiology and Recognition of Neuropsychiatric Disorders in Mental Health Settings."

> Overwhelming evidence shows that undiagnosed physical illness is prevalent in patients with psychiatric disorders. Medical conditions in this population are overlooked for many reasons, but in some cases these conditions directly cause the patients' psychiatric symptoms. Public mental health programs, especially programs for the seriously mentally ill, may be the patient's primary source of health care. Even with patients who have a primary care physician, the possibility of undetected, important physical disease remains substantial. (Yates & Koran, 1999, p. 41)

This Is a Common Problem

Everyone has had a firsthand experience with the effects of physical conditions on the mind. A night without sleep will make it more difficult to concentrate at work and easier for a someone to lose his or her temper at home. Too much coffee leaves people anxious and unable to fall asleep.

A few drinks at a party may bring out one's sense of humor, lend an unfamiliar measure of social confidence, or imperil good judgment and make a person argumentative. A high fever, the side effects of particular medications, and, certainly, psychoactive drugs may not only have an impact on alertness, mood, level of anxiety, mental agility, and attention but may also cause hallucinations, paranoia, or delusions, altering the very experience of reality.

In all of these situations, the mental effects are time-limited and their cause is apparent. You know that when your fever comes down, when the new medication wears off, when you sober up, or manage to get a good night's sleep, your mind will return to its usual state. This is comforting. But imagine what it would be like to experience these same changes in the workings of your mind with no obvious physical cause and no surety that you would ever be your old self again. That is akin to the experience of having a covert somatic disease that produces mental symptoms. Under these circumstances, patients are likely to believe erroneously that there is something troubling them psychologically or that they are going crazy.

If such a patient decides to seek help, he or she will most likely consult with a mental health professional. We all know that therapy would not stop the anxiety that comes from drinking too much coffee, the difficulty in concentrating that results from sleep deprivation, or the visual hallucinations that are produced by LSD. The same is true of the anxiety that is produced by an overactive thyroid, the difficulty with concentrating that results from disordered breathing during sleep as occurs with sleep apnea, or the visual hallucinations that may be produced by temporal lobe epilepsy, an extremely common type of seizure disorder that can occur without any loss of consciousness. Psychotherapy will have little to no impact on these very common medical diseases, but other treatment approaches might be effective.

Sometimes these physical illnesses are capable of persisting for years without worsening dramatically and without evolving into a crisis that would make it clear that an underlying organic disease is present. Yet without the correct somatic diagnosis, years of unnecessary suffering for the patient and frustration for the therapist are often inevitable. With medical treatment that is targeted at the patient's actual organic diagnosis, it is possible for the patient's symptoms to improve and, in many cases, completely resolve.

An Illustrative Clinical Vignette

Within the pages of this book, you will meet adult patients of all ages and be introduced to many different physical afflictions. This first clinical vignette is about an elderly gentleman with an important medical condition.

Joan was a social worker who had been seeing me in psychotherapy to work on her troubled marriage. In that context, she began to express concern about her elderly father's declining mental state. Joan's mother and father were both retired physicians who now lived in Chicago, many miles from their daughter.

Joan felt especially close to her father, Dr. Joe. She loved to hear him reminisce about having lived through that era of medical history when there wasn't much a doctor could do to help people who were sick; a physician could only make a diagnosis, provide emotional comfort, and prescribe medication that usually had little effect. In that time of mostly futile treatment, a diagnosis was virtually all there was, and back then it was a lot. A diagnosis represented not only the thoughtful engagement of the mind of an educated and respected clinician, focused squarely on the patient's condition, but it also foretold the future. Could you pass this disease on to others? Would you recover? How long might that take? Could you be left impaired? Would you die?

Joan's parents were retired from medical practice now, but they had hardly slowed down in this ninth decade of their lives. Their social and cultural calendar was astounding; their excitement about cutting-edge movies and trends in the art world was inspirational. This made it especially poignant to Joan when she noticed a change in her father's energy level. Dr. Joe began to move slowly and was increasingly unsteady on his feet. He ceased to be engaged by the activities that had animated him over a lifetime: He sat silently and still for long stretches of time; he no longer played the piano or even listened to music; he stopped reading the book review; and he had no further interest in the daily crossword puzzle. "It's *finito la commedia!*" he would say to his daughter.

Joan's mother Sarah was not unsophisticated in her diagnostic assessment. To Dr. Sarah the signs of depression were obvious: loss of interest in daily activities, absent zest for life, slowed physical and mental activity. Dr. Sarah also had noticed that her husband was having trouble with his memory, and she believed that he had the beginnings of Alzheimer's disease. With years of clinical experience under her belt, Dr. Sarah formulated that her husband was having a depressive reaction to early Alzheimer's disease, and she could readily envision the inevitable downhill course his mind would take, dragging the quality of their lives down with it.

Joan discussed with me how sad it was to think of her father having Alzheimer's disease. As therapists sometimes do, I became the hidden, long-distance consultant in the case. On my suggestion, Joan recommended to her parents that they consult with their geriatric primary care physician rather than simply assuming that these changes in Dr. Joe were the beginnings of an untreatable dementia. The primary care physician took a careful history, conducted a standard physical examination, and ordered some screening blood tests and a chest x-ray. A mini-mental status exam, which included screening tests of memory, was administered and, surprisingly, it was essentially normal for someone in his 80's. Joan's father did not appear to have a clear dementia like Alzheimer's disease. In fact, the doctor could find no obvious cause for Dr. Joe's decline.

It sounded as though Dr. Joe simply had a late-life depression. Clearly, he looked depressed, and he had reasons to be depressed. His physical capacities had declined; he could no longer play tennis or walk with a quick step; he still insisted on opening the door for the ladies, but really, it had become easier for the ladies to hold open the door for him. His self-esteem suffered. He had lived through the inevitable succession of deaths of good friends, colleagues, and relatives. Sarah and Joe going out with friends had come to mean Sarah and Joe going out with an assortment of widowed women. The men who had been dinner, concert, theatre, and museum companions for years were either deceased or in nursing homes. Joe said that he felt like the last one standing, but barely, and now with a cane.

In other words, it made sense that Joe was depressed. Joan and I pondered how to explain the atypical features of his presentation. Perhaps the mild, day-to-day difficulties her father was having with memory resulted from a depression that was affecting his ability to concentrate. As for the slight unsteadiness on his feet, perhaps this was orthopedic, the inescapable effects on bone and cartilage of a long life of stomping down hospital corridors and bounding across tennis courts, always going somewhere in a hurry.

No one knows for sure what would have happened if, at this juncture, Dr. Joe's doctor had referred him to a therapist. Likely, Joe would have been treated for the obvious diagnosis, depression. After all, he had essentially been medically cleared. In this case, the primary care doctor did not send Joe to a therapist. He sent him to consult with a neurologist. Joan was relieved to hear this, because she had learned from me that her father might have an early, treatable form of dementia called normal pressure hydrocephalus (NPH). This relatively uncommon condition occurs when the fluid-filled ventricles of the brain enlarge without an increase in spinal fluid pressure. As the ventricles gradually expand, adjacent nerve tracts in the brain are stretched and compressed. NPH presents with a triad of symptoms: apathy that can look like depression, a disturbance of gait, and, often, urinary incontinence.

But Joan's heart sank when her parents refused to see the neurologist. "What's the point?" asked Sarah. "The neurologist is only going to put your father through all kinds of tests and, in the end, there will be nothing they can do for him anyway!" "What's there to lose?" Joan spat back.

With encouragement from me, Joan persuaded her parents to give the neurologist a chance. NPH is treated by surgically installing a shunting tube that continuously drains small amounts of cerebrospinal fluid from the fluid-filled ventricles of the brain. A preliminary diagnosis is made by taking a history and performing a mental status examination. Only then does a physician conduct a physical exam and order brain-imaging studies. Often the diagnosis is confirmed by draining some fluid from the spinal column and noting whether gait or mental state improves.

It became clear that the diagnosis of NPH was correct when Joe called his daughter after the doctors had performed this test. Miraculously, it was Dad's familiar voice, animated and vital again. "Mom and I just had the most wonderful lunch!" he said, laughing. Joan cried—with joy. The diagnosis was everything!

This diagnosis of NPH told my patient a lot. It told her that her father had a covert physical problem that was likely generating many of the changes in his mental state as well as his unstable walk. It told her that a treatment could be targeted to this particular physical problem and that this treatment had a chance of being effective. It told her that there were risks, but also that there was the possibility of recovery, even at Dr. Joe's age. The diagnosis also gave her a glimpse into the future. She could imagine her father at the piano again, playing a little too loudly. She could picture him rejoining their traditional Thanksgiving game of charades. And that's what did happen. The correct diagnosis in this instance offered hope.

In the 1930s, a diagnosis was virtually all there was, whether it was hopeful or not. In the 21st century, a diagnosis is just the beginning. It still represents the thoughtful engagement of the mind of an educated and respected clinician, focused squarely on the patient's condition. It still tells the future. But now, once the diagnosis is known, in many situations the future can be altered. Effective treatment can begin.

Most readers have probably never heard of NPH, and many may worry, "What if Joe's doctor hadn't referred him to a neurologist but, instead, had sent him to see a therapist. And what if that therapist had been me?" Or "What if Joe had come to see me straightaway, without ever having seen his primary care doctor at all? Or, what about the possibility that this NPH might have emerged while I was seeing Joe for some other problem? It is very likely that I would have thought he was simply depressed. I would probably have missed the treatable diagnosis!"

At this point it is important to recall that Joe's primary care doctor did not send him to a therapist. He sent him to a neurologist, and he must have done so for a reason. I too had recommended that he see a neurologist. What did I know? What did the primary care doctor know? What did he see or sense? And what if you could learn to see or sense or know those things as well? When medical illnesses masquerade as mental conditions, they usually don't do a perfect imitation. Generally, they leave clues to the fact that there is some physical condition in the picture. With some work, it will be possible to learn the signs, symptoms, and patterns of presentation that indicate the presence of some organic disorder, though one may not know precisely which disorder.

Looking more carefully at the case of Joe will give the reader an idea of this book's approach:

- What were the clues to the presence of a covert medical condition in Joe?
- How were these clues disguised or camouflaged within Joe's presentation?
- What kind of investigation led to the disease's unmasking?

Three important clues pointed to the possibility of an underlying organic condition. The first was Joe's difficulty with walking, a clear physical sign. This clue was easy to overlook for several reasons: It came on gradually; it's not unusual for the elderly to have trouble with mobility; and there is a tendency to explain this kind of problem as simply a result of the ravages of time. But time takes its toll by causing actual physical changes. A clinical detective would need to be vigilant, careful to not dismiss this physical sign as simply a result of old age. It turned out that keeping this physical sign in mind while leaving open the question of its cause was important in eventually making an accurate diagnosis.

Clue number two was a marked change in Dr. Joe's behavior; this was noticeable to everyone. However, only careful and thoughtful inquiry ascertained that Joe was not precisely depressed. He was not happy about getting old, and he was not happy about having no energy, but he didn't actually feel depressed. What he was fundamentally experiencing was apathy, lack of motivation, and psychomotor retardation, which is a slowing in his physical and mental processes. This distinction between depression and apathy is difficult but important to make because apathy is more often associated with organic disease.

Clue number three was Dr. Sarah's observation that her husband had mild difficulty with memory in daily life. This symptom was frightening to Sarah. Given that her husband was elderly, she assumed that this was Alzheimer's disease. However, a simple mental status test performed by the geriatric primary care physician revealed that Joe's memory storage was not impaired. This implied that any difficulties with

Tolerate uncertainty

remembering were more likely because of problems with concentration or motivation.

In order to get to the right diagnosis, it was important to tolerate uncertainty about what was the matter. It was crucial to reject the easy idea that Joe was simply getting old. It was necessary to see that this was not a classic depression. One had to sweep aside the notion that Dr. Joe had Alzheimer's disease and open one's mind to other possibilities. Only then was it possible to see a pattern of signs and symptoms that pointed toward the actual diagnosis.

The geriatric primary care physician and I, as the background consultant in the picture, became aware that Joe's presenting problems could be part of that classical triad of signs and symptoms that comprise the presenting picture of NPH. Even without a history of urinary incontinence, it was still possible for Joe to have NPH, though I wondered whether Joan's father might have been uncomfortable sharing this potentially embarrassing symptom with his daughter. Untreated, NPH eventually leads to an irreversible dementia. If identified early on, this form of dementia is often treatable. In other words, NPH is one of those diagnoses you do not want to miss. This is why Joe's doctor sent him to a neurologist.

The story of Dr. Joe illustrates one further point—how difficult the road is to getting effective medical help. Even though Drs. Joe and Sarah were highly educated, motivated, and resourceful, and even with a trusted, caring, and competent family physician in the picture, they needed the support and encouragement of their daughter to make their way to the appropriate specialist. Their fear of Alzheimer's disease might have been paralyzing had it not been for their daughter's encouragement. For patients and families who are less educated, less motivated, less trusting, and less resourceful or financially able, the barriers to attaining top-quality health care are even more difficult to surmount. This is where an informed therapist, through support, encouragement, and active, informed referrals, can make a difference.

One of the many important obstacles to obtaining good health care that even blocks the best educated and brightest patients, families, and therapists is simply this: People do not know what they do not know! Joan and Drs. Joe and Sarah had never heard of NPH. The reason to consult with medical specialists is because they *do* know about conditions that others might never have heard of.

The goal of this book is to address needs that many therapists experience—to be more fully informed about physical diseases, to learn about how organic disorders masquerade as mental conditions and how to recognize when there is a need for a medical referral, and then to know how to work and collaborate with the patient, the family, and other health-care providers to see the referral through.

Medical Specialists Do Know about conditions never heard of

[handwritten margin note: Therapist Point of View]

In attempting to achieve that goal, this book has been written to be readable. It is filled with numerous narrative examples from a therapist's point of view. The book avoids the use of medical jargon while still presenting sophisticated, scientific clinical knowledge. And because there is a large amount of information to absorb about the numerous somatic diseases that can masquerade as psychological disorders, the book introduces that information in manageable portions and circles back to look at it from a variety of perspectives.

[handwritten margin note: adulthood] *[handwritten note: not secondary psychological reactions]*

What Is and Is Not Included

[handwritten note: information received from variety of perspectives]

This book focuses on organic disorders that present in adulthood. It does not cover pediatric illnesses, though it does include some medical conditions that might first be recognized in adulthood even though they have been present since childhood (e.g., attention deficit hyperactivity disorder and the autism spectrum disorders). Also, this book is not about the secondary psychological reactions that individuals may have when they are afflicted with a medical illness. Nor is this book about psychosomatic conditions in which an underlying psychological disturbance such as a depression or an unresolved conflict manifests with physical complaints. Psychosomatic disease is exactly the opposite of what I am writing about. With a psychosomatic disorder, the psychological component is hidden; the physical component, on the other hand, is "worn on the patient's sleeve."

Although *Unmasking Psychological Symptoms* aims to introduce many of the medical conditions that can masquerade as psychological conditions, it does not claim to be encyclopedic in presenting every disorder that a patient might have. The book also cannot cover every sign or symptom of organic disease that patients might experience.

[handwritten margin note: Real patients — Real Clinicians]

Disclaimers

This book cannot substitute for a formal consultation with a competent physician. The narrative cases in this book are based on the experiences of real patients and real clinicians. All identifying information has been changed, and often the narratives are composites of more than one clinical story. In all cases, the narratives strive to capture the complexity of actual practice and the essence of the therapist's clinical experience.

The contents of this work are intended to further general scientific research, understanding, and discussion only and are not intended and should not be relied upon as recommending or promoting a specific method, diagnosis, or treatment by physicians for any particular patient. The publisher and the author make no representations or warranties with respect to the accuracy or completeness of the contents of this work and specifically disclaim all warranties, including without limitation any implied warranties of fitness for a particular purpose. In view of ongoing research, equipment modifications, changes in governmental regulations, and the constant flow of information relating to the use of medicines, equipment, and devices, the reader is urged to review and evaluate the information provided in the package insert or instructions for each medicine, equipment, or device for, among other things, any changes in the instructions or indication of usage and for added warnings and precautions. Readers should consult with a specialist where appropriate.

The fact that an organization or Web site is referred to in this work as a citation and/or a potential source of further information does not mean that the author or the publisher endorses the information the organization or Web site may provide or recommendations it may make. Furthermore, readers should be aware that Internet Web sites listed in this work may have changed or disappeared between when this work was written and when it is read. No warranty may be created or extended by any promotional statements for this work. Neither the publisher nor the author shall be liable for any damages arising herefrom.

Chapter 2

Laying the Groundwork

Introduction

This chapter briefly discusses five key concepts upon which this book and much of our clinical work are based. As you begin to reflect on the process of unmasking the clinical presentations of organic disorders, it will be helpful to review these fundamental ideas.

Concept 1: The Significance of Psychological Symptoms

Even when a patient's problems look psychological, an underlying physical disorder may be causing them. This is a fundamental concept upon which this book is based. In other words, psychological symptoms are nonspecific.

Using an analogy, consider the nature of a fever. A fever is nonspecific. If you develop a fever, you know that you have some kind of medical problem. The most likely possibility is that you have some sort of infection, but without other information you wouldn't know whether you had the flu, pneumonia, an ear infection, urinary tract infection, or malaria. A fever is a nonspecific symptom. Psychological symptoms are also nonspecific; they tell you that something is the matter, but they don't tell you exactly what the problem is. And most important, they don't even tell you whether the problem is psychological or somatic.

This nonspecificity of psychological symptoms presents therapists with the challenging task of determining whether an individual who is seeking help might have an underlying physical condition. In some patients, there might be both somatic and psychological disorders operating, one complicating the other. In other individuals, a physical condition might be the sole cause of the mental symptoms.

The following three examples illustrate the point that physical disorders can look like mental disorders. All of these patients (about whom you will hear more in later chapters) reported symptoms of depression. When asked if they actually felt depressed, each one said, "Yes."

1. Laura and her husband came to see me for weekly psychotherapy soon after learning that Laura was pregnant; they wanted to explore their worries about becoming parents. A few weeks after the baby was born, Laura "dragged" herself into my office, saying that she was "bone tired" and "depressed." She thought she had postpartum depression, and she believed that she had made a terrible mistake in having had a child.

   An evaluation revealed that Laura had developed postpartum hypothyroidism. Thyroid hormone replacement cured her mood disorder, and she and her husband went on to enjoy a loving relationship with their newborn.

2. Ms. Rebecca McCartney's adult children had noticed a personality change in their mother and asked her to see me. The symptoms began just before Ms. McCartney's own elderly mother had died about one year earlier. Ms. McCartney had changed quite dramatically from being a lively, engaged, and sociable person to someone who was sluggish, passive, and "no longer enjoyed the springtime."

   Ms. McCartney's mental and physical slowing (psychomotor retardation) was being caused by a medication she was taking for her high blood pressure. She is back to her normal self now that she is using a different medication for her hypertension.

3. Peter consulted me just after his 60th birthday, saying that he felt "sort of depressed" and that he thought he was upset about "getting old." Of late he had found himself no longer interested in his career. He had been spending a lot of time on the Internet and was especially interested in Internet pornography.

   Peter had an early fronto-temporal dementia. Although it wasn't possible to slow the course of this degenerative brain disorder, it was helpful for the patient and his family to know why Peter had changed so much. Having identified this disorder while it was in its early stages allowed the patient and his family to have time to make thoughtful plans for the future.

Concept 2: The Process of Going From Signs and Symptoms to Diagnosis

The task of every clinician, with every patient, is to go from listening and carefully observing to figuring out what fundamental problems might be generating the patient's difficulties. In other words, each clinician begins by eliciting a patient's signs and symptoms in order to figure out what circumstances and diagnoses might be contributing to the presenting picture.

Signs and Symptoms Not Specific to Mental Disorders

Generally, when individuals believe they have a physical disorder, they seek help from their primary care physician or from pertinent specialists. And when individuals (or their families or doctors) believe they are suffering with a psychological condition, they seek help from us: psychologists, social workers, counselors, psychiatrists, and mental health practitioners from a wide variety of educational and theoretical backgrounds. The patients might be experiencing anxiety, depression, difficulty with getting things done, trouble sleeping, hallucinations, bad dreams, indecision, conflicts with a family member, so-called crazy thoughts, disappointments, heartache, rage, despair. You know the list!

As therapists, we use a variety of approaches in order to figure out what our patients' fundamental problems are and how to help. First, we listen. We try to understand the difficulties within the context of the patients' life histories. We work to conceptualize the dynamics of the problems and to diagnose and treat any underlying maladies such as mood, anxiety, or psychotic disorders, or character pathology. Unfortunately, during this process what is often underappreciated is that the kinds of difficulties that bring patients to us as mental health clinicians—namely signs and symptoms that lie in the psychological realm—are not specific to mental disorders.

nonspecific symptom

Let's look back at my three patients: Laura, Ms. McCartney, and Peter. Each had the *symptom* of a depressed mood, but a depressed mood is a nonspecific symptom. Also, each had additional symptoms that are commonly part of the presentation of a mood disorder of some kind: fatigue for Laura, psychomotor retardation for Ms. McCartney, and a lack of interest in usual activities for Peter. But fatigue, psychomotor retardation, and diminished interest in daily activities are also nonspecific symptoms.

A depressed mood and accompanying symptoms can be seen in many different diagnostic disorders. A depressed mood may be the major presenting feature of a dysthymic disorder, major depression, a severe psychotic depression, bipolar disorder, or schizoaffective disorder. Depression can also be seen in individuals who suffer from schizophrenia, posttraumatic stress disorder, borderline personality disorder, and other mental disorders. As a therapist, you've learned to make what are often very difficult distinctions between one and another of these diagnostic possibilities. But don't stop there.

On your differential diagnosis list for a depressive mood, be sure to include the possibility of a somatic disorder. Many different physical disorders can present with a depressed mood. My three patients represent only a sampling of the possibilities: thyroid dysfunction; the side effects of innumerable, possible medications including prescription drugs, over-the-counter formulations, illicit drugs and supplements; and a dementia affecting the brain's frontal lobes. Many other disorders can present with a depressed mood, including normal pressure hydrocephalus, multiple sclerosis, Parkinson's disease, lung cancer, pancreatic cancer, and so on. Using the DSM-IV-TR, each of these would be classified as a Mood Disorder due to a General Medical Condition (American Psychiatric Association, 2000).

A depressed mood isn't the only kind of psychological presentation of somatic disorders that you might encounter. Some physical disorders will present looking like an anxiety disorder, a psychotic disorder, a personality disorder, and so on. Depending on the presenting clinical picture, using the DSM categories, the diagnosis would be listed, for example, as Anxiety Disorder due to a General Medical Condition or a Psychotic Disorder due to a General Medical Condition (American Psychiatric Association, 2000).

Going back to the three clinical vignettes above, it is important to point out that it was possible to find a clear, psychologically viable precipitant for each person's change in mental state: Laura's conflict about having a baby, the death of Ms. McCartney's mother, Peter's late-midlife crisis. This information is crucial to understanding the experience of the patient, to understanding the meaning the illness has to the patient, and *possibly* to understanding the diagnosis. But, as you can see, one can't assume that these precipitants were directly related to the onset of the patients' problems. In fact, one can't assume that any patient's narrative about what is the matter with him or her is literally true. As a clinician, it is crucial to weigh all the data and investigate within a larger context.

Where does this leave us? As a mental health practitioner, what is the best way to approach the task of differentiating between psychological and organic diagnostic possibilities? I encourage you to take the skills that you already have and apply them in this broader territory. You already know how to establish a trusting relationship with a patient, how to inquire about the patient's experience and history, how to experience and convey empathy while maintaining yourself as an observer. It is possible for you to extend your knowledge base and to expand your awareness so that you become alert to more signs and symptoms and increase your diagnostic options.

Concept 3: A Word About Language

In common parlance, mental health professionals generally use the terms *physical, organic,* or *somatic* to refer to those disorders that affect mental state or behavior and have a clear causal basis in some structural abnormality (e.g., severe head trauma), toxic exposure (e.g., lead

Psychological or Functional Disorders [handwritten margin note]

poisoning), infectious disease (e.g., Lyme disease), malignant affliction (e.g., breast cancer that has spread to the brain), or metabolic derangement (e.g., alcohol withdrawal).

Psychological or *functional* disorders are usually considered to be a
disturbance of mental state or behavior that are caused by mental or
emotional phenomena. This realm encompasses reactions to life events
(e.g., stress reactions, grief), learned behaviors (e.g., passive-aggressive
behavior, avoidance of conflict), and most of the DSM mental disorders
other than those that are due to a general medical condition or to substances. Included as *psychological* or *functional* are disorders that mental
health practitioners regularly treat: obsessive-compulsive disorder, panic
disorder, schizophrenia, major depression, bipolar disorder, the personality disorders, and so on.

The semantic distinctions between the terms *psychological/functional*
and *physical/organic* have fascinating philosophic and historic roots,
and they also reflect our subjective experience of a duality between the
mind and body/brain. But the terms are problematic. Scientific study reveals that there are deep difficulties with the psychological/functional
versus physical/organic distinction. Modern thinking embraces the notion that everything that has been considered to be purely mental derives
from the physical brain. Real-time imaging has demonstrated that complex brain processes are involved in everything that is considered mind.
If one thing is clear, it is that these distinctions between psychological
and physical, functional and organic, mental and somatic, are blurred.

This book uses *physical* or *psychological* terminology because that language is familiar and closest to our subjective experience. Nonetheless,
keep in mind that the *physical* or *psychological* terminology is extremely
limited and presents a distorted picture of current scientific understanding. We now know that *physical* and *psychological* are interconnected,
deeply bound concepts. The so-called psychological, functional, or behavioral disorders all have a basis in the physical brain. Mood disorders,
anxiety disorders, and schizophrenia, for example, have complex, multi-
factorial biological determinants. In addition to looking at environmental factors, scientists are actively investigating the genetic, molecular,
structural, and physiological basis of these and other so-called mental
disorders. The psychological is physical.

And the physical is psychological. The brain develops and operates in
a context, including an interpersonal context. The contextual environment
is fundamental to brain development and functioning. We all understand
that environmental factors such as nutrition or viral exposure will influence the brain. All experience in the world influences the brain—all experience, every experience. When individuals suffer traumatic events,
their brains change. And when people undergo psychotherapy and learn

Psychological to Physical [handwritten margin note]

contextual environment [handwritten margin note]

Physical is Psychological [handwritten margin note]

Brains Change in Trauma [handwritten margin note]

new ways of understanding themselves or of relating to others, their brains change.

Physical and psychological are interconnected, mutually influencing, deeply bound concepts. The same is true for brain and mind, nature and nurture. Without certain experiences during crucial developmental time periods, brain capabilities are hindered. For example, if an individual is deprived of early visual input—for instance, because of cataracts that cloud the eyes' lenses—he or she will not learn to see, that is, to discriminate objects, to recognize edges, to understand that something appears small because it is far away. Learning is the process of brain change in interaction with the environment, and learning about the interpersonal world by experiencing relationships is as fundamental to normal development as being exposed to visual stimuli.

Diagnosis
is flawed
and complex

Concept 4: What Is a Diagnosis?

This book is also based on the idea that there is such a thing as a diagnosis. I am referring to discrete, well-described disease entities for which there is some scientific understanding of the underlying biological mechanism involved in what went wrong. In addition, often these disturbances can be diagnosed definitively by some objective x-ray, imaging study, or laboratory test. But, like the physical or psychological conceptualization, the idea of a diagnosis is also flawed and much more complex than it might originally seem.

The so-called acid test of a disease is that someone who has never seen the patient can perform a specific test and determine what is the matter with that individual. It may be that one disease entity cannot be discriminated from other similar disorders until such a test is developed. For example, the development of the Wasserman test made it possible to distinguish syphilis (which, in its late stages, causes psychosis) from gonorrhea and other diseases with genital symptoms. By using the Wasserman test, early detection of syphilis became possible, and appropriate treatment allowed clinicians to decrease the population of patients who developed the psychosis associated with late-stage syphilis. Currently, scientists have just developed a clinically available "acid test" that will distinguish Alzheimer's disease, even in its earliest stages, from normal aging, from other types of dementia, and from the cognitive difficulties caused by depression.

We do not have such acid tests for the mental disorders as yet, but the search is on. The holy grail of schizophrenia research has been to find a clear biological marker of this disease (or diseases). The same is true of research into depression, obsessive-compulsive disorder, and so forth. At the present time, the best we can do diagnostically is to group them into descriptive categories that have been agreed upon after a scientific vetting process. This is what diagnostic systems such as the DSM are. These do not reflect diagnostic categories that are based on known physiologic mechanisms or underlying causes. Many would argue that the DSM diagnoses are not diagnoses at all.

Yet the goal of refining these descriptive categories is important in working toward diagnoses that are based on some understanding of causality. A diagnosis that reflects a clearer underlying biological process is useful for many reasons, as I began to discuss in this book's introduction. This kind of somatic diagnosis helps predict the course of an illness and guides you in finding effective treatment approaches. This information is invaluable.

But, as useful as a discrete diagnosis and a definitive test might be, it is important to be cautious about the limits of the concept of a diagnosis. Even when the cause of a disorder is known, the manifestations of that disorder in a particular individual will vary based on a myriad of factors, including the individual's genetic inheritance, nutritional and immune status, cultural milieu, and access to health care. In addition, disease expression will be influenced by the meaning that being ill has to the particular person and his or her family. Thus, any disease entity can be highly variable in its presentation. Even when a disease is caused by a specific genetic mutation, two individuals with that same gene mutation may have different manifestations of the disease. Individuality matters. Environmental influences matter. What a disease means to someone matters.

This variability of disease presentation makes the process of clinical diagnosis challenging, even when there exists a laboratory test that could confirm or rule out a particular diagnostic possibility. Thousands of possible tests, x-rays, scans, biopsies, imaging studies, and so on are available to be ordered. Thus, before any definitive diagnosis can be made in a laboratory or an imaging center, first the diagnosis must be imagined in the clinician's mind. Many studies have shown that most of the data that is used in making a diagnosis is obtained during the interview process, through the history and mental status examination.

If the clinician who is actually seeing the patient does not think of the possibility of a somatic disorder, if no clinician thinks of the possible physical diagnostic possibilities, appropriate diagnostic tests may never be ordered, and a diagnosis may be missed. Nothing will replace a well-trained, experienced, empathic clinician talking to a patient while actively listening, observing, being reflective, and thinking diagnostically.

Diagnosis is a challenging cognitive task

Concept 5: The Magic of Making a Diagnosis

As a psychiatrist and psychotherapist, I see most of my patients on a weekly basis and often over many years. I feel that I know each of them very well. So, initially I found it difficult to believe that it was possible for me to *not* realize that a patient of mine had an underlying physical condition. Experience has taught me otherwise. Many factors can lead a practitioner to be unaware that an organic disturbance is playing an important part in the clinical picture. Potential impediments to recognizing a covert organic diagnosis may be introduced by dysfunctional clinical systems (such as the unavailability of medical records, too-short appointments); the patient or family (skipping appointments, withholding important information); and clinicians themselves (being sleep-deprived, inexperienced, distracted by problems at home).

In addition, crucial factors are introduced by the nature of the organic condition, the inherent complexity of any clinical situation, and the limitations of human perception. Cognitive scientists have studied the kind of complex problem solving that practitioners are engaged in every day (Croskerry, 2003). It turns out that making a diagnosis is a challenging cognitive task. In actual clinical situations, it is often difficult to see to the bottom of what is going on. That's part of what makes figuring out a diagnostic solution so interesting!

Four factors make clinical diagnostic problem solving especially challenging: (1) the amount of information, (2) the number of possible solutions to the clinical problem, (3) the clinician's mental diagnostic process, and (4) the limits of human perception.

THE AMOUNT OF INFORMATION

In many problem-solving tasks, the information is well defined. For instance, in solving a crossword puzzle, we have the 26 letters of the alphabet to work with; in doing a Sudoku problem, even a large and difficult one, the set of data is countable, for instance, 1 to 9. The data we deal with in clinical problem solving is much more complex. In our consulting rooms as we try to make a diagnosis, the amount of information approaches the infinite. Moreover, within this vast information field, it is not at all clear just which data are important.

For instance, one might argue that in making a diagnosis, it matters that Peter had just turned 60 years old. For one thing, turning 60 was meaningful to the patient and may have precipitated a depressive reaction. In addition, certain disorders are more likely to occur to individuals in their sixth decade of life. In fact, fronto-temporal dementia tends to strike people in their fifties and sixties, a younger age of onset than for

Alzheimer's disease. Therefore, knowing that Peter is 60 potentially helps to rule in and rule out certain kinds of problems. But in Laura's situation, does it matter that she was 35? It was much more important that she had just had a baby, because that would put her at increased risk for pregnancy-related disorders, including postpartum depression or psychosis as well as hypothyroidism. And in Ms. McCartney's situation, does it matter to the diagnosis that she was 61? Probably not, given that a medication side effect can happen to anyone at any age, though the elderly are more vulnerable.

Is there any diagnostic significance to the fact that Laura has been awakened multiple times each night since taking her new baby home? What about information that Ms. McCartney sleeps 10 hours per night and that Peter yells out in the middle of the night, probably during dreaming? Laura is originally from the Midwest and looks you straight in the eye when she talks; Peter is from Maine and has a shy manner; Ms. McCartney is from western Massachusetts and is quite formal (which is why I refer to her by her last name.) Does any of that data contribute to the process of making a diagnosis? As clinicians we gather infinite amounts of information about our patients, and, along the way, we often don't know the relative significance of much of it.

The Number of Possible Solutions to the Clinical Problem

Adding to the complexity introduced by the vast amount of data is the fact that, unlike crossword puzzles or Sudoku problems with their unique solutions, it is never really clear how many solutions there are in the real clinical situations we face. In other words, in trying to help a patient by first figuring out what is the matter, the number of possible, contributing factors to what is the matter is never clear; individuals may have one or more organic disorders, a mental disorder, more than one mental disorder, an important psychodynamic conflict, a socially dysfunctional situation, financial problems, and so on. In practice, this means that there is uncertainty about when the full solution to the problem has been found. How much better is it possible for the patient to feel?

Laura's symptoms were acute, and the diagnosis of postpartum hypothyroidism was made in a matter of days. In addition, her symptoms responded quickly to treatment with thyroid hormone replacement. I knew that I had found the solution to her problem. But Ms. McCartney's situation was altogether different. The true source of her change in personality—the medication she was taking for her blood pressure—wasn't clear for months. Initially treated with antidepressant medication, she did report some improvement in her mood, but her psychomotor retardation persisted, as did the quest for identifying

How good the patient can feel

another cause. And what about Peter's fronto-temporal dementia? In the first session, an underlying organic disorder was considered, and it was actively pursued along with psychotherapy. But Peter's diagnosis was not definitive for years.

THE CLINICIAN'S MENTAL DIAGNOSTIC PROCESS   *explicit implicit*

Clinical problem solving involves using both conscious (explicit) and unconscious (implicit) processes. In other words, we use explicit search criteria, such as asking patients about their symptoms or their family history, and we also use unconscious mechanisms such as having a gut feeling that this isn't the usual presentation of a depression. As a clinician, one goes back and forth between the two. Based on experience, you have a hunch. Then, you follow that up with questions to see if your hunch is correct, to see if your intuition bears up to logical scrutiny.

THE LIMITS OF HUMAN PERCEPTION

Some disorders are easy to pick up using these dual techniques—explicit problem solving and implicit processes. But other disturbances are not easy to identify, even under the best of circumstances, even for clinicians who know their patients well, who listen and observe carefully and who are knowledgeable about both somatic and psychological disorders. The reason for this is simply that clinicians are human. We are operating within the limits of our perceptual systems and the limits of our minds. We don't know everything. We haven't experienced everything. And we don't notice everything.

Think about how magicians trick us. They take advantage of certain predictable aspects of human behavior: We are easily distracted by a prominent diversion (the emotional meaning of significant life-changing events such as Ms. McCartney's mother's death or the birth of Laura's new baby); we tend to look where others in the audience are looking (family members thought Ms. McCartney was in protracted mourning); we can be readily misdirected by the magician's story (Peter thought he was having a midlife crisis); we see what we expect to see (we are used to seeing depression and don't expect to see patients with hypothyroidism or dementia), and so on (Macknik, 2008). Becoming aware of these susceptibilities will make it easier to pick up physical conditions that might be camouflaged in a patient's presenting picture.

Chapter 3

Characteristics That Make Somatic Diseases Difficult to Detect

Introduction

If you were planning a strategy by which to catch a thief, you would first consider the methods of deception that thieves tend to use. The same is true in formulating strategies that will pick up somatic disorders that are camouflaged in a patient's psychological presentation. The thieves who are most difficult to apprehend are those who slip in and avoid notice, use a disguise, create effective diversions, and then disappear into the crowd, leaving no witnesses and no physical evidence. Somatic disorders are similar. Becoming aware of these tricks of the trade will make it easier for you to identify patients who might have hidden organic afflictions.

This chapter is arranged in sections according to these tricks of the trade:

- The somatic disorder may come on gradually (slipping in without being noticed).
- A physical condition may seem to be part of the individual's basic nature (a very effective disguise).
- There may be a convincing alternative explanation for the symptoms (a diversion from the real nature of the problem).
- The organic illness may cause the individual to behave in ways that are unappealing (leading the investigator to put distance between him or herself and the case).
- The physical disorder may render the individual unable to communicate effectively (impeding your investigation).
- The patient may exhibit few, if any, physical signs or symptoms, especially at the outset (leaving no evidence and slipping into the crowd).

- The physical disorder may be disguised by an atypical presentation (an especially effective disguise).
- The only clue may be the absence of something that should be there (something that only an astute detective might notice).

The Signs and Symptoms of These Disorders Come on Gradually

Patients, families, and caregivers do not readily perceive changes that occur at a very slow pace. This is true for physical changes as well as for behavioral or mental status changes, any of which might be diagnostically salient. An individual's recognition of changes in mental status, in behavior, or in physical state over time is a complex matter that is influenced by many factors. For instance, people differ in their capacities for self-observation; some individuals will be aware earlier than others of a new symptom or a decline in some area of functioning. In addition, people vary in the psychological mechanisms they use when faced with something that is out of the ordinary, whether in the realm of the mind or the body. Some will tend to use avoidance or denial, which may delay recognition of a problem. Others may be hypersensitive and worried, but anxiety may interfere with their ability to clearly conceptualize exactly what changes are going on.

Quite apart from individual variations in psychological defense mechanisms or in the use of insight, all human beings have difficulty recognizing change when it comes on gradually. Likely this is because our brains are constantly and imperceptibly adjusting to small changes. What we notice are contrasts. Changes that are gradual tend to escape our notice.

GRADUAL MENTAL CHANGES

When changes in mental status occur very slowly, it may be a long time before anyone notices, including the patient. This phenomenon is familiar to therapists. Individuals often come to us in the midst of a crisis that *seems to them* to have come on quite suddenly. Only upon reflection does it become clear that, in fact, there had been gradual change occurring in the patient's mental state or behavior over weeks, months, or even years. Because of the insidious onset of symptoms, the changes will have escaped notice until they began to interfere with functioning or have led to an interpersonal crisis. The patient may have become more and more irritable or depressed, apathetic or suspicious, anxious or withdrawn, aggressive or distractible. Therapists know that these changes may be the markers of some psychological condition. In addition, given that mental status changes of this sort are not specific to any particular diagnosis, they may also signal the onset of a variety of organic conditions.

Another sort of gradual mental status change that is more specifically indicative of an organic condition is a slowly progressive decline in cognitive functioning or social behavior. The gradual onset of memory loss in early Alzheimer's disease is a good example of this. But many other neurological disorders also begin with mild cognitive deterioration (such as a loss of the ability for abstract thinking, difficulty with finding one's way around even familiar places, problems with calculation or with spoken or written language, and so on) or a change in personality (such as socially inappropriate behavior or remarkable passivity). These changes may come on so gradually that, at first, it isn't clear whether there really have been any changes at all.

Here is a classic and common situation of this sort.

Mrs. Trudeau was an elderly widow who lived alone in the Victorian house in which she had raised her children. She felt comfortable there. She was in good health other than having "a little arthritis" in her feet. So she "lived" in her pink, fuzzy slippers and said that she was happy to "stay in more" and "see people less." "I keep myself busy with TV," she reassured her children.

But her children worried that the house was too big for their mother to manage. Given her arthritis, they were concerned about the stairs, especially the flight of steps down to the washer and dryer in the basement. So, they convinced Mom to move to an assisted living facility, where they were sure she would be happier, surrounded by people and a potpourri of activities.

Surprisingly, Mom didn't make such a good adjustment. She had trouble learning the names of the new people she met; she couldn't keep the schedule of activities straight; it was even difficult for her to find her way around the new community. As her daughter put it, "She seemed, suddenly, a little demented."

The children dated the onset of Mrs. Trudeau's difficulties to the move. They figured that she was having trouble adjusting to the new residence and that she was probably depressed about losing her home. They were relieved that their mother was safer, but they had to admit that she wasn't happier. So they asked the social worker to stop by to see Mom.

The social worker had seen this kind of situation before. She wasn't surprised to find that a mental status exam revealed that Mom had substantial trouble with visuospatial skills and difficulty remembering items from a list. After a few interviews, the social worker referred Mrs. Trudeau to a neuropsychologist for testing and to a neurologist for a medical workup. The two clinicians agreed that Mrs. Trudeau had early Alzheimer's disease.

In looking back on what had happened, we can see that from the family's perspective, Mrs. Trudeau seemed to have had a sudden decline in functioning after the move. But actually, their mother's dementia had come on very gradually, only no one had noticed it creep in. While still living in the old familiar house, Mom hadn't had to learn anything new. Though her cognitive capacities had been failing, the changes were so gradual that everyone had accommodated to her declining capabilities without even realizing it. The children had shifted holiday events to their own homes; they accompanied their mother to her doctors' appointments; and "just to help out and be nice," they had taken over some of the more complicated life tasks such as bill paying.

Mom's withdrawal from social interactions, meanwhile, was probably not only motivated by her arthritis but also by a diminishing ability to handle the more complex outside world. And unobserved at home, over time, she probably watched less TV news and more soap operas, and she also probably followed less and less of the storyline. The dementia wasn't new. It's just that no one had noticed the gradual changes in Mom's ability to handle new information until after the move when adapting to the new living environment had taxed her declining cognitive functions.

GRADUAL PHYSICAL CHANGES

Gradual physical change is also difficult to recognize. This is familiar to all of us. When your child tries on last year's winter coat, you realize how much he or she has grown. When you look back at old photographs of yourself and your friends, you are able to see that the aging process has been taking place all along. Examples of the large number of physical signs and symptoms that may come on very gradually and initially escape notice include such things as tremors, weakness, fatigue, sleep disturbances, exercise intolerance, heat intolerance, and changes in sexual functioning, bowel function, skin or hair texture or dryness, voice quality, and so on. When a somatic condition presents with only slowly developing physical signs and symptoms such as these but accompanied by prominent changes in the mental sphere, it is easy to overlook the physical clues that would indicate that an organic source should be considered and mistake the problem for a mental disorder.

Disturbances of the endocrine system tend to begin in this way. The endocrine system consists of a set of organs (including the pituitary gland, the thyroid, parathyroid, adrenal, pancreas, ovaries, testes) that secrete a complex variety of hormonal substances; these hormones travel through the circulation and influence the functioning of cells at distant sites throughout the body. Disturbances in the functioning of the endocrine system are capable of producing physical transformations that come on very slowly and thereby escape notice. However, the psychological manifestations of these disorders may appear early, thus leading a patient to seek out psychotherapy and/or psychotropic medications, while the true nature of the illness may escape detection until the accompanying physical signs have become prominent.

Here are a few classic examples of disorders of the endocrine system and some of the physical symptoms they might display that come on gradually. Note that the early psychological symptoms of these disorders are nonspecific, but that many of the physical symptoms are diagnostic. Diseases of the thyroid gland are the most common of the numerous endocrine disorders. Hypothyroidism results when there is insufficient thyroid hormone. The common, early mental changes that accompany hypothyroidism may include such nonspecific symptoms as depression, lack of energy, slowed mental processing, and poor concentration. The slowly developing physical manifestations, however, are more specific: a gradual weight gain, the development of dry and thickened skin, cracked nails, coarse hair, constipation, intolerance of cold temperatures, loss of hair on the outer third of the eyebrow, swelling of the feet, and/or a lowering in the pitch of the voice.

Hyperthyroidism, an excess of thyroid hormone, generally leads to a gradual loss of weight, intolerance of heat, increased sweating, a coarse tremor, increased heart rate, and, in one form of this disorder—Graves' disease—bulging eyes. The early psychological symptoms of hyperthyroidism may include anxiety, irritability, restless hyperactivity, emotional lability, depression, insomnia, and difficulty with concentrating.

Some years ago, a colleague told me the following story about how she discovered that she had a thyroid condition.

Anne was having a wonderful winter. At the annual checkup with her primary care physician (PCP), Anne reported that things were going very well in her life. She had lots of energy and was especially proud of having made really good progress on stepping up her exercise and losing weight. She felt strong and healthy. Everything was fine except for an odd and persistent sense of anxiety. Anne had discussed this at length with her long-term therapist, and quite honestly, she couldn't identify any particular reason for being anxious. The primary care physician asked more about this anxiety. "Well," Anne told her, "It's kind of like an inner racing."

Then the PCP asked about other symptoms. Had her temperature sense changed? Well, actually, yes. She had come in to the doctor's office that mid-February day without a winter coat! And, come to think of it, she had barely worn the coat at all that season. And, did her weight loss seem proportional to her dietary restrictions and increased exercise? Well, not really. She was

> *going to the gym more often, but truthfully, the pounds had just seemed to*
> *melt away, even as she helped herself to seconds of her favorite foods. Did she*
> *have palpitations, a sense of awareness of her heart beating in her chest?*
> *Why, yes, she did. Anne had the symptoms of hyperthyroidism; the diagnosis*
> *was confirmed by laboratory tests.*

Anne hadn't been aware that the characteristic symptoms of hyperthyroidism had slipped into her life. She hadn't really noticed that she was always feeling warmer than others; it had been liberating to be comfortable without a heavy winter coat, and she just didn't think about it. Also, she hadn't thought of her weight loss as coming from anything other than her new exercise program.

Anne had only been aware of her problem symptom, the free-floating anxiety. She had brought this up for discussion in her ongoing therapy. It was only in retrospect that she considered the possibility that she may have been misinterpreting the sensation of a rapid heart rate and a slight tremor as signifying that she was anxious. Whether that was the case or not, her anxious feeling was a symptom of a thyroid in overdrive. It had no psychological roots.

There are many other complex and fascinating endocrine conditions that can present as psychological disorders. Three are outlined as follows; although these are less common than disorders that involve the thyroid gland, they have characteristic features that are important to be able to recognize.

Cushing's syndrome is a consequence of excessive amounts of the hormone cortisol. You may be familiar with many of the features of this syndrome because individuals who are on long-term treatment with cortisol or related medications exhibit the same kinds of signs and symptoms as those who have the disorder as a result of excessive hormone secretion from the adrenal glands.

Excessive cortisol causes a gradual shift in the distribution of body fat, leading to a characteristic rounded face, obese trunk with thin arms and legs, and a fat pad on the upper back (called a buffalo hump). Cushing's syndrome may also be associated with other physical manifestations that come on gradually: thinning of skin, easy bruising, and purple streaks on the abdomen. But often the symptoms that are the most prominent and distressing to the individual are changes in mental status: depression that may be severe, fatigue, irritability, emotional lability, anxiety, apathy, insomnia, and possibly even psychosis.

Addison's disease, a disorder in which there is insufficient production of adrenal gland hormones, causes a gradual bronzing of the skin. Addison's disease was responsible for President John Fitzgerald Kennedy's perpetual "tan" (Kurtzman, 1967). Symptoms in the mental sphere include depression, apathy, fatigue, loss of libido, irritability, mood lability, anxiety, and problems with memory.

Acromegaly is a rare disorder in which excess growth hormone, secreted by the pituitary gland in the brain, leads to the slow enlargement of the jaw, hands, and feet with an actual increase in glove, shoe, and hat size. These changes are accompanied by the mental symptoms of depression, apathy, irritability, loss of libido, instability of mood, and trouble with recent memory.

Disorders Considered Part of the Individual's Basic Nature

Some constellations of symptoms are incorrectly conceptualized and considered to be part of the individual's essential nature rather than being seen as a physical condition. The symptoms of these disorders may be obvious and even overtly problematic, but they are misunderstood to be part of the individual's basic character or temperament. This kind of misdiagnosis is particularly likely to occur when the symptoms of the condition appear to be voluntary or controllable, when the disorder is longstanding, and the manifestations do not worsen substantially over time.

A good example of an organic condition of this sort is narcolepsy. Individuals with classic narcolepsy have chronic daytime sleepiness and the irresistible urge to sleep multiple times during the day ("sleep attacks"). This condition is not only a source of chronic distress, but it may also interfere with academic or occupational performance as well as with social relationships. Yet, even in the face of these significant disabling symptoms, individuals with narcolepsy are frequently not perceived to have an organic condition at all. Rather, they are often considered to be unmotivated, lazy, unsociable, or perhaps depressed. It frequently takes years before an accurate diagnosis of narcolepsy is made. Here is an example:

> *Melissa came to see me for therapy after her marriage fell apart. Her husband, Jeffrey, had left her for a younger woman who worked for him in his business. Melissa felt "hurt," "rejected," "unworthy," "furious," "lost," "jealous," and more! However, after 2 years of psychotherapy, she began to realize that the loss of Jeffrey, this energetic, exciting, entrepreneurial, "whirlwind of a man," actually had been a blessing. Yes, she had loved their winter gambling trips to the Caribbean, and she had "had a blast" at the raucous autumn dinner parties and summer pool parties they had hosted. But she realized that she had actually felt "always pushed to do more" by Jeffrey and had been quite miserable with his fundamentally critical attitude toward her.*

During the marriage, Melissa had been devoted to their four children; she had loved "just taking care of the kids and running the household." But Jeffrey saw this attitude as "lazy." He would grumble that she couldn't keep up with his pace. He found her "boring," and he told her so.

It was only when Melissa's life settled down following the divorce that she began to complain about feeling inefficient in getting things done. On reflection, it turned out that this was really nothing new. In fact, Melissa wondered whether this might have been a trait that Jeffrey had been respond- ing to, even in the early days of their marriage. Now Melissa was fully aware of how her inefficiency thwarted her own goals.

I began to wonder what Melissa really meant by inefficient. Was she depressed? Melissa said her mood was fine. Her attitude was optimistic. I wondered whether Melissa's difficulty in getting things done might be a result of distractibility. Did she have ADHD? I asked questions to assess this possibility. Melissa had been an excellent student, straight through graduate school; her fundamental problem didn't seem to be distractibility or having difficulty with directing her attention.

Several factors ultimately led me to another hypothesis. Melissa fre- quently complained of fatigue, even when she got to sleep early. She liked to take afternoon naps and found that even short siestas were very refreshing. In addition, when she described her mother and sisters, she called them "chronic couch potatoes." They all still lived together in the big, old family house where her mother took frequent naps, while her sisters "lived on No-Doz."

I was beginning to think that Melissa had narcolepsy and that her fam- ily members might have it as well. So I asked Melissa about whether she ever had three symptoms that people with narcolepsy sometimes experience (though these are not diagnostic of narcolepsy): hallucinations, cataplexy, and sleep paralysis. I explained to Melissa that the hallucinations of people with narcolepsy are essentially dreams, intruding into waking life. I told her that cataplexy involves a sudden loss of muscle tone that might lead to fall- ing or dropping things, often at emotional moments. And I described sleep paralysis as the state in which "your mind awakens before your body—for a brief time you are fully awake but cannot move." This is a very frightening experience at first, but individuals come to relax about it as they learn from experience that it always dissipates in a few moments.

Melissa said that she had none of these symptoms. But a few weeks later, Melissa came to therapy and told me that she had changed her mind about one of my questions. Upon reflection, she had realized that she did have sleep paralysis. In fact, the experience of awakening and initially not being able to move was so common that it was "just a part of life." She had never named it; it was just something that she assumed happened to everyone.

I referred Melissa to a sleep specialist. A thorough evaluation revealed that Melissa indeed had narcolepsy. Medication was transforming. Melissa became peppier; she tore through the piles of papers that had been accumulating around her house; she cleaned out closets; she made plans with friends. Melissa had thought of herself as a smart but "inefficient, low-energy person," for most of her life. And her husband had reinforced that self-image. It had never occurred to Melissa or to her husband that she had a medical condition.

Learning that she had narcolepsy shifted the way Melissa thought about herself, both in the present and in the past. Now she began to wonder whether she was attracted to active, exciting, highly stimulating men like her former husband, in part, as a way of trying to compensate for her chronic, low-level fatigue. Those traits in men were so important to her that she would overlook their lack of kindness. Now she began to seek a different kind of partner.

Attention deficit hyperactivity disorder (ADHD) is another example of a condition that is frequently camouflaged within the individual's life and comes to be regarded as simply who the person is. ADHD symptoms such as fidgeting, interrupting, impatience, procrastination, and repeated tardiness are frequently interpreted to be evidence of laziness, bad manners, or lack of self-discipline.

Chronic alcohol or drug abuse also may become so much a fixture in an individual's life that the patient and the patients' friends and family members may be unaware that the use of these substances is producing the individual's irritability, apathy, outbursts of rage, chronic exhaustion, and so on. They may have come to think that this person is simply someone who is mean, impossible to get along with, a curmudgeon, "a loser," unable to hold down a job or to effectively function in the world.

Other disorders that may infiltrate an individual's life such that the symptoms do not stand out include sleep apnea and other sleep disorders such as restless legs syndrome, certain seizure disorders, and the side effects of some medications that are taken over many years. Common medications of this sort are those for allergies, birth control, elevated blood pressure, seizures, or psychosis.

Emma, the friend of a former patient, consulted me because she wanted help with leaving her boyfriend. She was having trouble disentangling her life from his. They owned a home together, and, even worse, he was the major client of her struggling public relations business.

Emma had a mildly depressed mood and no trouble with appetite. But she did have prominent difficulties with sleep, including excessive daytime sleepiness. "I've had problems with sleep all my life. This is just the way I'm built!" she told me. "I'm always wrestling with being tired. My siblings can get twice as much done in a day." She had had a life of struggles with school and work, while her siblings had advanced degrees and successful careers. This had taken its toll on Emma's self-esteem.

In a systematic way, I asked Emma to tell me more about her sleep: Did she have difficulty with falling asleep, staying asleep, or waking up early? Did she feel rested in the morning upon awakening? Emma told me that she had a terrible time falling asleep and that her best sleep was in the morning hours. I knew that this pattern might be seen with restless legs syndrome, because restless legs have a diurnal variation—worse at night, better in the morning.

So I asked if she ever had funny or uncomfortable feelings in her legs. "Yes! How did you know?" was her startled reply. At the end of each day, she felt "like hot worms are wiggling up and down inside my legs." And the only way to rid herself of this sensation was to jiggle her legs.

Emma then proceeded to tell me an extraordinary story. When she was a child, she had slept in the prized, top bunk bed in a shared room with one of her sisters. This allowed her to kick her legs against the ceiling, which she would do every night. But the upstairs neighbors complained. A lot! Her parents scolded her for doing this, even punished her. But she couldn't stop. She confessed that she had thought of herself as out of control and bad ever since. And she had never told anyone about this before.

She had needed to keep her legs in motion in order to fend off those horrid "hot worm" sensations. No one, not even the patient herself, had ever considered the possibility that she might have had an organic condition, a sleep disorder. No one, not even the patient, had considered that her chronic fatigue might have had substantial daytime effects on her school and work performance and, certainly, on her sense of self. All her life, she had believed that she was just "built" to be "bad."

A Convincing, Alternative Explanation

Human beings have been called meaning-making machines. People construct narrative explanations for just about anything, including for bad weather, swings in the stock market, premature births, and certainly for changes in mood, feelings of anxiety or fear, and physical illnesses. This meaning-making process has survival value in negotiating the world. If you think you got sick from eating certain berries, you won't try those again! If you think that a wind from the north predicts a storm, that theory will allow you to prepare for the bad weather. If your narrative hypothesis is correct, you will be better off.

Looking at this process through a psychological lens, explanatory notions also serve as a way to cope with fear, uncertainty, helplessness, and hopelessness. But it is important to keep in mind that these ideas about

causality
coincidence
fantasy

causation that we human beings generate may reflect causality, coincidence, or pure fantasy. Our theories are driven by combinations of the rational and the emotional, the supernatural and the scientific, the spiritual and the psychological, the impulsive and the thoughtful. And this is true for patients as well as for clinicians.

When faced with a set of symptoms, the patient and the clinician automatically will generate explanations for what is going on. On the clinician's side, this often takes the form of a dynamic formulation and/or a diagnosis. As a therapist, it is crucial to keep in mind that one's initial understanding of the clinical situation may not necessarily reflect the true etiology of the patient's problems. When a patient has a hidden organic condition, a flawed but compelling psychological explanation may become a diversion, directing attention away from investigation of possible, underlying, physical factors.

subtleties

It is cognitively challenging for practitioners to shift their thinking to new diagnostic possibilities once they have settled on some way of understanding a patient's symptoms. This tendency to stick with one's original diagnostic impression is ubiquitous and contributes to delays in diagnosis.

Four kinds of situations tend to lead to faulty psychological explanations and then to premature closure:

1. Physical conditions that come on at the same time as a major life event
2. Physical disorders with intermittent symptoms
3. Physical disorders in which the symptoms are precipitated by emotion
4. Disorders that have prominent symptoms in the mental sphere and physical signs and symptoms that are readily misattributed to a second disorder

PHYSICAL CONDITIONS THAT COME ON AT THE SAME TIME AS A MAJOR LIFE EVENT

A clinician's attention may be diverted away from a physical condition when a major life event takes place around the same time that an organic disorder with behavioral symptoms begins or becomes prominent. When a physical condition manifests itself around the time of a job change, a move, a marriage, or the illness or death of a loved one, or in concert with other meaningful life events, the natural, psychological explanation that comes to mind is that the individual is having difficulty adjusting to the new situation or to the loss. Unfortunately, this explanation may not reflect the actual cause of the patient's symptoms.

Changes in mental status or behaviors that come on during pregnancy or after the birth of a child are frequently assumed to be related to the challenging, psychological demands of new motherhood. But, in addition to the emotional challenges of becoming a parent and integrating a new baby into the family, there are seismic shifts in bodily functioning during pregnancy, birth, and nursing. It is possible for endocrine dysfunctions or other physical problems to emerge during a pregnancy or in the postpartum period. Here is more about Laura, whom you met in the last chapter.

Laura and Bill were both high-powered lawyers. They came to see me together after Laura became pregnant. They were used to planning ahead and being "in control" of their lives, so they wanted to talk about making the transition to becoming a family of three. How were they going to juggle work and parenting? Laura was especially worried that the bulk of responsibility for the care of their newborn would fall to her, and she did not want to sacrifice her career goals "at the altar of motherhood."

The therapy went well. Laura and Bill negotiated their schedules and hired a nanny. But they also faced the deeper issue of how becoming pregnant had opened them to a world of uncertainties. What if Laura had complications and needed to stop work early? What if something was wrong with the baby? Airing their sense of vulnerability in the face of so much hope for a healthy child seemed to quiet many of the anxieties and tensions that Laura and Bill had been experiencing.

We decided in advance that after the baby was born Laura and Bill would take a four-week hiatus from the therapy. Bill called me with good news about mother and child soon after the delivery. All had gone well. Mother and daughter were healthy. Surprisingly, however, at their first appointment after the break, Laura seemed remarkably depressed. In fact, Laura believed that she was suffering from a postpartum depression. She said that she had had to "drag" herself to the session; she complained of "utter" exhaustion. She clearly resented being repeatedly awakened by the baby during the night as well as being perpetually interrupted with "basic necessities" during the daytime. "I do nothing all day but breast feed and change diapers." Laura was also angry with Bill for not helping her more. "Just what I anticipated," she said.

During the session, Laura tearfully confessed that she was also furious with her new daughter and afraid that she didn't love her baby. Secretly, she believed that this was really why she was depressed and irritable. Laura painfully remarked that she had never felt so bad before: "My body literally aches with disappointment and self-recrimination. The entire day goes by and I don't get a thing done. I'm too tired to exercise; I haven't lost my extra pregnancy pounds; I am completely inefficient, ineffective. This is mother-hood! What was I thinking? How will I ever get back to work?"

Laura had never been depressed before. I wondered why Laura was so profoundly and quite suddenly depressed now. It was certainly possible that I was witnessing a postpartum depression, a serious condition needing urgent intervention for the sake of the mother as well as for the sake of the baby who needs an emotionally available mother. But what struck me were Laura's physical complaints, specifically her body aches and her truly overwhelming fatigue. It had been weeks since her delivery. These physical symptoms were not what one would expect this long after the baby had been born.

It was not easy to convince Laura and Bill that what was needed was an expeditious referral to Laura's primary care physician. She couldn't imagine how she would find time to get to the doctor's office. Phoning the primary care physician and emphasizing the prominent symptoms of concern—overwhelming fatigue, muscle aches, first-time depression, post-delivery onset—facilitated the arrangement of a convenient appointment time.

As it turned out, Laura was not simply having a problem in adjusting to motherhood, nor did she have a classic postpartum depression. Laura had hypothyroidism. This diagnosis largely explained why someone who had never been depressed before had become so "undone." It accounted for her depression, irritability, intense fatigue, body aches, her difficulty with losing weight, and the post-delivery onset—not uncommon for thyroid conditions.

After Laura's condition was correctly diagnosed, Bill, Laura, and I were all relieved. We now had a crucial new way of understanding what had gone wrong. Although psychotherapy alone would not have lifted Laura's depression, therapy was certainly useful now that this biological diagnosis had been made and a treatment had been instituted. Therapy helped Laura and her husband through this very difficult transition to parenthood. Therapy helped both members of the couple to see how Laura's overwhelming fatigue, depression, and irritability had complicated her early attachment to her daughter. The therapy supported Bill in being more patient, empathic, and available. It facilitated Laura developing a loving relationship with her little daughter and contributed to her eventual integration of work and motherhood.

Laura's depression did take a uniquely "Laura" form. This insightful, high-powered lawyer was indeed in conflict. Unrelentingly demanding of herself, fiercely self-critical, efficient, ambitious, she wanted to be a "successful mother." She worried that her professional strivings would interfere with her mothering and that motherhood would keep her from attaining her professional goals. But, as alive and vital as this conflict was, it was not the cause of her depression. It was a distraction from the organic condition.

PHYSICAL DISORDERS WITH INTERMITTENT SYMPTOMS

When somatic disorders present with intermittent behavioral symptoms that come and go without obvious cause, it is especially common for individuals to come up with faulty psychological explanations for the episodes. This is understandable. Anyone with a distressing symptom will quite instinctively try to figure out what is bringing it on—if you can figure out the cause, maybe you can figure out a cure. Not knowing the full variety of possible causes or how to weigh them scientifically, patients will reach for a handy folk explanation or psychological interpretation.

Consider my patient, Suzie, who experienced episodes of slurred speech on rare occasions. Her latest was a brief episode of slurred speech while talking to her mother on the telephone. She interpreted that episode of slurred speech as a manifestation of her inner conflict between "saying" and "not saying" the angry, emotionally charged words she had on her mind. I listened to Suzie's observations and her psychodynamic explanation with interest. She was telling me what this symptom meant to her.

But this was not the causal explanation of her symptom. In fact, slurred speech is almost always produced by a medical condition of some kind, a seizure disorder, a drug reaction, a transient ischemic attack (TIA) in which a focal area of the brain is briefly deprived of sufficient blood flow, a stroke, brain tumor, and so on. It was meaningful to explore Suzie's thinking about her symptom, including her discomfort with strong feelings, her conflicts about verbal confrontation, and her difficulties with letting another person in on her emotional life, especially her mother. But, it would have been a mistake to assume that this would necessarily be a discussion about the actual etiology of her symptom. Indeed, the appealing psychodynamic explanation could easily have diverted attention away from the exploration of possible physical causes for the slurred speech. Patients who are in psychotherapy are especially prone to assign psychological explanations to phenomena—so are psychotherapists.

What was the cause of Suzie's slurred speech? Suzie had a focal seizure disorder that was effectively treated with anticonvulsant medication. This is a common organic disorder that can present with episodic, physical and/or psychological symptoms. The psychological symptoms vary from feelings of fear and doom, to an altered sense of reality or time (such as a déjà vu experience), to visual or auditory illusions or hallucinations.

The general public's concept of epileptic seizures is usually confined to disturbing images of major motor seizures in which an individual loses consciousness, thrashes about, and may bite his or her tongue, or become incontinent. These major motor seizures involve synchronous electrical firing of neurons throughout the brain. But seizures that are confined to focal areas of the brain (called focal or partial seizures) may not disturb consciousness at all and may manifest only with what appear to be psychological symptoms. If a focal seizure does cause a change in consciousness, that change might be a clouding of consciousness or a short period of being out of touch. Then the focal seizure is called a complex focal seizure.

Disorders that are linked to the menstrual cycle also present the practitioner with an intermittent symptom picture. It is not uncommon for therapists and patients alike to fail to make the connection between the timing of symptoms and the hormonal changes that have induced them. This is especially likely if the disorders do not occur every month or if the individual has an irregular menstrual cycle. Premenstrual syndrome and premenstrual dysphoric disorder are tightly linked to the menstrual cycle, producing symptoms that may be emotionally disabling in the time period before but not after menstruation: irritability, anxiety, depression, emotional lability, difficulty concentrating, and so on. Hormonal changes during the menstrual cycle may also precipitate seizures in individuals who are prone to have them; these menses-linked seizures are referred to as catamenial seizures.

Other disorders can present with episodic psychological or behavioral symptoms and are open to misinterpretations of this kind. Acute intermittent porphyria, a genetic disorder of hemoglobin metabolism, can present with periodic episodes of psychosis. Multiple sclerosis is characterized by symptomatic episodes that may be separated by as many as 25 years. The physical symptoms of multiple sclerosis are often vague and fleeting, while depression or euphoria may be prominent in the clinical picture. Individuals who are eventually diagnosed with multiple sclerosis have often gone for years, even decades, without a correct diagnosis having been made.

SYMPTOMS ARE PRECIPITATED BY EMOTION

Other clinical situations that readily lend themselves to psychological misinterpretation are those in which the physical symptoms of an underlying somatic disorder are precipitated by emotional upheaval. Stress or intense affect will play a part in worsening most neurological symptoms, including tremors, headaches, disturbances of balance or speech, and so on. In all of these situations, the emotional component operates in the context of an underlying organic condition. The emotion is not the cause of the symptom, only the precipitant or a complicating factor.

Consider cataplexy, mentioned earlier in the case of Melissa who had narcolepsy. Cataplexy is a symptom that is seen in about 10% of patients with narcolepsy. Individuals with cataplexy will suddenly lose muscle tone in some or virtually all of their voluntary muscles. They may drop objects without warning; their knees may buckle, or they may collapse to the floor with no change in alertness and no clouding of consciousness. What is most remarkable about these cataplectic attacks is that they are usually brought on by strong emotion in the moment. The husband tells an embarrassing joke and the wife, quite literally, collapses to the floor. Either consciously or unconsciously, individuals with cataplexy may try to avoid intense emotions, including sexual arousal, for fear of having an attack. It probably wouldn't surprise anyone to learn that these incidents are not uncommonly assumed to be caused by hysteria. The prominent emotional precipitants in each case divert attention to the psychological diagnostic possibilities.

Stress and intense affect also play an important role in several other disorders that are frequently mistaken to be psychological. In Tourette's syndrome, patients experience building tension and eventually an irresistible urge to perform some action, be it touching, twitching, barking, and so on; these actions are called tics. Stress may worsen Tourette's syndrome such that individuals with this disorder may be less able to hide their symptoms under emotional circumstances.

Myasthenia gravis is a disorder involving abnormal signal transmission between nerves and muscles that leads to muscles tiring with repetitive use (e.g., muscles used in exercise, chewing, blinking). Stress is such a crucial determinant of symptom severity in myasthenia gravis that therapy for stress reduction is frequently considered an essential part of treatment.

Stress also makes it more likely that an individual who has a seizure disorder will actually have a seizure episode. Focal seizures are frequently mistaken for psychological disturbances.

Symptoms That Are Readily Misattributed to a Second Disorder

Another sort of organic disorder that creates an effective diversion is an illness with signs and symptoms in the spheres of mental functioning and behavior that also has physical manifestations that match the pattern of a second, more common diagnosis. Under these conditions, clinicians will tend to diagnose two disorders rather than realizing that one fundamental diagnosis has manifestations in both body and mind.

Here is an example: A wildly psychotic patient appears in the emergency room with excruciating abdominal pain. The doctor's preliminary diagnosis is schizophrenia and acute appendicitis. If the surgeons rushed the patient to the operating room, they would find nothing amiss in the patient's abdomen. This patient could have a genetic disorder called acute intermittent porphyria. This presentation is considered to be so classical that the diagnosis of acute intermittent porphyria is put high on the differential diagnosis list in any patient who comes to an emergency room in an acute psychotic state and with multiple abdominal surgical scars.

The fundamental problem in the porphyrias, actually a group of disorders, is a disturbance in the metabolism of heme, the central molecular component of hemoglobin. Acute intermittent porphyria can cause a variety of episodic psychiatric disturbances that may range from depression to an atypical psychosis, from anxiety, agitation, and insomnia to hypomania and confusion. At the same time, patients will exhibit a variety of physical symptoms such as severe pain, headache, nausea, vomiting, elevated blood pressure, and possibly seizures. Though the presentation of this disease is highly variable, it frequently looks like an acute medical disease (such as appendicitis in the previous case) in an individual who happens to be psychotic or who is delirious from the medical disease.

Here is another example: A therapist thinks a patient is in the early stages of dementia. The patient has some memory loss and a mild depression. He also carries the diagnosis of severe chronic colitis and has been losing weight; in the background is also a long-standing arthritis. In fact, the patient may have a very uncommon disease that is responsible for all of these problems. Whipple's disease is a rare, potentially lethal, but entirely treatable infectious disease that tends to affect men more often than women. It presents as a chronic disorder that affects multiple systems, including the small intestines, joints, heart, and central nervous system, and is usually misdiagnosed for years.

Many other physical disorders affect the brain as well as multiple other organ systems. When these illnesses first present themselves, it is not uncommon for the liver, heart, or kidney disturbances to overshadow the impact that the underlying metabolic disturbance is having on the central nervous system. For instance, hemochromatosis is a genetic disorder in which excess iron is deposited in body tissues and leads to organ dysfunction (for instance, diabetes from pancreatic involvement, liver cirrhosis from liver involvement, heart failure and arrhythmias from heart involvement). Hemochromatosis also leads to iron deposits in the brain with symptoms of fatigue, loss of libido, poor attention, and then declining intellectual functioning, memory loss, disorientation, and lethargy. The same kind of pattern is seen with Wilson's disease, a less common genetic disorder of metal metabolism, this time copper.

Some malignancies may present initially with a prominent depression or other neuropsychological symptoms. In these tragic situations, the significance of any associated physical manifestations only becomes clear over time. Pancreatic cancer may present with a profound depression and only vague abdominal symptoms and gradual weight loss. At first, these physical manifestations may be attributed to the depression. Only later does it become clear that the depression and the physical symptoms have a common, underlying cause. Certain types of lung cancer may also begin with a depression, while an insidious weight loss, worsening smoker's cough, or hoarse voice may only eventually rise to the level of notice.

The Organic Illness Makes the Individual Unappealing

If an organic disorder transforms a patient so that he or she is unappealing in some way, it is common for clinicians to distance themselves from the situation. Unfortunately, there are numbers of organic conditions that may render patients uncooperative, belligerent, crude, unkempt, seemingly unintelligent, socially inept, impulsive, violent, sexually inappropriate, smelly, or appearing to be intoxicated or high on drugs. The danger is that diagnostic thinking will be short-circuited when these presentations elicit the likely negative reactions in clinicians.

Therapists are familiar with the tendency to use dismissive pseudo-diagnostic labels when patients stir up negative reactions in the caregivers. The patient may be perceived as simply being someone with character pathology, or called "self-destructive," "a druggie," "an alcoholic," "passive-aggressive," "manipulative," or "*just* a psych patient." Though these terms may at times be accurate descriptions of one aspect of an individual's behavior, they are also commonly used in a judgmental, distancing fashion that may impede further psychodynamic or diagnostic thinking and even cut short any further engagement with the patient. Rather than seeing the patient's unappealing behavior as a symptom, the cause of which needs to be discerned, the symptomatic behavior is used as a reason to slow or even stop further investigation. Dismissive labeling is problematic under many circumstances but is especially perilous when the patient's unappealing behavior is actually the manifestation of an underlying organic illness.

Unfortunately, one feature in a patient's presentation that tends to be found unappealing is a psychiatric history. When, for instance, the diagnosis of schizophrenia or bipolar disorder or borderline personality disorder is found in the chart, it is particularly easy for clinicians to jump to the conclusion that the psychiatric history explains all of the patient's current symptoms.

Here's another kind of unappealing patient. A divorced man in his late fifties was referred for neuropsychological testing by his male therapist. The patient had been in therapy for several years for a mild depression, but over the past 6 months, the patient seemed to be going downhill. The patient and his wife had been fighting more, and the patient had been fired from his job as a computer software engineer for reasons that weren't clear to the therapist.

> *Dr. Meredith Shah, a neuropsychologist, went to the waiting room in order to meet the patient and escort him to her office. She called out the patient's name. He whistled at her from across the room. Dr. Shah found herself wondering whether the patient was drunk, but she noticed that he walked confidently across the waiting room and that he did not slur his speech, nor did he smell from alcohol. But the patient did have an unpleasant body odor and was quite disheveled in his appearance. Also, throughout the testing session he interrupted her with provocative, off-color remarks. All of this made Dr. Shah feel that she wanted to get through the testing as quickly as possible.*
>
> *The results of the neuropsychological battery of tests revealed frontal lobe dysfunction, the likely explanation for the patient's disinhibition, poor social judgment, and difficulty with self-care. Imaging studies confirmed that the patient had a frontal dementia, possibly Pick's disease.*

Many different organic disorders can cause a dementia, just as many kinds of infections can cause a fever. The term *dementia* refers to deterioration in cognitive abilities without a disturbance in the individual's level of consciousness or alertness.

Dementia may lead an individual to be unappealing in a variety of ways, depending on which areas of the brain are being affected. When the frontal lobes are involved, one may see the sort of uncensored behavior that was evidenced in this case. Other examples of loss of comportment and failure of inhibition would include individuals who urinate in public, take food from the plates of diners at adjacent tables, eat with their hands, make insensitive remarks to others, and so on.

Other kinds of disorders also may lead patients to present in ways that are unappealing. Individuals with certain acute brain infections (such as Creutzfeld-Jakob disease, related to mad cow disease) may have gait disturbances and a rapid mental decline that might be mistaken for intoxication.

The tics of Tourette's syndrome may include touching other people, grunting, making inappropriate remarks, or sometimes cursing. These behaviors may be off-putting even if they are understood.

Here is another situation in which a clinician is likely to feel judgmental.

> *The moment I walked into the waiting room I noticed the purplish bruise on my patient's left cheek.*
>
> *"What happened?" I asked right away.*
> *"My husband. He punched me in the middle of the night."*
> *"Tell me more."*
> *"It was the craziest thing. He didn't really seem awake. And he seemed to think he was fighting off some attacker."*

Clinicians are likely to be disbelieving and judgmental when they hear such stories: middle-of-the-night assaults on a bed partner, possibly even the infliction of significant injury. The patient was not covering up an incident of spousal physical abuse, and her husband did not have posttraumatic stress disorder. PTSD may cause nightmares, but not the "acting out of dreams during sleep." PTSD may cause flashbacks, but these occur when the individual is fully awake. No, this patient's story is consistent with REM sleep behavior disorder, a condition that may be brought on by particular medications or is reflective of the onset of certain underlying organic brain disorders such as Parkinson's disease.

Normally during REM sleep, a temporary loss of muscle tone, called atonia, keeps all of us from acting on our dream content. If this atonia fails to kick in, individuals will not lie still during their nightmares but will be free to act on their dream impulses *while still asleep* and altogether lacking in judgment. During these episodes, patients with REM sleep behavior disorder may seriously injure their bed partners or themselves. They believe they are chasing away robbers or fighting aggressively to defend themselves and their families from invaders, monsters, and so on, all while in REM sleep. (Sleepwalking and/or talking occurs in a different stage of sleep.)

Physical Disorders May Make the Individual Unable or Less Able to Communicate

Individuals differ considerably in their baseline abilities to communicate with a clinician and actively engage in the diagnostic and therapeutic process. Therapists expect to encounter variations that are based on innate capabilities or cultural and educational influences. But, in addition, some underlying physical disorders can subtly or profoundly impair people's ability to effectively communicate what has happened to them over the course of their illness or even to convey what they are experiencing in the present. Patients who are thus affected may be incapable of full, effective participation with a clinician in working toward identifying the source of their problems.

When this occurs, clinicians are more apt to miss a somatic diagnosis. A practitioner may simply not be able to obtain enough information, or the information the clinician is able to gather may be inaccurate. In addition, the difficulties with communication may make the work of history taking so difficult that clinicians may find themselves worn out, confused, and tending toward giving up. All therapists have encountered patients who are considered to be poor historians or unreliable informants. These individuals are readily assumed to have a psychological affliction, especially when the impairments in communication are subtle, intermittent, or appear to be voluntary.

Problems in the following areas of mental functioning might contribute to difficulties with communication: motivation, memory, alertness, attention, articulation of speech, the production of language, finding words to describe an experience, and/or insight.

MOTIVATION

An organic disorder may interfere with motivation, rendering individuals less able to be active participants in treatment planning. If the patients' impaired motivation is subtle, and especially if it is not clear that the apathy or lack of motivation is new, a clinician may simply assume that these patients have always been passive or have always had a "whatever happens, happens" attitude toward life. Under these circumstances, it would be easy to overlook these symptoms as a signal of organic disease.

In some cases, patients who are lacking motivation may delay in seeking help or altogether fail to initiate contact with the health-care community until their families make an appointment and "drag them in to see you." When asked about any problems, they may say that "everything is just fine." In more extreme cases, patients may initiate no activity whatsoever, including conversation. There may be a "failure of discourse," in which patients answer questions with only short phrases or a simple "yes" or "no." Or patients may be altogether mute.

Disorders affecting the frontal lobes of the brain are renowned for presenting with apathy (one of two major frontal lobe syndromes, the other being the uncensored, disinhibited presentation demonstrated by the patient who whistled at the neuropsychologist from across the waiting room). Here is an unforgettable narrative, illustrating an amotivational syndrome.

After an extensive evaluation, the team scheduled a meeting with Mrs. Anderson and her family to present what they had found. They explained that Mrs. Anderson had fronto-temporal dementia, a degenerative neurological disease that tends to affect people earlier in life than Alzheimer's disease. As the name implies, it particularly affects the frontal and temporal lobes of the brain. They said that Mrs. Anderson's condition would gradually worsen and that probably, within five to eight years, she would die. The family was understandably distraught. Mrs. Anderson's two sisters and her brother asked lots of questions. The sisters cried and hugged one another. Throughout the meeting, Mrs. Anderson simply picked her nose.

MEMORY

Memory difficulties may also interfere with effective communication between the patient and a clinician who is trying to piece together what might be the matter. When an underlying organic disorder causes problems with memory, the patient may distort the time course of the problem or may omit crucial data, such as a personal medical history of hypertension or cancer, a family history of a genetic disease like Huntington's or Wilson's disease, a recent infectious illness or auto accident that might have been a precipitating event.

Some patients are aware of memory problems they are having and may report this to the clinician. But in many instances, individuals are unaware of any memory difficulties and will simply present their version of the present illness with substantial omissions or even confabulations. Particularly in these latter situations, the disturbances of memory may not be apparent to the interviewer and may lead to mistaken diagnostic impressions.

Mrs. Van Dorn, a 70-year-old woman, came to the mental health clinic, saying she had been feeling "out of sorts" and had been having trouble with her memory for about two months. The intake psychologist asked whether anything particular had happened two months ago.

"Come to think of it," Mrs. Van Dorn said, "I've been feeling this way ever since I fell on the ice while carrying my groceries home."

She reported having struck her head but not having lost consciousness. After taking the history, the clinician's working hypothesis was that the patient probably had a straightforward, post-concussion syndrome that would likely resolve in a matter of months.

The therapist hadn't yet started her cognitive exam when the patient's son knocked on the consulting room door. He had been delayed in traffic. He was very sorry to be late. The son reported that he had talked with other family members, his sisters and his father, and they all agreed. The patient's memory had been deteriorating for at least two years, and the fall was entirely incidental.

Mrs. Van Dorn's mental status testing during the appointment showed that she had substantial loss of the ability to store new memories. After 5 minutes, she recalled only one item out of the three that she had been asked to remember; she recalled none after 20 minutes. Clues did not help her to retrieve any memory of the items. A further workup, including formal neuropsychological testing, a neurology consult, and an MRI, revealed findings consistent with early Alzheimer's disease.

ALERTNESS

In addition to the other parameters we have discussed, communication may be impeded if an individual is not fully alert. Indeed, mental status abnormalities in the areas of arousal or state of consciousness are common and very significant clues to the presence of a covert somatic condition. An individual may have his or her alertness impaired by being sleepy or by having impaired consciousness.

An individual may be *sleepy* if one has simply not had enough sleep. But having excessive daytime sleepiness might be caused by an underlying physical condition such as an infectious illness (Lyme disease, HIV) or a sleep disorder (restless legs syndrome, sleep apnea) that interferes with the restorative effects of sleep.

Or a patient may have *disturbance of consciousness*, running on a spectrum from being lethargic to obtunded to comatose. An individual in a lethargic state, especially in a mild and fluctuating lethargic state, may be difficult to distinguish from someone who is extremely sleepy. The distinction is important to make, because a clouding of consciousness is always extremely significant and indicative of organic pathology, sometimes of a life-threatening nature.

One might think that disturbances in these areas of mental functioning would be obvious in any clinical interview. However, when an individual's impairment is mild or fluctuating, it may be misinterpreted or missed entirely. First let's look at a disturbance of consciousness.

Rose was a 24-year-old patient with bipolar disorder who had been on the psychiatric inpatient unit for about five days when she was given her first day pass to visit home. When Rose returned at about 9 p.m, she told the nurses that she had had a fight with her mother but that she "didn't want to talk about it." She said, "I'm sleepy and just want to go to bed."

> *Rose looked worn out. The nursing staff members could understand how Rose might be exhausted from the stress of dealing with her flamboyant and volatile mother. Rose's mother had become a legend on the unit after Rose's first hospitalization there several years earlier; Rose had tried to hang herself, using her hair dryer cord, but the cord had broken during the attempt. Rose's mother had come to the hospital for a visit and had brought with her a replacement hair dryer for her daughter.*
>
> *The nurses were busy checking in other patients, so they suggested that Rose get into her pajamas and then come back to the nursing station to talk about what had happened at home. After 15 minutes, Rose had not returned to the nursing station, so they sent an aide to check on her.*
>
> *The nurse's aide found Rose lying across the bed, fully clothed and breathing as though she was in a deep sleep. When the aide called Rose's name, the patient roused herself with great difficulty and told the aide to leave her alone. But Rose's speech was slurred, and, immediately, she slipped back into that deep, faraway state. The aide had to shake her to get her to respond more fully. Now it was clear that the patient was more than sleepy.*
>
> *"What did you take?" The nursing aide insisted.*
>
> *"Sleeping pills."*
>
> *"How much?"*
>
> *"A bottle."*
>
> *A short while later, the patient could no longer be aroused.*

This situation could happen to any practitioner working with patients who act out or are suicidal. It illustrates the obvious, that a mild lethargic state, such as the one that develops soon after a drug overdose, might not be recognized for what it is. However, on the other end of the spectrum, as a drug is absorbed (or in cases of a covert medical condition, as that condition worsens), a more obvious stupor or coma might follow, rendering all communication about what has happened impossible. At this point it would be obvious that one was dealing with a physical disorder, indeed, a medical emergency.

A very important takeaway message is that one of the most commonly missed presentations of an organic condition is a state of minimal or fluctuating lethargy. Innumerable organic conditions can present with mildly impaired or fluctuating levels of alertness, including chronic subdural hematomas (the slow accumulation of blood between the two outermost membranes that surround the brain), liver failure, kidney failure, infections of all sorts, and so on. A fluctuating or clouded state of consciousness will present a challenge to the clinician who is trying to obtain cooperation from a patient, but if there is any good news in the situation, it is that this sort of mental status change is a clear signal that an underlying organic condition is present.

Extreme sleepiness may also interfere with patient-therapist communication. The quiet, soothing environment of a therapist's consulting room can be soporific, and this effect may be accentuated if the appointment is at the end of a long day and if the therapist's style tends to allow lulls in the conversation. Some patients with organic conditions may have difficulty maintaining their state of arousal under these circumstances, including patients with a variety of covert sleep disorders. These patients might appear to have difficulty generating ideas to discuss in therapy; they may seem not fully engaged in treatment. Patients with serious sleep apnea or with narcolepsy might even fall asleep in the office, sometimes in mid-sentence.

ATTENTION

Enduring or repeated episodes of difficulty with attention, whether mild or serious, are also indications of an organic condition. Inattention may present difficulties in the flow and interchange of information during an interview.

When inattention is mild, as with many cases of ADHD, the problem might be subtle. A patient with ADHD might have difficulty fully attending if the therapist speaks at some length, or the patient might get distracted in couples therapy while the partner is talking. This inattention might take the form of eyes glazing over, increased fidgetiness, frequent checking of the clock or cell phone, for example. These sorts of behaviors are easily interpreted as having a purely psychodynamic meaning, namely that the patient doesn't care what the other person is saying. In these instances, the biological disorder is easy to overlook as a contributing factor.

On the severe end of the spectrum, wild distractibility and inattention may occur, for instance, with alcohol withdrawal and the development of delirium tremens, and this could impede virtually any effective communication. In fact, in addition to impaired consciousness, distractibility and inattention are other important features of a delirium, a very common and important syndrome indicating an underlying somatic disorder.

The unit social worker stopped by to introduce herself to Mr. Stevens a day before his liver transplant. The interaction was difficult. Mr. Stevens would seem engaged, but then a random stimulus in the environment would distract him, and he would lose the thread of the conversation entirely. This happened repeatedly. He noticed the doctors going by on their daily rounds. He turned his head when he heard a patient walking down the corridor with her noisy IV pole. He was distracted by his roommate's phone ringing and by the chatter at the nursing station across the hallway. He commented on an airplane that was flying overhead. He stopped to listen to the ambulance sirens coming from the street below. And when the cloudy day cleared and the sun came out, Mr. Stevens was distracted by the glint of sunlight on his stainless steel water pitcher. Mr. Stevens was in liver failure, and it was affecting his brain. He had hepatic encephalopathy.

Articulation of Speech

Many clues to organic illness may be discerned by listening carefully to an individual's speech articulation. But once again it is easy to overlook or misinterpret the significance of any findings as well as to let them get in the way of effective communication. For instance, a low volume of speech is common in Parkinson's disease. Not only is this difficult for the interviewer who must strain to hear what is being said, but also it may be misinterpreted to be voluntary on the part of the patient rather than a somatic difficulty with projecting one's voice.

Probably the most commonly encountered difficulty with articulating speech takes the form of slurred speech, which may range from mild and barely interfering with communication to severe and rendering speech virtually unintelligible. Perhaps the most common cause of slurred speech that therapists encounter is intoxication with alcohol or other drugs such as opioids, but, when evaluating a patient with articulation difficulties, it is important not to assume that substances are the cause. Difficulties with speech articulation may be caused by head trauma, strokes, transient episodes of insufficient blood supply to the brain, seizures, brain infections, and so on. In fact, individuals who use drugs and alcohol are also more prone to head trauma, seizures, and other medical conditions. Thus, even if there is evidence of drinking or drug use, assuming that the individual's slurred speech is only the result of the drinking or drug use may become the source of a missed diagnosis.

Production of Language

Difficulties in the use of language (as distinct from difficulties with the articulation of language) may be mild and have almost no impact on communication or may be so severe as to block the flow of virtually all information between patient and therapist. Mild word-finding difficulties may be simply a part of normal aging, but they also may be a side effect from antidepressant medications or, rarely, an early sign of a primary progressive aphasia.

Aphasias are disturbances of language and, when severe, they can render a patient incapable of producing grammatical speech or unable to understand the content of what another individual is saying. There are many kinds of aphasia, but they all result from either a transient dysfunction or a permanent injury that affects the language areas of the brain.

> *John came into his therapy session one Monday and told me that his 42-year-old girlfriend, Samantha, had had a 30-second episode of "talking gibberish" over the weekend. It was just after the dinner guests had arrived.*
>
> *John asked Samantha about it as soon as their friends had departed. Her explanation of the episode was simply, "It was the alcohol." Apparently, just before the dinner party had begun, Samantha had quickly downed a large-bowled, salt-rimmed margarita. "I was really stressed about the meal preparations."*
>
> *Samantha had no headache, no change in vision; she reassured John that she "felt fine." Samantha wasn't worried, but John was. The guests, who had witnessed the meaningless string of utterances, dismissed the episode as just odd and teased John about being a worrywart.*
>
> *I had a different reaction, especially when my questions revealed that Samantha actually had had a small stroke while in her twenties when she had been on birth-control pills. With my encouragement, John prevailed upon Samantha to see her primary care physician. An MRI established that she actually had had multiple small strokes in the past. Very likely this recent episode represented a transient ischemic attack (TIA), in which a small area of the brain that is crucial for the production of language was briefly deprived of sufficient oxygen.*

In addition to aphasias being misinterpreted as psychologically driven events, at times it may be difficult to distinguish aphasia from a thought disorder of the sort that might be seen in an individual with schizophrenia. Thought disorders also render patients less effective at communication.

TROUBLE FINDING THE RIGHT WORDS

A different sort of language difficulty may arise when the patient has difficulty finding words to describe the quality of the experience he or she is having. This is an extremely common problem, even when the patient has intact attention, language, speech, clarity of consciousness, orientation, motivation, memory, insight, and reality testing. If the subjective symptoms of a disease are outside the patient's usual experience, the individual may simply not know how to accurately communicate the problem. Therapists are used to helping patients to find words to describe feelings and experiences they have never before articulated. Here, when the experiences are somatic, cognitive, or neuropsychological, the task is similar.

For instance, patients with sleep disorders ranging from restless legs syndrome to sleep apnea may report simply that they "have insomnia" or "can't sleep." Patients with visual disturbances of all kinds may say that they "can't see" or have "blurry vision." Individuals may use the word *fatigue* to refer to what would more accurately be called depression or apathy, daytime sleepiness or lack of stamina, and the term *anxiety* might be used to refer to a set of bodily sensations, such as a rapid or irregular heartbeat, that might have an underlying physiologic cause, not an emotional source.

Individuals with focal seizures commonly struggle to articulate the unusual sensations they have experienced; this may be akin to trying to describe the vivid experience of a dream. Words simply don't capture some of the truly terrifying, spiritually ecstatic, profoundly revelatory, or eerie otherworldly sensations that may comprise the experience of a seizure. Karen Armstrong, best known for her book *The History of God* (Armstrong, 1993), has written about her own seizure experiences and how difficult it is to communicate what they are like:

> I am trying to describe an experience that has nothing whatever to do with words or ideas and is not amenable to the logic of grammar and neat sentences that put things into an order that makes sense. Maybe I could explain it better if I were a poet. (Armstrong, 2004)

As a clinician, it is crucial to actively work to understand the vocabulary of the patient; it is important to help the patient find the words to accurately describe his or her experiences; and it is especially worth the clinician's and the patient's time to investigate any experiences that seem particularly resistant to being captured and communicated in words, for these may in fact be representative of underlying physical illness.

INSIGHT

Therapists are familiar with patients who have impairments of insight, whether mild or severe. For instance, individuals with personality disorders may regularly use defensive externalization and have little awareness of their own contributions to a difficult relationship, whereas patients with psychotic disorders will have no insight about the lack of veracity of their paranoid beliefs. In fact, the lack of insight helps to define these latter notions as delusional in nature. These problems with insight regularly create challenges to establishing communication and maintaining a therapeutic alliance between patient and clinician.

Physical illnesses may produce a variety of different sorts of disturbances in insight. In some instances, the difficulties with insight will mimic the kinds of impairments that one sees in the psychological disorders, ranging from garden-variety externalization to paranoia. When evaluating a patient, it may be impossible for the clinician to ascertain how much the individual's use of externalization or paranoia is a defense that is characteristic of the individual and how much it is the effect of some underlying physical disorder. The rule of thumb is that when the individual's problems with insight represent a change from his or her usual mode of behavior, they may be a significant clue to the presence of an underlying physical problem.

Innumerable organic conditions may cause a frank psychosis with a lack of insight. This has been a subject of interest for centuries. The mad hatter was probably suffering from a toxic psychosis because of exposure to the mercury fumes that were used in making felt for hats. *Myxedema madness* is an old term for a psychosis associated with hypothyroidism. Tertiary syphilis may cause a schizophrenic-like psychosis or megalomania, a grandiose, manic psychosis. Psychedelic drugs, speed, phencyclidine (PCP), and other street drugs may generate psychotic states, as may withdrawal syndromes from alcohol and other substances. Delusional beliefs are often seen in patients with dementias. The list of organic psychotic states goes on and on.

With patients who are frankly psychotic, the disruption in communication is obvious. These individuals may be profoundly disorganized, agitated, and out of touch with reality. They may be preoccupied with incidents that are clearly delusional or hallucinatory, and, in addition, they may be terrified. Any of these mental status changes that commonly accompany psychosis are capable of interfering substantially with effective communication.

A failure of insight also may take the form of profound denial or apparent lack of concern (*la belle indifference*), even in the face of an obvious physical disability such as the paralysis of a limb. Contrary to the once-popular belief that *la belle indifference* is a sure sign of hysteria or of a conversion disorder, in fact, denial and lack of concern may be diagnostically highly significant for organic disease. Frontal lobe brain involvement is strongly associated with a lack of insight. Typically, certain brain disorders are also associated with a fairly characteristic timeline of changes in insight. For instance, insight about a loss of cognitive functions (such as memory or the ability to orient in space) is generally lost after the early phases of Alzheimer's disease, whereas insight is often preserved until fairly late in another common form of dementia, called Lewy body dementia.

Another dramatic organic syndrome in which patients are entirely lacking in insight about their deficit is called *neglect*. These individuals display complete inattention to half of their spatial environment. If you were to approach these patients from their left, they would have no

La Belle Indifference

awareness of your existence, but if you were to enter their visual field from their right, they would respond entirely normally. At first, you might not notice that these individuals were having any trouble, but if you asked them to fill in a clock face, they would place all the numbers, 1 to 12, crowded along the right circumference of the circle. And if you happened to be with them during dinnertime, you could observe them eating only the food that was on the right side of their plate and displaying no awareness at all of the food on the left side. This syndrome of unilateral neglect may be seen following strokes that involve the right parietal lobe of the brain.

A lack of insight may not only be a manifestation of an underlying physical condition but may also indirectly mask that condition by rendering the patient unaware of his or her symptoms. Any failure of insight, whether in the form of denial, absence of concern, lack of awareness, externalization, or frank psychosis, reflects some distortion of reality. This presents a challenge for the clinician in establishing a working relationship with the patient, because the patient and the therapist do not agree on the nature of the problem. There is an elephant in the room. Failure of insight may also interfere with the patient's trust in the clinician or the patient's sense of safety within the health-care institution. These possible consequences of impaired insight are all potential obstacles to effective communication.

Few, If Any, Physical Signs or Symptoms

Because of a paucity or absence of physical clues at the time of presentation, some somatic disorders will look like purely psychological conditions. Initially, patients with these conditions may exhibit none of the usual signals to alert us that we are faced with an organic illness. In other words, nothing makes these conditions stand out as different from the multitude of patients with garden-variety mental disorders. These are the disorders that leave no physical evidence and get lost in the crowd. Statistics work against the clinician in identifying them.

Consider your chances of catching a culprit who is described by witnesses as being "a young woman, about 5 feet 4 inches tall, with brown hair." Now contrast that with your odds of finding a criminal who is "a young woman, 6 feet 4 inches tall, with red hair." You could fairly easily round up for questioning all the over-6-feet-tall, red-haired young women in Boston, because there wouldn't be that many of them. But don't even think about trying to bring in all the women who are 5 feet 4 inches tall with brown hair. There are tens of thousands! You simply can't question them all.

The same is true of somatic disorders whose characteristic psychological symptoms mimic garden-variety anxiety disorders, affective disorders, psychotic disorders, and the like. Here, too, it is impractical to thoroughly scrutinize every patient who presents with these kinds of symptoms. There are so many patients with these disorders and, comparatively speaking, so few in whom the cause is an underlying physical condition. It is simply not practical to medically investigate every patient in depth, if there is nothing at all atypical or suspicious about the clinical situation.

Here is how Dr. E. K. Koranyi put it in his important paper on this subject in 1979:

> Nonspecific behavioral and mood alterations often represent the very first and, occasionally for prolonged periods of time, the one single and exclusive sign of an undetected physical illness. Flagrantly and convincingly "psychological" in nature on presentation, such masked physical conditions frequently mislead the examiner and obliterate any further medical consideration, resulting in misdiagnosis and thus, inevitably, in treatment gone astray. (Koranyi, 1979, p. 414)

What is a practitioner to do? The key is to maintain awareness that sometimes what appears to be a garden-variety mental disorder is actually the early onset of a somatic condition. Also, keep in mind that someone who seems to have an uncomplicated mental disorder may possibly develop a new physical problem while under your care. It is important to maintain your flexibility. If the patient does not respond as expected to the usual treatment, if new mental status symptoms emerge, or if physical signs or symptoms develop, be prepared to rethink your diagnosis or diagnoses, to extend your investigation by asking more questions or seeking consultation.

Three types of disorders that commonly fall into this category of somatic conditions that present with mental symptoms but without physical symptoms are (1) organic conditions that begin with mental status changes and, only after some period of time, go on to cause overt somatic manifestations; (2) disorders that involve discrete brain regions that result in mental status changes but no physical symptoms; and (3) side effects of medications and other substances that also may be confined only to the realm of behavioral or mental status change.

ORGANIC ILLNESSES THAT BEGIN WITH MENTAL STATUS CHANGES ALONE

Mental status changes may be the initial signs, the harbingers, of certain organic illnesses. In other words, early on in the course of these diseases, the only clue that something is amiss may be depression, anxiety, or some other neuropsychological symptoms. Only later (sometimes years later) do clear, prominent, physical signs and symptoms emerge that make it clear that the individual does not have a straightforward psychological disorder. Here is an example:

> *For the first time in his life, Roy was depressed. Although he had felt neglected during his childhood, this 56-year-old, self-made businessman had not let those difficult early times stop him. He found pride in having learned to find strength within himself.*
>
> *"I was going strong, until I was hit with this. I used to be oblivious. I had no idea what people with depression went through," he said. "Now I know. It saps all the life out of you."*
>
> *The usual therapy and medications helped, but only somewhat. But everyone had to admit that it wasn't at all clear why now, for the first time in his life, Roy was depressed. An entire year passed before the reason for Roy's depressive state became clear. It was first noted on a routine annual visit to his primary care doctor. When Roy walked from the waiting room into the office, there was a bit of rigidity in the way he held his body, and he didn't have much natural arm swing. Roy also had a very mild tremor characterized by "pill-rolling" hand movements, as though he was fidgeting by rolling imaginary wads of paper into little balls. The primary care doctor knew that Roy was not on any medications that might have produced these findings, such as certain antipsychotic drugs. Within moments of first seeing his patient, the primary care doctor knew that Roy had Parkinson's disease.*

Patients who eventually develop Parkinson's disease will frequently report that they had experienced long periods of depression and/or fatigue before they were diagnosed.

There are other diseases with prominent psychological symptoms early on. Cancer of the pancreas can present initially with severe depression and anxiety. These psychological symptoms may or may not be accompanied by minor gastrointestinal complaints at the outset. A severe depression may also be an early prominent symptom of lung cancer, while the long-standing smoker's cough may receive less notice.

Huntington's disease is a devastating genetic disorder known to produce prominent involuntary writhing movements and dementia. However, years before any of those obvious manifestations appear, Huntington's disease may begin with alterations in behavior that appear to be purely psychological: irritability, changes in personality, increased alcohol intake, anxiety, depression, suicidal behavior.

Wilson's disease is a treatable, genetic disorder involving the body's handling of copper. This disorder can initially manifest with changes in personality, depression, and other alterations in mental state that appear to be psychological. Eventually, without treatment, deposits of excess copper in body organs, including the brain, will lead to physical symptoms and death.

ORGANIC DISORDERS THAT INVOLVE CERTAIN BRAIN REGIONS

Disturbances that involve certain regions of the brain may also present without physical symptoms, making it easy for clinicians to think that the fundamental problem is purely psychological. The specific areas of the brain affected will determine the neuropsychological symptoms that surface. In some situations there may be only changes in personality or memory, social comportment, spatial orientation, or higher levels of cognitive functioning, such as abstract thinking and problem solving. A great variety of physical conditions that affect specific areas of the brain may present with defined changes of this sort. Following are some common examples.

When the frontal lobes of the brain are affected (e.g., by tumors or certain degenerative neurological diseases), the patient may present with only a change in personality and few, if any, physical symptoms. Many types of dementia, Alzheimer's disease being the most common, will affect memory and other high-level, cognitive abilities but will cause no apparent bodily disturbance for many years.

Focal seizures are also common and frequently masquerade as psychological disorders because they may produce only short-lived, purely experiential disturbances. The symptoms of a seizure will depend on which parts of the brain are triggered when the abnormal electrical discharge that constitutes the seizure is taking place. Fear is the most common symptom, especially feelings of dread or impending doom. But a very long list of other disturbances that may seem psychological can be caused by seizures, including fleeting hallucinatory smells, tastes, visions, or sounds; a sense of someone standing nearby or that the world is uncanny; or a feeling that one has been in an unfamiliar situation before (déjà vu) or that one has never been in a place that is actually familiar (jamais vu).

Transient ischemic attacks (TIAs) also involve short-lived disruptions of function in limited regions of the brain. That these are episodic, passing phenomena makes it easier to mistakenly interpret the symptoms they produce as being psychologically driven. To understand this somewhat better, let's look back for a moment at the case in which Samantha started "talking gibberish" at her dinner party.

In reconstructing the events of that evening after the fact, it was clear that Samantha had had a TIA. But, at the time, it was easy for her friends to dismiss her symptoms, given the circumstances. If Samantha had been

70 or 80 years old and had had a history of cardiovascular disease, the context would have been altogether different and, likely, the response of the group would also have been different. But Samantha was young. She had been feeling fine before she started "talking gibberish." She had no physical symptoms at all. "Talking funny" was considered by the group to be a psychological matter, not a physical one, especially since it had been so transient. Also, Samantha had no ill after-effects following the brief episode, and she had an alternative explanation for the incident, namely her alcohol intake.

Samantha was someone who didn't like to worry. In fact, everyone at the dinner party had a strong wish for nothing to be the matter; everyone wanted to have a good time. And group pressure led Samantha's boyfriend to suppress all but a mild expression of his worries. When he told me about the dinner party in therapy, he was burdened with concern that perhaps he had made too much of the incident. In this case, with no obviously physical symptoms, the role of wishful thinking and denial is laid bare.

Side Effects of Medication and Other Substances

Of all the covert organic sources of psychological symptoms that hide out, undetected in the lives of patients, medications and substances of all kinds are arguably the most common. Prescription and nonprescription medications, including herbal preparations and nutritional supplements, are capable of causing depression, anxiety, or other mental status changes as lone side effects. Sometimes these side effect symptoms are easy to diagnose: when they are dramatic (such as visual hallucinations); when they are noted to follow closely on the heels of starting a new medication; and when the symptoms are widely recognized to be side effects associated with the particular drug that was taken. But more often than we like to think, a depressive picture, a state of anxiety, or even psychosis may emerge gradually following the introduction of a new drug or as more drugs are added. The patient, the patient's family, and, most significantly, the patient's caregivers may not realize what the true source of the problem is. Let's revisit Ms. McCartney's story from Chapter 2.

A dear and trusted colleague called to ask if I would be willing to help a family she had met at her gym. The family consisted of Mrs. Rebecca McCartney (the mother), Kevin (the father), and their two grown children, Frank and Alexandra. The problem was that Rebecca McCartney had changed. Kevin, Frank, and Alexandra all seemed to notice and agree, but none of them had talked about this to Rebecca.

My colleague arranged for an extended consultation. Initially I spoke with Alexandra, the daughter, on the phone. Here is what she told me: Her mother used to be a talkative, energetic woman, filled with "positive energy," busy with friends and community activities. Now she simply sat at home. "Who knows what she does all day!" Alexandra stated. Mother also had little to say when her daughter called her on the phone. Initially, Alexandra had thought her mother was angry with her. In fact, she even called her brother and asked, "Do you know what Mom is mad at me about?" Frank replied that he had been thinking their mom was mad at him!

The family was spurred into action after they received outside validation of their worries. Rebecca and her husband attended a spring wedding at which they saw old friends after a hiatus of 2 years. After the wedding, those friends tactfully wrote to the children. They said that they hadn't wanted to intrude, but they were terribly concerned about Rebecca, who seemed so different from her usual self, so much less talkative, so withdrawn.

After helping the family members to think through how they would talk to Rebecca about their worries, it wasn't long before Rebecca herself called to make an appointment. Here is what she told me: She said that she had been aware of feeling like she was "slogging through water," slowed down physically and mentally. "I feel old," she confessed. She added that as a child she had thought to herself, "I'll know when I'm old, because, only then, will I no longer enjoy springtime." Now she felt that she was getting close to that.

Rebecca did not volunteer that she felt depressed, but when I asked her if she did, she readily assented. I was puzzled as to why Rebecca hadn't complained or sought help on her own. I found myself thinking of this as a lack of motivational drive. I thought of her as exhibiting a failure to initiate. And I conceptualized Rebecca's "moving slowly" as psychomotor retardation combined, perhaps, with this apathy.

Though Rebecca did not have a classical depression, I started her on an antidepressant medication. This helped her mood, but her psychomotor retardation did not get better. In subsequent consultations I began to search for more clues to answer the question of what had happened to Rebecca. Was this simply an atypical depression? Or was an underlying medical problem leading to a change in Rebecca's personality including a depressive mood?

Rebecca could identify no precipitant for her depression. Her mother had died about 18 months earlier, but Rebecca was sure that the changes she felt had begun before her mother had died. In fact, she remembered clearly that she hadn't visited her mother very much in the few months before her mother's death. "I just couldn't get myself going. And that wasn't like me," she added with insight.

All the same, I wondered. Maybe Rebecca had anticipated her mother's death, couldn't quite face it, and now felt guilty about not having visited her sufficiently often during those last months of her mother's life. With careful inquiry, we began to hone in on exactly when the changes in Rebecca had started. We got everyone in on the detective work. Rebecca recalled that she had developed hypertension around the time that things took a downturn. Her husband, Kevin, who was a patent lawyer and a very reliable observer, was sure that the changes started after she began the medication to lower her blood pressure.

Even though depression, apathy, and psychomotor retardation were not listed as side effects of the blood pressure medication Rebecca was taking, her internist was willing to try changing this antihypertensive medication to something different. Sure enough, when the medication was changed, Rebecca regained her spontaneity, her zest for life, and her ability to initiate activities. And she no longer needed the antidepressant I had prescribed for her. Everyone in the family agreed, "Rebecca was back!"

There are many reasons that medication side effects are readily overlooked as covert causes of psychological symptoms. Often there is a lack of knowledge about the many possible side effects of any particular medication. Some side effects are rare or even undocumented. Also, elderly patients frequently require lower doses of medications and may have side effects from standard doses.

In addition, for patients who are on more than one medication, unanticipated drug-drug interactions may emerge. A lack of coordination and communication in the delivery of medical care often makes this problem difficult to sort out. Several physicians may be caring for the patient, each of whom could be prescribing medications, unaware of what the others are giving the patient, or even in the dark about the fact that other physicians are involved. Or patients simply may not tell their traditional doctors about the nontraditional preparations they are taking. Frequently there is no updated, master list of all the medications and herbal remedies that the patient utilizes on a regular basis.

Many clinicians have a story like this one:

"I had a patient with thyroid disease who was quite depressed and anxious. But, for some reason we couldn't get her thyroid replacement medications right. So, one day I asked the patient to bring all her medications with her to the next appointment. She arrived with a shopping bag, filled to the top."

"It took us quite some time to get her off all the supplements and herbals and unnecessary medications, some prescribed by other physicians. Eventually, we sorted the situation out and got the patient better."

Individuals commonly believe that herbal or organic preparations, folk mixtures and tonics, dietary supplements or nonprescription remedies aren't really drugs at all and that they certainly couldn't cause profound mental changes. Unfortunately, this is not true. Think of it this way: It is inconsistent to think that an herbal might be strong enough to cure but not strong enough to cause side effects or problematic interactions with traditional prescription or over-the-counter medications.

Moreover, scientific studies have shown that the manufacturing of these dietary supplements is not scrupulously controlled and that consumers cannot count on what is actually in the bottle that they buy (Cohen, 2009). Dosages vary and contaminants abound, including toxic metals, pesticides, microorganisms, and even prescription medications. On occasion, folk remedies have been found to contain arsenic or radioactive substances. Of course, none of these components are found on the label; nonetheless, these ingredients may lead to neuropsychological symptoms, either alone or in combination with other substances the patient is using.

This section would not be complete without mentioning the plethora of potential mental status and behavioral changes that one may see in individuals when they withdraw from or use and abuse substances such as alcohol, tobacco, caffeine, or the large variety of illegal drugs commonly consumed. Given that use of these substances is widespread and that their presence in the clinical picture is often underreported or entirely covert, it is crucial for clinicians to be aware of the power of these psychoactive substances to produce psychological symptoms.

Disguised by an Unusual Presentation

Common diseases that present in an uncommon fashion are known to be commonly misdiagnosed. Put another way, it is easy to miss a diagnosis when a practitioner thinks that the diagnosis "couldn't be X" because "X doesn't look like this clinically." Although diseases do have typical presentations, they do not always arrive in classical form, and when a disorder presents in a disguised or atypical fashion, it is especially challenging to make an accurate diagnosis.

One obvious reason for a missed or delayed diagnosis in these cases is that, in the clinician's mind, the actual diagnosis has been ruled out early on. A breadth of knowledge and experience are needed for a clinician to be familiar with the variety of disguises in which a single disorder might arrive. The following are examples of some common somatic disorders and the atypical mental presentations that might fool clinicians and throw them off track.

The patient is depressed and lethargic; her diagnosis is *hyper-thyroidism*. How is that possible? After all, as the name implies, hyperthyroidism is associated with increased metabolism, with being restless, anxious, having a racing heart, feeling hot (even in the winter), and so on. But, some patients with hyperthyroidism, especially the elderly, may present with an atypical, lethargic picture.

The patient has mild depression, chronic daytime fatigue, and difficulty with concentration. He does not snore, but his diagnosis is eventually found to be sleep apnea. How is that possible? In *obstructive* sleep apnea, as an individual enters deep sleep there is increasing muscle relaxation that leads to the partial collapse of airways; snoring occurs when air is forced through these narrowing passageways. But *central* sleep apnea is caused by a different mechanism. For reasons that are not known, the central nervous system simply signals pauses in breathing during sleep. In central sleep apnea, there may be no snoring at all.

A first-year student in a top-ranked psychology PhD program is in academic trouble. The instructors note that the student turns in his reports well past their due dates and that his writing is "sloppy." Faculty members theorize that perhaps the student is depressed or that life circumstances are making it difficult for him to perform at his highest level. But it turns out that this student has a significant verbal learning disability that had gone undetected until now. How is that possible? Learning difficulties of all kinds, including problems with attention, are often masked in individuals who are very bright and who work hard. These individuals may have performed well in other situations in the past by finding ways to compensate for their cognitive inefficiencies, but if they enter an arena in which the demands exceed their capacity for adaptation, their disabilities may become apparent. This may occur when individuals ramp up to the expectations of college-level work, graduate school, full-time employment, or a promotion. Even PhD students or CEOs may have learning disabilities or ADHD.

The patient has fluctuating difficulties with erectile dysfunction over the past year, and the problem has been getting worse. Sometimes he is unable to sustain an erection, but then, at other times, he has no problems at all with arousal or sexual performance. The patient and his partner believe there must be deep-seated psychological reasons for these difficulties. Why else would there be times when everything goes just fine? Well, impotence is not necessarily an all-or-none phenomenon, especially early on in the development of an erectile dysfunction that is caused by the very common maladies of diabetes and atherosclerosis. And that is what this patient had. While the dynamics of his relationship contributed to the clinical picture, a gradually developing, underlying physical vulnerability was the stage on which the psychodynamic drama played out.

These are just a few examples of how common disorders might not arrive in the packaging that one expects.

The Absence of Something That Should Be There

A particularly elusive clue is the absence of something that you would expect to find. Practitioners refer to this as a significant negative finding. For instance, the diagnosis might seem obvious when a new patient staggers into the emergency room, looking disheveled and slurring his speech, but what if there is no odor of alcohol on his breath? The absence of this piece of corroborating evidence might be the first clue that tips the clinician off to the fact that this patient is not intoxicated. Perhaps he has a subdural hematoma from a recent episode of head trauma; perhaps he has an infection affecting his brain.

The absence of certain historical clues can be significant. Consider an individual who presents with a first manic episode late in life. Mental health clinicians are familiar with mania as one phase of bipolar disorder, but it is important to keep in mind that manic episodes may also be associated with a variety of medical conditions, including multiple sclerosis or the use of corticosteroid medications. If a patient has made it through much of adulthood without a depressive or manic episode, and if there is no family history of bipolar disorder, it would be wise to rule out other diagnostic causes for this individual's current symptoms. The absence of a personal or family history of bipolar symptoms would be crucial data, indeed.

The following scenario is yet another example of the sort of clinical situation in which the absence of some expected finding is a most important clue. A primary care physician refers a patient for psychotherapy after a medical workup has failed to identify a physical cause for the patient's somatic symptoms. The patient might have unexplained abdominal discomfort, tingling of the feet, blurry vision, loss of appetite, fatigue, weakness of an arm, or any of a myriad of other possible problems. The patient has been told that his or her symptoms are caused by stress or anxiety or that he or she has somatization disorder. Sometimes this is accurate. We know that masked depressions are common and that anxiety and stress-induced symptoms are rampant in the climate of modern life. But the literature abounds with warnings that somatization disorder, conversion disorder, depression, or anxiety disorder are not diagnoses that should be made simply on the basis of ruling out an organic condition. Rather, these diagnoses should be made only when the actual criteria for that particular diagnosis are met.

As the therapist, you may find that your patient doesn't seem to be under a lot of pressure (other than perhaps from having unexplained medical symptoms) and doesn't appear to have an underlying depression or anxiety disorder (even when psychological testing is performed). You may even find that after a good try at psychological exploration with your patient in psychotherapy, you honestly can't find a substantial, persuasive psychodynamic explanation for the patient's symptoms. This is a situation in which the most important clue you have may be the absence of an emotionally cogent, psychological explanation that is also powerful enough, meaningful enough, to be the cause of the patient's symptoms.

It is common for patients to suffer for years with certain diseases before they are correctly diagnosed: narcolepsy, Huntington's disease, temporal lobe epilepsy, Lyme disease, syphilis, multiple sclerosis, to name just a few. Many patients are in therapy during this lag time. Often they are trying to work on psychological problems in the hopes of ameliorating their physical symptoms. Though their psychotherapy may be helpful in many ways, it is futile to expect these sorts of physical diseases to respond to a talking cure. Indeed, in these situations it is far more useful for the clinician to squarely face the lack of evidence for a psychological etiology and help the patient to seek another medical opinion.

Here's a short, but dramatic story in which the most important clue was the absence of something that should have been there.

> *Evelyn Crabtree was a fastidious 35-year-old woman, an accountant who owned a two-family house and kept it, as the saying goes, neat as a pin. When Evelyn's physician friends, Jim and Shana, were visiting from out of town, they were shocked to encounter an intense smell in the hallway from the downstairs tenant's cats.*
>
> *"What a terrible odor! You must be upset about it," they remarked.*
>
> *Well, their dear friend Evelyn hadn't noticed the smell. This was truly astounding to Jim and Shana. After the visit, Jim and Shana strategized and sensitively discussed their concerns with Evelyn. They encouraged her to find out what was the matter with her sense of smell since it seemed to be absent. A medical work-up revealed that Mrs. Crabtree had a benign frontal lobe brain tumor.*

As you might surmise, congestion, polyps, or other problems in the nasal passages are usually the reason for a disturbance in the sense of smell. And these sorts of difficulties are generally reversible and are not significant as indicators of brain dysfunction. But, in other cases, the olfactory (smell) centers of the brain may be affected by organic disturbances. It is known that the sense of smell may be impaired in Alzheimer's disease, following some instances of head trauma, in Huntington's disease, multiple sclerosis, as well as in schizophrenia. And, as with Mrs. Crabtree, these patients may not be aware that they have lost this capability.

Chapter 4

Patterns in Time

Introduction

Often the most important information you can gather in deciding whether your patient has an underlying organic condition is the manner in which an individual's symptoms have emerged and developed over time. All illnesses have a time course. They begin and then evolve, usually in some fashion that is characteristic for the disorder. That evolution may take place over minutes, days, weeks, years, or, when one looks at family histories, even over generations.

Unfortunately, rather than having the opportunity to observe a patient as his or her illness begins and then advances, we clinicians are virtually always walking into the theater some time after the play has begun. We might arrive only after the situation has escalated to crisis proportions and propelled the patient and family into the emergency room. We might pick up the story when the patient has for some reason decided to seek psychotherapy or couples counseling. Or perhaps we will walk in when a colleague finds that his or her patient is not getting better and seeks consultation. But in every situation, much has transpired before we begin to learn about what has been going on.

Taking a careful history helps us catch up on the beginning of the story. Deciphering the narrative timeline of an illness and its evolution within the context of the patient's life is at the heart of all clinical care and especially at the heart of making a diagnosis. It is crucial to take an excellent history and find out what happened before the moment of your first clinical encounter with a patient. You want to know when and how it all started and what has happened along the way.

In addition, because you have walked in during the play, you also do not know how the story is going to end. As you watch the production unfold, you might find yourself confused at times. Or you might think that the story is leading in one direction, but after awhile the plot might twist and turn and lead to an outcome altogether different from the one you had anticipated.

Looking Backward

The Nature of the Onset Helps Differentiate Physical From Psychological

Learning how a patient's difficulties began will give you crucial data as you try to decipher the complex factors that may be contributing to the clinical picture, including the possible role of somatic disease. A careful history of the onset of the present illness, often including information from knowledgeable individuals other than the patient, can give an invaluable perspective.

It is important to go back to the very beginning of the story. Often you will first hear from patients about the latest episode or crisis or about what is most upsetting them at the moment. But the earliest symptoms of an individual's disorder may have begun years before, and you want to turn your attention to those very first signals that something was amiss.

Getting a Baseline Picture

Looking back to the onset of a patient's illness means returning in your inquiry to that point in time when the person was "doing just fine" or "felt like his or her self." In this way it is easier to see the contrast between what the patient was like *then* compared with how he or she is *now*. What was your patient really like before he or she got sick? How have life circumstances and illness taken their toll? This information helps give you a crucial broad and empathic perspective on your patient's life and also provides you with clues to the nature of the problems that have led to the current clinical picture.

It is often difficult to establish an individual's baseline level of functioning, but this is a challenge worth pursuing. Consider the following common situation.

> *A college junior named Sofia comes in to see you for therapy because she's "struggling in school and feeling kind of unhappy." She's failing two of her four courses and is considering dropping out of college. What is causing Sofia to be in this kind of difficulty? And how will you help her? The answer to these questions will depend a lot on how the Sofia who is now in your office compares with Sofia when she was at her best.*
>
> *Let's say that you learn that things got worse for Sofia just 6 months ago. The pivotal event may have been an automobile accident in which she sustained a head injury; or it may have been learning that her parents were getting divorced or that her boyfriend was killed in a military operation; or it*

may be that Sofia doesn't really know why she started to have trouble, in which case you would need to search for the causative factors, including covert organic disorders.

Whatever the precipitant, overt or covert, your whole understanding of the problem would be affected by what you learned about the kind of person Sofia was prior to 6 months ago. If Sofia had always been an honors student as well as a social butterfly, someone with good long-term friendships and a devoted family, you would know that she had fallen very far indeed from her baseline. And you would have to search for a diagnostic and dynamic understanding that would have the power to entirely destabilize a bright, effective young woman with a good social network.

On the other hand, let's say that Sofia had been a C student with ADHD who always had to "work hard to get those Cs." And perhaps this Sofia had been a loner who tended to feel left out socially. Perhaps she was the first person in her family to go to college and she sensed that her parents didn't understand the stresses she was under. Now you would begin your thought process with the knowledge that, whatever happened 6 months ago, it happened to a young woman who had few psychological reserves or social supports. This Sofia was already using all of her coping skills and was just getting by. She was already in a fragile state of equilibrium. It wouldn't take as much to destabilize this second Sofia.

The two different baselines would inform your diagnostic thinking. It would influence which therapeutic approaches you would try. The meaning of any precipitating event would be unique for each of the different Sofias. Their natural network of social supports would be vastly different. And the type of academic and administrative support they would each require would have to be tailored to their very different situations.

THE NATURE OF THE ONSET HELPS TO CLEARLY SEE THE DISORDER

Another benefit of making a careful inquiry into the nature of a disorder's onset is that different disorders will make their entrances into the lives of patients in ways that tend to be characteristic for the illness. If you are seeing a patient for the first time after a long and protracted deterioration in functioning, you may only be able to figure out the patient's diagnosis by looking back at the onset.

Aamir was a psychology student who worked part-time on the night shift in a residence home for chronic mental patients. This was a good opportunity for Aamir to earn some extra money while simultaneously learning firsthand about chronic mental illness. Aamir found that he was especially interested in one particular resident, a 32-year-old man named Allen. Although Allen kept mostly to himself, sometimes he would wander out of his room and engage in long conversations with Aamir about deep topics like "how mind emerges out of the brain" or "the eerie feeling of knowing how infinitely small and irrelevant one's life is in the giant universe while simultaneously experiencing one's own life as all important."

During these conversations, apart from some pressure of speech and tendency to be fidgety, Allen seemed pretty normal. But, there were other times when Allen was obviously psychotic. He would talk to himself in mumbling tones; his facial expressions and gestures would shift rapidly from angry to exuberant; he seemed to be actively engaged in conversation with an invisible someone. Allen also had a strong belief that his suffering was God's way of helping the world. "My suffering is necessary so that the world will be healed." This seemed to help Allen by giving meaning to his psychic pain.

From Aamir's perspective, Allen seemed exceptionally intelligent and somewhat different from most of the other chronic patients. It was difficult for Aamir to articulate what exactly was different about Allen. Perhaps it was that Allen was more emotionally animated and more interpersonally connected—when he wasn't overtly psychotic.

One night when things were especially quiet and Aamir didn't have much reading to do for school, he leafed through Allen's chart. The various entries agreed on Allen's mental status. He had grandiose delusions. He was suspicious. He had auditory hallucinations. He was psychotic. Also, he did not have flat affect. He could be circumstantial, giving too much information before getting to the point in conversations, but he did not have loose associations.

Although most of the notes agreed that Allen had chronic paranoid schizophrenia, a few diagnosed him with organic brain syndrome. This made Aamir curious. So, the next time Aamir talked with Allen, he slipped in questions about how Allen's illness had started. He also took the opportunity to chat with Allen's mother when she came to drop off some brownies for her son and the residence staff.

Here is what Aamir's inquiry turned up. Allen's illness truly began when he was 5 years old. Before that time he had been a vibrant, vivacious, bright, inquisitive, simply delightful little boy. But then, on one bright autumn afternoon, everything changed. Allen's mother said she would never, ever forget what happened. She had kept "Allie" home from school because he had a bad cold. He was taking a long nap, too long. Mother checked on little Allen and simply could not wake him. After a panicked call to the pediatrician, she rushed him to the hospital, where he was treated for acute meningo-encephalitis. He survived, but he was never the same again.

> *Allen and his family had been on a long and tortuous journey before arriving at this residence for chronic mental patients, but it was not the usual road that individuals with schizophrenia take. Allen did not have schizophrenia. His illness had started at an earlier age than patients with schizophrenia. His psychosis had resulted from the early effects of a serious infection in his brain.*

ACUTE OR CHRONIC?

To differentiate a psychological from an organic disorder, it is often helpful to think about whether the illness onset was acute or chronic. In other words, did the individual experience a rapid change or even one that was altogether sudden? Or was there a slow, gradual onset to the illness? When there is a gradual onset of symptoms, a disorder may be organic or functional. But when the patient's mental state or behavior changes suddenly, the disorder is more likely to be organic.

With many organic conditions an individual may be in fine health one day and experience profound mental deterioration the next day. Some examples of medical disorders of this sort include meningitis, seizures, head trauma, bleeding into the brain, poisoning, a medication side effect, toxicity, withdrawal, or a drug-drug interaction. These are conditions with an *acute* onset; they come on suddenly and generally have very prominent symptoms in the mental sphere.

The clinical picture of these acute medical conditions is in stark contrast to those organic diseases with a *chronic* course. The latter have a gradual onset and are generally more difficult to distinguish from the so-called functional disorders that also have a gradual onset.

Other than an acute psychological reaction to traumatic news or events, psychological disorders almost always manifest with a gradual, even insidious, emergence of symptoms in the mental sphere, which may worsen and eventually reach a crisis. The onset may appear to be sudden, but careful inquiry will reveal that, actually, there has been a gradual evolution of the disorder over time, not simply an abrupt crisis. When asked, individuals will reveal that they have been experiencing such things as mounting tension, a buildup of stress, an increasing sense of alienation, or growing, inner conflict. They may have shared these feelings with no one, until the crisis point.

In summary then, as a rule of thumb, a truly acute change in mental status and/or behavior is likely to have been generated by an organic condition, whereas a disorder that began with gradual changes might be psychological and/or organic.

AGE AT ONSET

The age of an individual when symptoms first began is crucial information, because disorders of all kinds have typical ages of onset. This means that, statistically speaking, most people who get a specific disorder, whether it is psychological or organic, are likely to be between certain ages. This knowledge can be a great help in making a difficult diagnosis. It can help you to know which organic disorders your patient is most likely to have, given his or her age. And it can put you on alert for a psychological masquerade if a patient seems to have a disorder that is unusual for his or her age.

As an example, typically multiple sclerosis begins during young adulthood or early middle age. Keep in mind that these data are statistical. *Most* individuals with this disorder will have their first symptoms beginning in young adulthood or early middle age, *but not all individuals*; some will have a younger or older age of onset. Nonetheless, being aware of the usual age of onset is one important factor in helping you to figure out *how likely* it is that your patient has multiple sclerosis.

Multiple sclerosis may be a difficult diagnosis to make, because the clinical presentation lends itself to misinterpretation. The symptoms result from randomly scattered damage to the fatty sheaths that insulate nerves, making the neural pathways inefficient at transmitting electrical signals. Multiple sclerosis begins with discrete but transient episodes that may seem to be purely psychological in origin, especially because they may be spaced out over years, even decades, and often are accompanied by depression or euphoria. The random, scattered, and fleeting nature of the patient's tingling sensations, weakness, fatigue, clumsiness, blurred vision, and other neurological symptoms are easily misread as conversion reactions. So, the next time you see a young woman in your office who is working in her first job out of college, having a hard time adjusting, feeling depressed, and complaining of odd and transient physical symptoms, don't think "hysteria." Think, "This is a *young* woman. I have to consider the possibility that she might have multiple sclerosis."

Another possible tip-off that you are dealing with a psychological masquerade is when an individual has what appears to be a psychological disorder with an inappropriate age of onset. Keeping in mind the natural history of the psychological disorders, especially the usual age of onset, will make it easy to recognize this important clue to the likely presence of an organic condition.

As an example, a first episode of what looks like schizophrenia at age 55 is much more likely to be the result of a covert medical problem. Although schizophrenia can present later in life, it much more typically begins before age 40. Numerous organic conditions can produce psychotic episodes later in life. Here are just a few examples: partial seizure disorders; Lewy body disease (a common dementia) may produce hallucinations and delusions; systemic lupus erythematosis may produce psychosis when it affects the blood vessels of the brain.

Similarly, mania presenting for the first time in a 52-year-old individual with no history of a mood disorder is quite atypical; this should make you suspicious that this manic episode is not the expression of bipolar disorder. There are other causes of mania-like presentations; perhaps the patient has been given corticosteroid medication, or has been taking amphetamines or cocaine; perhaps this is a manic episode secondary to a brain lesion, Cushing's syndrome with the production of excessive cortisol, or multiple sclerosis. The take-home message here is that a psychological disorder that presents at an unusual age of onset should lead you to wonder about whether you have the correct diagnosis.

When it comes to age, it is also important to be aware of another set of statistics that reflect the natural tendency for clinicians to think about younger patients and older patients in different ways. When younger individuals have physical problems that are generating a psychological picture, these underlying diagnoses are more likely to be missed. Clinicians are aware that younger patients are less likely than older patients to have organic disorders, and thus they are more prone to assume that a young person with mental status changes has a psychological disorder. This may lead to settling on a psychological diagnosis without a thorough investigation, as exemplified in this next case.

When Shari came to see me for a consultation, she told me about how irritated she had been with her first therapist. Shari was an especially bright 25-year-old when she sought psychotherapy for the first time. What had prompted her entrance into therapy was a sense of "desperation" about finding a man. She wanted to get married and have children, and, although Shari had many good friends and was beloved at her job as a personal assistant to a wealthy woman, she had been feeling lonely and worried that she would never find someone who would truly love her.

In the therapy, she had complained of "always feeling tired." Her therapist believed that Shari was mildly depressed and that her prominent fatigue was a consequence of this depression. Shari wasn't so sure about this theory, though she had no better explanation for her fatigue. But her therapist's hypothesis did not address why Shari also had begun to experience increasing numbness and tingling in her feet.

Because Shari was a long-standing vegetarian, her internist decided to check her vitamin B12 level as part of her routine annual exam. "The level was virtually zero!" Shari reported. Vegetarians may deplete their vitamin

B12 stores if they don't either eat enough foods containing this necessary vitamin or take supplements. But Shari's problem had a different source. It seemed that Shari had pernicious anemia, an impaired ability to absorb B12 from her gastrointestinal tract. B12 injections resolved the patient's fatigue as well as the tingling in her feet, two typical symptoms of B12 deficiency.

Shari's sense of joy in life returned. Could the B12 deficiency have led to a mild depression? We'll never know for sure. But here's what Shari observed to me: "I'm usually a very active person. I hated the fatigue! I think I was depressed about being so tired."

Shari's therapist had clung to his depression diagnosis, even after Shari had developed abnormal sensations, a neurological symptom called paresthesia. But all of Shari's symptoms were explained once the primary care physician made the correct diagnosis. Adopting the simplest scientific explanation, the one that requires the fewest assumptions, is referred to as following Occam's razor. In clinical practice, this translates into the goal of finding a single cause to explain the multiple facets of the individual's presentation. In Shari's case, B12 deficiency explained her fatigue as well as the tingling in her feet. It also might have led to Shari's mild depression either directly or as a secondary psychological reaction.

In a younger population of patients, when patients have multiple symptoms, utilizing Occam's razor can be very helpful; it drives the clinician to search for a unifying explanation. However, this approach must be somewhat modified in dealing with the elderly. Older individuals are more likely to have multiple medical problems, including some conditions that will affect the mental sphere. Older individuals are also more likely to be on multiple medications and to have numerous clinical caretakers who are not necessarily communicating effectively with one another. One diagnosis is not likely to explain the full set of symptoms one sees in elderly individuals.

The Evolution of Symptoms Over Time

Once you have fully explored how the story began, it is time to look at the unfolding of the narrative. Keep in mind the big picture, the pattern of evolution of the individual's symptoms over time. Disorders of all kinds tend to generate typical patterns of entering and exiting, waxing and waning, or building to a crisis. This is true of those conditions we consider to be psychological as well as those that are organic. With increasing experience and a growing fund of knowledge, clinicians develop a mental picture of the kinds of patterns that are associated with different diagnoses.

As you look carefully at the narrative of your patient's illness, think about two questions. First, does your patient's illness actually following the time course that is expected for the psychological diagnosis you have in mind? Second, do any physical disorders follow this same narrative time course, and might they be imitating a psychological disorder? Let's look at an example of each.

First, during the natural course of a grief reaction, after a significant loss, you expect someone to go through an intense period of emotional disruption. But after 6 months had passed, you would be surprised if the individual wasn't beginning to have some periods of feeling back to normal. By a year or so, you would expect that the person's sense of loss would have taken a background place in life, even if the grief had not entirely resolved. But, let's say your patient is still emotionally overwrought and somewhat dysfunctional after a year has passed; you would have to consider the possibility that your understanding of the situation and your diagnosis are incomplete. Perhaps this individual has a pathological grief reaction. Before coming to that conclusion, it would be important to rule out numerous other diagnostic possibilities. You know that it is possible that some other disorder may have slipped in under the cover story of mourning. Does this individual have a major depression? Could a drug or alcohol problem have been exacerbated with the experience of loss? Does your patient have a dementia that is being revealed by the absence of the loved one who died? Has your patient simply developed some other medical condition during the year of mourning?

Here's another example, illustrating the second question: Could you be dealing with an unfamiliar physical disorder that is simply following the same time course as a more familiar psychological illness? In this example, the familiar psychological illness is panic disorder. You expect patients who have panic attacks to have symptoms that come and go. You expect each episode to be relatively short-lived and leave no lasting effects beyond a fear of the same thing happening again. But consider that some organic conditions might follow a somewhat similar time course. Partial seizures, transient ischemic attacks, and hyperventilation syndrome are also short-lived, episodic disorders. Also consider hypoglycemia associated with taking too much insulin or from rare insulin-secreting tumors, or the episodic release of epinephrine-like substances from tumors of adrenal gland tissue (pheochromocytomas), or the bursts of serotonin emitted from certain tumors that are most often found in the gastrointestinal tract (carcinoid syndrome). Although these disorders do have characteristic features (headaches in the case of pheochromocytomas and flushing with carcinoid syndrome), nonetheless, they may follow the same time course as panic attacks and mimic panic disorder in their presentations.

You can see how expanding your mental library of illness patterns is a skill that would be especially helpful in discerning an organic condition that might be masquerading as a psychological one. Here are some questions to keep in mind as you see patients and listen to their stories. Is this patient describing an episodic disorder? If so, what seems to bring it on? What are the associated symptoms? How often does it occur? Does it come and go and always leave the individual pretty much back at baseline? Or has this patient been gradually deteriorating or changing over time, a little worse after each bout? Is this a disorder that began slowly and that has worsened inexorably over time? Has the individual deteriorated and, if so, in what way? Or has this illness simply been a part of the patient's life, sometimes waxing, sometimes waning, but ever-present since it began. Is there any rhyme or reason to the waxing and waning? Could there be an even longer time pattern here? Is there a family history of this disorder?

Expanding the Timeline—Family History

Expanding your timeline to include the patient's family history can be enormously helpful in your search for possible organic factors. Many disorders have genetic roots, and, if you are able to identify patterns of inheritance through a multigenerational family history, this will contribute invaluable information toward making an accurate diagnosis.

Generally, when taking a family history, one inquires about the family history of both medical diseases and mental disorders. Both are important. However, keep in mind that often these are not easily separable. For instance, just because Granny was in a mental hospital for the last 10 years of her life does not mean she had a psychological disorder; she may have had a dementia. If 50 years ago Uncle Joe had electroshock therapy or committed suicide, one should not assume that Uncle Joe had major depression. He might have had any of several possible organic disorders that were not diagnosed properly at the time.

Also, when taking a family history, be sure to inquire not only about parents, grandparents, aunts and uncles, and siblings but also about children of the patient and children of the patient's siblings. It is not uncommon for genetic diseases to be first diagnosed in a child or through pre-pregnancy genetic testing or amniocentesis once a baby is conceived. Any abnormal findings in these situations may raise the issue of a genetic disorder for older members in that family for the very first time.

There are some important concepts to keep in mind as you look for disorders with genetic determinants. Inherited factors are present and influence health and disease in everyone. In most cases, these factors are numerous, complex, difficult to differentiate from environmental effects, and influenced by life experience. However, there is a spectrum of diseases with neuropsychiatric symptoms in which the role of causative genetic factors has been well studied and can be described.

At one end of the spectrum, there are diseases with a pattern of inheritance that is fairly straightforward, such as Huntington's disease, hemochromatosis (which causes a buildup of iron in body organs), and Wilson's disease (in which copper metabolism is abnormal). Once the diagnosis is made, a knowledgeable clinician will be able to predict the course of the illness in the affected individual with a good deal of accuracy. However, with some genetic diseases, such as neurofibromatosis (which is associated with learning disabilities and possible brain tumors), acute intermittent porphyria (which may lead to acute psychotic episodes), or the mitochondrial diseases (with fatigue and seizures running in the maternal line), though the pattern of inheritance is clear, the symptomatic expression and course of the disease will vary considerably from individual to individual, even if individuals have the same gene defect. The family history and genetics may be straightforward, but the symptom presentation and course of the illness are not.

At the other end of the spectrum are diseases with complex patterns of inheritance. In these disorders, such as schizophrenia, bipolar disorder, attention deficit disorder, Alzheimer's disease, narcolepsy, and fronto-temporal dementia, it is clear from statistical analysis that genetic factors play an important part in causing the disease; however, multiple genes are likely involved, and these heritable factors interact with multiple, nonheritable elements, including possible infectious exposure, environmental toxins, nutritional deficiencies, psychological trauma, and so forth in producing the disorder. Here even experienced practitioners are less able to trace a clear pattern of transmission within the family history or to predict with accuracy the chances that any particular individual will inherit the disorder.

If you are able to uncover a family history of a disorder with some genetic determinants, keep in mind that this does not prove that your patient has that disorder. It does, however, constitute one statistical piece of evidence pointing in that direction. If the individual's symptoms and the course of his or her illness do fit the picture of the genetic disease, then you have a stronger case for this diagnosis.

On the other hand, you may identify a patient as having a genetic disorder but be unable to elicit a history of that disease in the family. There are several possible explanations for this: Family members may have died before the genetic disease expressed itself; diagnoses that family members received in the past may have been inaccurate or imprecise; the genetic disease may be a new mutation; or the person who the patient believes to be his or her father may not be the actual, biological father. Historically, as a rule of thumb, physicians have generally assumed that many people have false knowledge about who their biological fathers actually are. With more widespread use of assisted reproductive technologies, including insemination with donor sperm and the use of donor eggs and surrogate mothers, the problem of determining an individual's genetic roots, both paternal and maternal, has become still more complex.

Looking Forward

It takes time for even the best practitioners to figure out what is the matter with a patient. It takes time when you are seeing a new patient, especially if the situation is complex. It takes time to gain the trust of your patient and to hear the full story. It takes time to obtain permissions and to contact family members and friends. Also, you may need to talk with previous therapists and obtain old records. It is likely to take awhile to stitch together all of this information into a complete picture.

In addition, sometimes it is only by getting to know a patient well over a period of time that you will come to some clarity of understanding. For instance, you may realize that the person's symptoms are too severe or intractable to be reasonably explained by the psychodynamics of the situation. Or you may learn some new information that the patient didn't reveal initially. Perhaps there is some important piece of family history or early head trauma. Or you might even discover that the patient actually has a known medical condition that could be contributing to or causing the symptoms you've been observing. Unless patients are specifically asked, they may think that information about their medical illnesses or their medications are unrelated to the problems for which they are seeing you in therapy.

There are other reasons why it might take time to figure out what is the matter with your patient. It may take time for a covert organic disorder to become apparent. Specific or definitive symptoms may only develop with the passage of time. Examples of this include the characteristic movement disorders associated with the genetically transmitted Huntington's or Wilson's diseases; the moon-shaped face, thin arms, and obese trunk associated with Cushing's disease; the necklace-shaped rash of niacin deficiency, also called pellagra; the severe loss of weight and characteristic associated infections that occur in individuals with HIV.

Or a subtle difficulty that, initially, is just subjectively experienced by the patient may become worse over time and only then able to be objectively documented. This is often the case with early changes in cognition, especially in individuals who are bright and who initially are able to find adaptive strategies. These individuals may notice a slowing of their mental processing speed or subtle difficulties in memory or word retrieval before these changes are apparent to others or easy to document on neuropsychological testing. The same is true for symptoms in other realms of functioning. If your patient is a tennis player, for instance, he or she may be aware of subtle alterations in response time with early Parkinson's disease before the symptoms worsen and tennis partners notice. When an individual is in the early stages of an autoimmune disorder, he or she might feel tired, but others might only notice a change once the fatigue becomes more extreme.

Though time is an important factor in uncovering masked physical disorders, it is not enough to simply accept that time will tell. We want to use time to *actively* observe whether anything is changing. As clinicians, we need to keep an open mind and remember that our working diagnosis is only a theory. Over time, it is important to stand ready, willing, and able to incorporate into our thinking any new clinical data as it presents itself. Shari's story told earlier is a good example. If her therapist had been able to shift his diagnostic thinking once Shari began to experience tingling in her feet, he might have been able to realize that a medical consultation was in order. This would have more quickly led to the diagnosis of vitamin B12 deficiency.

The following narrative illustrates how important the factor of time is. This story is a bit unusual in that, I metaphorically walked into the theater only a short time after the play had begun. The story is about Peter—the gentleman from chapter two. The first time I saw Peter, I told him that I thought it was possible that he had a covert organic condition, but it was many years before we knew what that condition was.

Peter was a computer software engineer who consulted me just after his 60th birthday. "I haven't been feeling like myself. I'm sort of depressed, but not really." he said. "Maybe it's because of turning 60 and worried about getting old." Even though this chief complaint was vague, it was clear that something was bothering Peter.

Peter was good at problem solving, so he had put together a coherent, psychodynamic formulation of his midlife loss of zest and motivation. He revealed a profound, tortured dissonance in his life. He recalled a salient moment during adolescence when he had been sexually turned on by the cowboy belt and tight blue jeans of his friend Bobby. From then on, he had known that he was gay. Nonetheless, he had married after college and now had three wonderful, mature children, and a wife whom he dearly loved. But periodically, over the years, when times were stressful, Peter would have clandestine liaisons with strange men, usually at "the rest stop between exits 6 and 7 on the eastbound freeway." Eventually, he told his wife.

Now that he was 60, he had begun to regret that he had never fulfilled his dream of having a long-term relationship with a man. He was torn apart by this desire, on the one hand, and a deep attachment to his wife and family on the other. He felt longing, sadness, and grief, uncertain about what to do and completely stuck. Recently, he had become obsessed with gay Internet pornography, and this was getting in the way of his work. It was increasingly difficult for him to concentrate at his job, and he was less motivated to do the work. Mental tasks required more effort. He had multiple awakenings during the night; his wife said that he talked in his sleep and, at times, kicked violently.

The psychodynamic roots of Peter's current state seemed clear, but I was troubled by another possibility. I was worried that Peter might have an underlying medical condition. Primarily, I was concerned that he may have contracted acquired immune deficiency syndrome (AIDS). Perhaps his symptoms were the organic manifestations of brain infection with human immunodeficiency virus (HIV): apathy, slowed mental processing, disturbance of concentration—a subcortical dementia syndrome. I referred Peter to a neurologist, who performed a thorough neurological examination, including tests of cognitive functioning and an electroencephalogram (EEG). Everything seemed normal. And, we were both relieved to learn that Peter's HIV test was negative.

The therapy moved on. We explored many psychodynamic aspects of Peter's distress. I did not lose sight of the other clue in Peter's story—his disturbed sleep. A sleep study revealed possible nocturnal myoclonus, a sleep disorder that can cause nonrestorative sleep because of disruptions to the normal cycling of the sleeper in and out of deep sleep during the night. I wondered whether this might be contributing to Peter's mental slowing, difficulty with concentration, and loss of motivation.

We proceeded with the work of psychotherapy, exploring Peter's feelings and conflicts, assuming that fundamentally Peter was depressed. Peter worked hard in therapy, but his unhappy state did not really change, and I could not rid myself of a nagging feeling that there really was something organic the matter with him. On the other hand, I was also well aware that from the start Peter had not wanted to try a powerful tool I had to offer him in combating his depressive state. Peter's initial reluctance to take medications gave way as the other treatment modalities failed to make him feel any more at peace, any more motivated or engaged in his life.

Antidepressant medication led to the first positive change in Peter's depressive state. He wasn't entirely back to his old self, but he was able to stay away from the Internet more easily and to feel a bit happier. At this point, 2 years after first consulting me, Peter decided that he was comfortable enough to stop weekly therapy and to come see me just for periodic visits to monitor his medication. But, within a year, news from the family was not good. When Peter's son visited from the West Coast, he was shocked to see how his father had changed. He was a different person! He had "lost all his stuffing." Peter's wife had begun to notice deterioration in Peter's memory. "He needs a lot of reminding," she told me over the telephone.

The next time Peter checked in with me, I did some quick cognitive testing and was surprised to find that this intelligent man could recall only one of three objects after 3 minutes. I sent him back to the neurologist. This time the news was grim. Neuropsychological testing and magnetic resonance imaging (MRI) documented that Peter had a progressive dementia, probably of the fronto-temporal type. Now it was finally clear what had been the matter with Peter when he had walked into my office 3 years earlier. Yes, he had been in a depressive state. The painful dynamics of his life were clear and real, but they had not been the fundamental cause of Peter's deterioration.

Peter's sense from the outset that he was "sort of depressed, but not really" and my sense that this was not a typical depression proved accurate. We had been witnessing the early stages of a dementia. It was only over time that the underlying neurological diagnosis and full complexity of the clinical situation had become clear.

Peter's story is a good illustration of how important the dimension of time is in the unfolding of an organic disorder, in this case fronto-temporal dementia. It also demonstrates something else about time. Often, it is only over the course of time that a therapist can begin to tell whether the psychodynamics of an individual's situation are actually causative of the clinical signs and symptoms as opposed to being the milieu in which the somatic disease expresses itself and by which the patient makes meaning of his or her experiences.

To be more specific, it is intuitively clear that if a patient's symptoms do not appear to make psychological sense, one needs to consider the possibility that those symptoms may be manifestations of a covert physical condition. What Peter's case teaches us, however, is that the converse of that is not necessarily true! Just because an individual's symptoms make psychodynamic sense does not mean that they are causing the patient's symptoms. In Peter's case, it appeared that his depressive feeling, his loss of motivation, his obsession with Internet pornography, his difficulties at work, and his sleep disturbances could be explained by his nearly lifelong, deep inner turmoil about his gender identity and partner choice, emerging now as a crisis upon his turning 60 years old. But the situation was more complex that that. Peter was experiencing the early manifestations of a degenerative brain disorder in which the functions of his frontal lobes, his executive brain, were slowly breaking down.

His motivational gusto was fading, his ability to generate new ideas for work was drying up, his capacity for concentration was slipping away (except when the material was highly stimulating—the way pornography is), and these are all symptoms of early fronto-temporal dementia.

We know that the manifestations of clearly documented physical diseases will be given meaning by a patient and a patient's caregivers; these meanings will be secondary and interpretive. It would be a mistake to assume that these explanations are accurate descriptions of the forces that have actually caused the individual's symptoms. A disease takes shape within the life of an individual, just as water assumes the shape of its container. It is wise to be humble about our psychological interpretations, knowing that we might be able to discern the true cause of a patient's symptoms only over some span of time.

As for Peter's sleep disorder, his preoccupation with pornography, and his depressive feelings, it isn't altogether clear what mixture of physical and psychological forces led to these symptoms. This important matter of whether, or if, or how much an organic condition is contributing to a patient's mental symptoms is often difficult to assess. Frequently it is only with time, and often only after a physical condition has been treated, that this question can be answered. If, following treatment, the patient returns to his or her previously healthy mental state, one will strongly suspect that the physical condition was the cause of the mental disturbance. The case will be especially strong if the somatic condition is known to produce the kinds of mental status changes that the patient exhibited.

But if we are completely scientific in our thinking, even a full recovery is not 100% definitive proof that the physical condition was the sole cause of the mental derangement. For instance, one cannot know for sure how much the patient's psychological reaction to being sick contributed to the clinical picture.

One factor that makes it difficult to know how much an organic condition is contributing to a patient's mental state is that in some situations it may take quite a long time for the patient's mental status to clear following appropriate medical treatment; this makes the correlation between the physical illness and the mental disturbances less obvious. A common example of this phenomenon is seen in patients who have a dementia (such as Alzheimer's disease) when they develop a urinary tract infection. Frequently, this will lead to a sharp deterioration in their mental condition; for instance, a patient with significant impairment of recent memory but who has been fully conversant all along might become mute. When the urinary tract infection is treated, even though this infection was the precipitating factor for the patient's worsened state, it might take months for the patient to fully recover the capacity for discourse.

On the other hand, if you have seen an individual who becomes psychotic every time she gets a urinary tract infection, or every time her autoimmune disease flares up, or only after having a seizure, those repeated episodes add weight to the notion that the underlying physical disorder is the causative factor for the mental status changes. The same is true for repeated episodes of irritability and depression that are in sync with a particular phase of the menstrual cycle or with rounds of infertility drug treatments. These recurrent episodes are like natural experiments: When the offending factor is in play, the symptoms emerge; when the offending factor is gone, the symptoms remit. A clinician may be able to elicit a history that reveals these patterns, but often it is necessary for the practitioner to observe a patient over time in order to make connections between the patient's mental status changes and the factors that are actually causing those changes.

Despite all our best efforts, it is important to recognize that there will be many times when we will not be able to know for sure how much, or even if, a physical condition is contributing to an individual's mental state. This was the case with some of Peter's symptoms. Here is another example:

> *Josh served in the military in Iraq, where his vehicle was hit by a roadside bomb. Now that he is back in the United States his primary care physician and his wife have urged him to consult with a therapist. Josh complains, "My wife has had it with me. What she wants me to get help for is my temper." The patient sheepishly admits that he has been yelling at his children and even got into a fight in a bar the month before. But Josh's chief complaint is trouble with memory.*
>
> *When asked about the bombing incident, Josh reports that he felt "stunned" when his vehicle was hit and that he did have bruises on his face, but he had no actual loss of consciousness. Memory testing in the office doesn't reveal any problem with memory storage, though he may be having difficulty with memory retrieval.*

Will we ever know how much of this man's irritability, impulsivity, and aggressive behavior are caused by the head trauma he sustained in Iraq versus the psychological trauma of combat? And how much of his current behavior, including his difficulty with memory retrieval, is simply a reflection of the person he was when he first enlisted? Is there any element of secondary gain complicating this presentation, for instance, the hope of receiving a service-connected disability? In situations like this, in which there are complex psychological and possible organic factors, we often can never know for sure how much each of the various elements is contributing to the full clinical picture. Even so, it is best to keep in mind the question of how the pieces of any complex clinical puzzle might be interacting with one another and to be observant over time. This will help generate a more comprehensive understanding of the patient and will reduce the likelihood of missing some important, contributing element.

HOW PSYCHOLOGICAL DISORDERS AFFECT PHYSICAL CONDITIONS

Although the focus has been on physical conditions that affect mental processes, keep in mind that the reverse is also true. Of paramount importance are the powerful and lasting effects that the mental disorders have on health (e.g., the negative effects of depression on cardiovascular disease). In addition, treating a psychological condition may be an important part of preventive care or may help improve a coexisting physical disorder. For example, think of the individual with an untreated psychosis who cannot manage his or her diabetes; the patient with unregulated bipolar disorder who neglects to follow up on an abnormal mammogram; the patient with intermittent explosive disorder who had three car accidents last year; the depressed young adult who feels that she doesn't have much of a future, so who cares if she has unprotected sex with inappropriate sexual partners?

In principle, we know that every patient presentation results from a combination of somatic and psychological factors that are intertwined and inseparable. With each patient encounter, it is our job to perform a full diagnostic evaluation and then to treat, to our best ability, whatever conditions we find, however complex the situation. Along the way we need to keep our eyes, ears, and our minds open, as time will provide an opportunity to learn more.

TREATMENT RESISTANCE

The term *treatment resistance* is not a judgmental label but an important, descriptive concept. It refers to the lack of response or actual worsening of an individual's condition with standard treatment. The presence of treatment resistance may simply mean that the best treatment for this particular individual has not yet been tried, but treatment resistance may also signal that there is a missed diagnosis or mistaken diagnosis.

The key here is to ask: Why aren't the patient's symptoms responding to treatment? Why is this patient getting worse? Has the best treatment for the individual's condition been tried? Perhaps a more intensive psychotherapy, a different psychodynamic formulation, higher doses of a medication, a different medication or combination of medications, electroconvulsive therapy (ECT), or repetitive transcranial magnetic stimulation (rTMS) would be more effective? Or is it possible that the treatment approaches that have been used have not been targeted for the diagnosis or diagnoses that are actually causing the patient's symptoms?

Psychotherapy and/or antidepressant medications will not effectively treat a depression that is caused by or aggravated by hypothyroidism or pancreatic cancer. Antipsychotic medications will not effectively treat hallucinations that are generated by seizures. In fact, certain medications such as clozapine or bupropion may lower seizure threshold and actually facilitate the occurrence of seizures. Keep in mind that, when an individual's mental symptoms worsen with ECT or psychotropic medication use, it may be because the treatment has had a negative affect on an undiagnosed, underlying medical condition.

Consider the story of Mr. Benoit, as an example of treatment resistance. Time worked in favor of problem solving the true source of his difficulties.

> *It began as an unremarkable therapy. Mr. Benoit had consulted me, saying, "I want to work out any personal issues that might get in the way of an important creative project I'm about to begin." He was a psychologically minded, sophisticated middle-aged man with deeply intense feelings. Yet Mr. Benoit's chief complaint struck me as so purely cognitive that I hypothesized it was only the surface reason for his seeking treatment. With time I learned that although Mr. Benoit was outwardly composed, inwardly he exerted considerable effort to contain anxiety and irritability. He had frequent nightmares that made him fearful about going to sleep, and he felt emotionally distant from others, even his wife.*
>
> *Twice each week, Mr. Benoit arrived by taxi to my office and worked hard in therapy, trying to elucidate the psychological dynamics that might be generating his symptoms. He was intolerant of any hint of incompetence in people he wanted to rely upon, and his high standards left him feeling isolated, with no one he could fully trust. He was the only child of a narcissistic, alcoholic mother and a father who worked multiple jobs in order to make ends meet and was often absent. As a youngster he couldn't depend on either parent; moreover, he had felt responsible for keeping his mother safe during her alcoholic binges while his father was at work. The patient was furious that throughout his mother's life he had remained tied to her by virtue of her incompetence and his own sense of responsibility.*
>
> *This dynamic linked many of the threads of Mr. Benoit's past with his current experiences. However, the elucidation of such an explanatory life narrative is generally curative, and Mr. Benoit was not getting better. A year of intensive psychotherapy had not provided Mr. Benoit with*

much relief. In fact, if I was honest with myself, I had to admit that Mr. Benoit's anxiety was actually getting worse. Moreover, the intensity of his symptoms made less and less psychological sense to me; his anxiety seemed too pervasive, and I couldn't find an explanation for his disturbing night-mares despite an exhaustive search.

I decided to prescribe an anti-anxiety medication for Mr. Benoit to take at bedtime; this was somewhat helpful for his sleep. But a small dose of an antidepressant surprisingly sent him into a brief but disabling depression. This was unusual. It was possible that Mr. Benoit was sensitive to antide-pressant medications on the basis of the biological levels of his metabolic enzymes. But in light of the concomitant failure of the talking cure, I began to wonder whether there might be some underlying physical problem that I was missing.

Then one day the patient called me in a state of panic from a vacation in South America. He had suddenly been overcome with the feeling that he was about to die. Even in the midst of experiencing this intense episode of fear, Mr. Benoit was theorizing that his terror had been brought on by identifying with the statues in a church near his hotel that "depicted Jesus, the son, dy-ing for the sins of others." He was a master at psychological thinking, and together we had theorized many similar explanations. By now I had come to doubt that these dynamics were the fundamental cause of Mr. Benoit's most disturbing symptoms.

In my state of doubt, hearing the terror in Mr. Benoit's voice triggered a new thought in my mind. I knew that intense fear was the most common symptom of focal seizures involving the tempo-limbic regions of the brain. Terror that is generated by these localized electrical storms in the brain comes on randomly and is often accompanied by a feeling that something terrible is about the happen. I also knew that when seizures happen noctur-nally, they could manifest as nightmares.

Now I had a better explanation for Mr. Benoit's nightmares, atypical reaction to medication, and his worsening anxiety with no entirely convinc-ing psychological etiology. Focal seizures also explained other aspects of Mr. Benoit's remote history that had been at the back of my mind, but that had never been the focus of serious inquiry because the patient and I thought we understood them: an episode of loss of consciousness (attributed to alcohol toxicity rather than a seizure triggered by alcohol withdrawal), nearly driv-ing off the highway (attributed to extreme fatigue rather than a seizure trig-gered by sleep deprivation), and his reliance on taxis (his irritation at the hassle of parking covering up for an unconscious fear of another car acci-dent), a very brief episode of slurred speech while trying to speak calmly even though he was very angry (psychological conflict rather than a momentary seizure symptom), and the list went on.

When Mr. Benoit returned from his trip, he was open to entertaining this new diagnostic possibility. I referred him for a seizure workup. An EEG confirmed that he had a partial seizure disorder with a temporal lobe focus. Anticonvulsant medications eliminated Mr. Benoit's nightmares, his anxiety, irritability, and episodes of fear. His social world has expanded, and his work has never been more successful.

Chapter 5

The Clinical Interview

Introduction

This chapter discusses matters that are often sidelined in writings about the clinical encounter. It emphasizes the centrality of a clinical interview in making any diagnosis. While effective interviewing techniques help patients to articulate their experiences, be they emotional or physical, therapists face many challenges in translating the patient's language into clinical language and in utilizing their observations and inner experiences to gain clinically valuable insights.

The Clinical Interview—Fundamental to Making a Diagnosis

As a therapist you already understand the nature of a clinical interaction. You know how to establish a trusting relationship with the patient. You have mastered the complex process of actively listening to the patient's experience while formulating a clinical understanding of the underlying nature of the individual's problem. This chapter simply expands on these skills.

The clinical interview is not only the first step in the process of uncovering a somatic diagnosis; it is also the key element. I cannot stress this enough. Studies of the various elements of a medical workup (history and mental status, physical exam, laboratory tests, imaging) have consistently shown that in the vast majority of cases, information from the history (i.e., from the clinical interview) is the most important element in making an accurate diagnosis. This makes sense, because it is during a clinical encounter that the most raw, as-yet-unfiltered data about a patient's condition is available to the practitioner. This is akin to using primary rather than secondary sources when doing historical research.

From the very first moment of every clinical interaction, a therapist begins to get information about a patient and starts to piece together a narrative and diagnostic understanding of what the individual's problems might be. It is also through the process of actively listening to the patient's story, through history taking, that the clinician establishes a working relationship with the patient; and it is within the context of this relationship that diagnostic and problem-solving thinking takes place. The therapist and the patient begin to talk. The clinician begins to generate diagnostic hypotheses and asks the patient more questions; the patient begins to realize that there's more story to tell. The patient comes to find words to describe what he or she has been experiencing. During the clinical interview, a therapist begins to formulate the nature of the patient's problem, begins to think in a certain direction, to go down a certain investigative trail.

When I first glimpse a patient from the waiting room doorway, I see a lot. The patient is or isn't reading. The patient has chosen from the overflowing pile of magazines on the table a copy of *National Geographic* or *Art News*. He or she may be standing by the window, pacing or talking too loudly on a cell phone. When I appear in the doorway, she looks straight at me, rises, and extends her hand in greeting. Or he is slow to look up and hesitates until I begin to introduce myself. She smiles or doesn't. He looks worried or suspicious, frightened or sad. She is attired in black, or red, wearing unmatched socks or too much perfume. And all of this happens within moments.

The patient may have trouble rising from the waiting room chair or perhaps has failed to notice that he dropped his keys between the sofa cushions. She may walk to my office with a shuffle or list toward one side. Her eyes may be bulging or her ankles swollen. He may have a tremor or lack a natural arm swing on one or both sides. Her face may have a yellowish hue, acne, or perhaps a rash. And the patient may have an odor about him or her. I make special note of such findings; they may be important clues.

Along with these sorts of observations begins a process of mentally proposing conceivable scenarios of what might be causing the patient's problems. Automatically, I begin to hypothesize about diagnostic possibilities. As the clinical encounter unfolds, I have an opportunity to gather more data, make more observations, and ask pertinent questions to test out those hypotheses. Everything else follows from this initial encounter.

It would be natural to assume that advances in medical technology over the years have decreased the errors in diagnosing organic conditions. On the contrary, research data shows that somatic diagnostic error rates seem to be stable across hospitals, countries, and perhaps most surprisingly, eras of practice. When the organic diagnoses listed in patient charts are compared with those discovered at postmortem, the error rate is the same now as it was 20, 30, or even 50 years ago (Kuhn, 2002). Moreover, the negative impact of diagnostic errors on patients' outcomes has hovered around 10% over the years; this statistic has not been affected by advancements in medical diagnostic technology during this time frame (Kuhn, 2002).

Undoubtedly, many factors contribute to these statistics, but this simple fact is a given: Before any diagnostic test or imaging study can rule a diagnosis in or out, first a clinician and a patient have to sit together and talk. First, there needs to be a clinical interview during which the therapist helps the patient to articulate what he or she has been experiencing; first there needs to be a clinician who is observant and thoughtful and who generates ideas about what the patient's diagnoses might be. In other words, even with all the advancement in technology, the real key to diagnostic accuracy remains the clinical encounter.

This important lesson was brought home to me years ago. I was trying to figure out why my patient, Annie, was having chronic headaches. Annie was a 58-year-old single woman with a history of having been raped by her uncle when she was a child. She had been quite depressed when she first came to see me. She also had hypothyroidism, high blood pressure, chronic obstructive pulmonary disease, possible congestive heart failure, chronic pain from having fractured her spine in an automobile accident during college, and arthritis in numerous joints that she simply said were "wearing out." She had a primary care doctor, a pulmonologist, a cardiologist, and an orthopedist. She was on a lot of different medications, and she was obese.

Two years into psychotherapy, Annie also developed headaches. She had them every day for months. The question was why? Were these tension headaches related to stress? It was easy to make a case for stress; Annie had recently changed jobs and broken up with her boyfriend. But there were so many other possible organic sources for Annie's headaches. I felt overwhelmed by data; I didn't know where to start. I considered whether the culprit was the fluoxetine that had "chased away" Annie's depression. I suggested that she try tapering the antidepressant dose; her headaches remained unchanged.

Perhaps Annie had a dental problem; maybe the prescription for her eyeglasses was now slightly off; possibly she was having muscle spasms in her upper back or grinding and clenching her teeth at night. After checking out all of these possible minor problems, I began to worry that I was missing something serious. So I referred Annie to the chairman of a neurology department at an internationally acclaimed hospital in the area; we are lucky to have several in Boston. The neurologist conducted a thorough physical exam, including an extensive neurological exam. Then he ordered several tests, including an MRI of Annie's brain. Nothing was revealed.

But Annie and I were determined to figure this out, so we tried yet another path. It was Annie's idea. She consulted with the endocrinologist who had originally diagnosed her hypothyroidism and who had a reputation for being a great diagnostician. Annie took this doctor's advice, and her headaches—the ones she had had every day for months—disappeared by the next time I saw her.

"How did he figure it out?" I asked.

"It was magic," Annie replied.

And how did he perform this magic? He took a careful history. That's all. He asked Annie to tell him in detail about what the headaches really felt like. He asked her whether she had ever felt anything like this before. Did she have any other symptoms, accompanying the headaches? And, of course, he inquired about when the headaches had begun and whether anything else had changed at about that same time. He asked the standard questions. He didn't order any tests. At the end of the interview, he simply told her to stop using the nitroglycerine patch that her cardiologist had prescribed.

It wasn't magic. It was good history taking. The key to finding the solution had been in eliciting the quality of Annie's headaches and when they had begun. This ordinary magic had involved establishing a relationship with the patient, committing oneself to figuring out the problem, listening carefully, using one's knowledge base and experience, and thinking scientifically. It was good detective work. I could have done the same thing. (So could you.) Only I hadn't.

Helping the Patient to Find Words

A central part of your job as a therapist is to help your patients to become team members with you in trying to figure out the possible sources of their problems. You have a complex diagnostic situation to figure out. Who has the pertinent information? The patient! Even close family members and friends will not be privy to certain kinds of details or to subjective experiences that only the patient knows. In trying to understand what has happened to your patient over time in order to figure out what the sources of the difficulties might be, you need to help the patient to fully articulate his or her experiences. This is what Annie's endocrinologist did. This is what all good clinicians do.

Individuals come to see you because they are having difficulties of some kind. These difficulties are experienced in the context of the patient's own world, articulated in the patient's unique personal vocabulary, and imbued with suppositions inherent in the patient's private, deep, and nonverbal understanding of causality. Therapists are familiar with helping individuals translate their private experiences into words. We do this every day when we ask patients to tell us about their families, their jobs, their aspirations and fears, the traumatic experiences they have suffered, the grandparent who "loved them to pieces." Therapists are especially used to helping individuals find language for nonverbal experiences, to express ideas that are not yet fully formed, to put emotions into words. Expanding this skill to include the nonverbal arena of bodily sensations is of central importance when you are on the lookout for covert organic disorders.

There are three important aspects of helping individuals who are in your care to put their experiences into words. The first is to work with patients in such a way as to promote the process of self-observation. You want to encourage individuals to become aware of what they are experiencing. How do they behave in the world, and what is the nature of their inner life? What has happened to them, and when did it happen? Your aim is for each patient to become a co-investigator with you, a partner in problem solving. The second part of your task involves facilitating the process of reporting. You want to help patients to say in words, in their own words, what they are experiencing nonverbally. And the third of your jobs is to mentally translate patients' language into clinical language.

This process may sound easier than it really is. For one thing, the entire enterprise is based on very careful, active listening and empathy. I will never forget the lesson I learned during my training from a gifted fellow resident. It was a simple moment in an offhand conversation. He was talking about a patient of his, a 20-year-old single mom who would spend hours each day washing her hands. Everyone on the inpatient unit was worried about the patient's baby. I was focused on speculating about her unconscious motivation. He, on the other hand, was naturally and deeply curious about the patient's conscious experience. The patient would lock herself in the bathroom and spend hours washing. What was she doing? What kind of soap did she use? Did she lather? What did she think about? What state of mind was she in? And in what struck me as a leap fully into the patient's mind, he asked her another question. When she was satisfied that her hands were really clean, how did she ever get out of the bathroom? I never forgot that question, because it took his therapy with this patient into a new realm. In fact, this young woman had been having terrible difficulty in getting herself out of bathrooms; this had been a significant problem for her, but one that she had never articulated, even to herself. She had struggled with the issue all alone until her therapist empathically asked that simple but important question.

The patient in the previous anecdote had a well-known condition: obsessive-compulsive disorder. But the same rule applies to evaluating a patient's symptoms when the situation is murkier and especially when there is a possibility of covert organic illness. One needs to get inside the patient's experience in order to understand enough to ask about things the patient hasn't thought to tell you.

Being deeply empathic is not some esoteric skill known only to the best diagnosticians. It is, or should be, the bread-and-butter skill of all therapists in all clinical disciplines. The point is that the array of abilities one needs in order to make a differential diagnosis begins first with a facility that lies very close at hand: understanding what the patient's experience is like.

HELPING PATIENTS TO BECOME AWARE OF THEIR EXPERIENCES

An individual comes to be seen by a therapist because someone thinks that individual has a mental health problem. That someone may be the patient him or herself, another clinician, or someone in the patient's family system or community. What is that someone noticing? What do they think is the matter? This becomes the starting point of any practitioner's inquiry.

It is important to keep in mind that this starting point, or chief complaint, is not the problem; it is simply the place to begin one's investigation. To use an analogy, the chief complaint is like the surface of a lake, and your job is to see to the bottom. Sometimes the water is clear; the chief complaint is classic, and right away you think you can see what the source of the problem is. Sometimes the pattern of ripples on the surface of the lake will give you clues to what probably lies below. But, at other times, algae has bloomed, and the water is murky.

What do I mean by a murky chief complaint? Here are some examples: "I feel like I'm losing it." "I don't know, Doc, I just don't feel well." "I had one of my dizzy days." "Everything just goes out of my head." "I feel crappy." "Everyone is just bugging me." "I feel jiggy." "My brain is swelling."

What do these individuals mean? Their statements don't make it easy for a clinician to see to the bottom. Rather, they invite a lot of questions. And so an exchange begins between practitioner and patient, and an important consequence of this exchange is that it encourages the patient to be observant.

What do you mean by jiggy? Is this an emotional feeling? Or are you describing a physical sensation? Do you feel it all day long or only at certain times? And when you experience this jiggy sensation, is it associated with anything else, anything you eat or drink, anything you feel inside, anything that might happen to you during the day or night?

Your questions essentially shine a flashlight on the lake. Then you dive in and take your underwater light with you to search beneath the water's surface. "What's that?" you say to the patient. You point to something. "And, what about that?" The patient hadn't necessarily paid any attention to those things before. Now the patient begins to wonder, to ask friends and relatives for their input, to look at old pictures, to search memories. And eventually you hope to come across something important, something the individual may not have focused on before, something that's on the bottom, something that helps you make a diagnosis of the patient's difficulties.

The following case illustrates how murky the waters can be, even when the patient is bright and entirely engaged. In psychotherapy, she and I swam around in murky water for a long time, shining a spotlight here and there. It was a long time before she could make out the salient experiences that were clues to the diagnosis at the bottom of it all. My patient, Heather, was having discrete, stereotypical emotional experiences, but she didn't recognize them as being any different from the usual ups and downs of her inner feeling life. She also had no idea how diagnostically meaningful they were.

Heather came to see me because she had been having some difficulty with her academic work in graduate school. She also suffered with painful self-consciousness and interpersonal sensitivity. During college she had retreated from friendships by entirely reversing her wake/sleep cycle. She would take early morning classes and then go to sleep for the day. In the evening she would wake up, have breakfast in her room, and study all night. She told me that in order to avoid encountering fellow students outside of class, she would buy dinner at a local drive-through restaurant and eat in her car.

It wasn't at all clear why Heather was so vulnerable to social slights. She was an attractive, intelligent, and thoughtful young woman from a supportive and loving family. Yes, her parents were "old-fashioned," "proper," and "a bit judgmental," but they were devoted and loving. The patient was highly motivated and a full participant in the psychotherapy. I liked her. She was articulate and able to talk about her inner life, her thoughts, feelings, and fantasies. And what she communicated was that she felt utterly despairing. This was puzzling because, even though I believed that I knew Heather really well, I couldn't see how her psychological dynamics explained her profound pain. I couldn't figure out what was fundamentally the matter.

I decided to send Heather for neuropsychological testing. The report noted latent suicidal ideation; that was not a surprise, but there was one puzzling finding. Heather's IQ had dropped a small but significant amount when compared with testing she had had during her freshman year of high school when she was experiencing headaches and "school phobia." One year into psychotherapy, I referred Heather to a neurologist in an effort to figure out what might account for her drop in IQ. I also hoped that this consultation might shed some light on Heather's social and academic difficulties. As part of a full neurological evaluation, Heather had what turned out to be a very revealing electroencephalogram (EEG). It showed right temporal spiking activity that is characteristic of a focal seizure disorder.

Chronic focal seizures could certainly have accounted for Heather's lowered IQ, but there was a problem. Heather didn't seem to have any symptoms of a seizure disorder, and neurologists don't want to commit to treating a patient with anticonvulsant medication on the basis of a laboratory finding if that patient has no symptoms to follow. How would they know if the treatment is necessary or working? They do not want to treat an EEG; they want to treat a patient.

During his first meeting with Heather, the neurologist had gone through the list of standard questions about seizure symptoms. Heather didn't endorse having any of them. But now the neurologist went over the list again and in great detail. Did she have frequent déjà vu experiences? No. Did she episodically have strange sensations or pains in her chest or abdomen? No. Did she have hallucinatory experiences of tastes or smells, visions or sounds? No.

The list of possible focal seizure symptoms is long; this is because focal seizures lead to manifestations that depend on precisely which areas of the brain are firing during the seizure episode. The neurologist went down his long list until he got to, "Do you have fears? Do you ever feel like something terrible is going to happen?" No. "How about feelings of dread or doom?" Well, yes, she did have feelings of dread. She had short bursts of them, many times each day. And she had had these feelings since she was a child. "Doesn't everyone?" Now we had really gotten to the bottom of the problem.

Over the ensuing months, Heather and I talked a lot about these feelings of dread. They were intense. But nonetheless, for her they were just an everyday (dozens and dozens of times a day) experience. She hadn't realized that they resulted from the random electrical firing of neural circuits in her brain. Quite naturally, she had assumed that her feelings of dread signaled that she was fearful about some upcoming event. For instance, as a child she would wake up virtually every morning and feel overwhelming dread. She thought this was because she didn't want to go out of the house. Clinicians at the time said that she was school phobic. While in college, she interpreted her intense feelings of dread as a reflection of her complex feelings about engaging in the social relationships of her dorm. This was what her inner life had been like for almost as long as she could remember.

Remarkably, antiseizure medications made these feelings of dread virtually disappear. Heather had thought that her fears were caused by her discomfort with being out in the world. Now she knew that the fear feelings were not specifically linked to anything outside of her brain. And now, on medications, whenever she would experience breakthrough dread she had *different ways of explaining her symptoms: Perhaps she had forgotten to take her medicine; perhaps she was under a lot of stress, sleep-deprived or premenstrual. She had learned that these are the kinds of factors that can make it more likely that someone with a seizure disorder will actually have a seizure.*

Heather was able to move on to establish a successful career, marry, and have children. But first, she had to learn that the world was a safer place than she had believed it to be when she first came into therapy with the chief complaint of difficulties with academic work in graduate school.

Helping Patients to Articulate Their Nonverbal Experiences

Individuals differ substantially in their ability to put experiences into words. For some this task is natural and easy; for others it is difficult, akin to learning a foreign language. For everyone, certain kinds of experiences, by their very nature, are a challenge to translate from the experiential arena into the world of verbal communication. Think of pain. At some point in your life you've probably encountered a clinician who wanted you to articulate what kind of pain you were feeling. "Was it sharp? Stabbing? Dull? Throbbing? Aching? Searing? Burning?" The clinician was introducing you to a new vocabulary, one that perhaps you had never before needed to acquire. "And, on a scale from 1 to 10, with one being the least painful and 10 being excruciatingly painful, how bad is your pain?" This has become a standard question in trying to understand the individual's subjective degree of discomfort. All of this information could be important in making a diagnosis.

When it comes to new physical experiences, it may be very difficult for people to find words. A few years ago, I was afflicted with acute viral vestibular neuritis. This illness came on quite suddenly, and not sure what was the matter, I went to the emergency room. Even though as a doctor I am familiar with the vocabulary options for describing numerous bodily sensations, I found myself struggling when I tried to explain what I was experiencing to the physician in the ER. It wasn't exactly dizziness or lightheadedness, though I did feel that I was vulnerable to falling. And neither was it vertigo, in which the world feels like it is spinning. But what exactly was I feeling? Though I was used to medical lingo as a clinician, I simply did not know what all of those words felt like from the inside, experientially. I was unable to translate my sensations into descriptive language. And I knew that the subtle distinctions were important because they had diagnostic implications.

Then the neurologist consultant came by. She asked if I would describe my sensation as disequilibrium? And that was it, exactly! This doctor had given me a way to express what I was going through. Not only did I feel a reassuring sense that the neurologist understood my experience, but I was also more optimistic that she might be able to figure out what was the matter. The desire to be heard and known, understood and then helped, is at the heart of every clinical encounter in every field of practice.

In addition to physical sensations, it is also very difficult for individuals to find words for a whole world of mental experiences that lie outside the bounds of usual, everyday feelings, thoughts, and sensations. Dreams fall into this realm, as do spiritual experiences. Others include hallucinations of all kinds, illusions, déjà vu experiences, out-of-body experiences, and feeling that the world is uncanny. The list is long. Even the most highly educated and articulate patients will have a hard time putting these sorts of experiences into language. If you are seeing an individual who is generally comfortable with conveying thoughts and experiences, and he or she tells you that it is simply impossible to put some quality of an experience into words, that in itself is important data about the nature of the experience.

Translating From the Patient's Language Into Clinical Language

As a therapist, you need to think in two different languages simultaneously, the everyday language of the patient as well as the descriptive and diagnostic language of the clinic. When patients come to see you and describe whatever symptoms they might be experiencing, they do not use proper clinical terminology—and they shouldn't. It is your job as a therapist to listen to an individual's narrative and to converse in that person's native tongue, metaphorically speaking. In this way, you enter the patient's world. Simultaneously, it is also your job to stand back in order to carefully and thoughtfully listen and observe. It is also your job to mentally translate what you hear from the patient into clinical terminology.

For instance, patients do not come in complaining of "psychomotor retardation." Patients might say they feel "sluggish" or "draggy" or "don't manage to get anything done" or that they feel like they're "walking through molasses." You might notice that a patient takes forever to get from the waiting room into your office and also seems to process your questions slowly. The patient is saying "molasses"; you are thinking "psychomotor retardation." You are translating from the patient's native tongue into clinical terminology.

Even when individuals do use diagnostic or clinical terms, it is important to not assume that they are using those words in the same way that you would. Let's assume the patient says, "I think I'm depressed." Does she mean that she thinks her diagnosis is depression? Is she saying that she feels depressed, or is she trying to describe a lack of motivation or apathy? Or, is she interpreting the fact that she feels like sleeping all day as a sign of depression? Perhaps she is actually experiencing fatigue. In other words, when your patient uses these kinds of terms, you want to be sure that you understand exactly what he or she means when using them.

TRANSLATING YOUR OBSERVATIONS INTO CLINICAL LANGUAGE

In addition to translating from the patient's language into clinical language, it is also your job to observe signs that the patient may not talk about or might not be aware of; it is your job as a therapist to observe any such findings and define these in clinical terms as well. Here are some examples of what I mean.

Patients will certainly never complain of flat affect, but the moment you see someone you might notice the blandness of expression that is clinically referred to as flat affect. Initially you might interpret this as a withholding look, or you might wonder whether you are seeing depressive affect, but then you watch more closely and realize that the patient's expression doesn't change much during the interview, except perhaps with extremes of emotion. And you realize that there is an absence of the usual small muscle movements that animate a normal face. You think to yourself, "Ah, this person has flat affect or a masklike face." This helps you to move on to thinking diagnostically: schizophrenia? medication side effects? Parkinson's disease? congenital facial muscle paralysis— Moebius syndrome?

Your patient filled out a clinic form, providing his contact information. You notice that he has written a number 3, but it has three loops instead of two, and the patient has written his address as "Stevens Road Road." You think to yourself, "Oh my, this patient is perseverating." And perseveration is a strong indication of the presence of an organic disorder.

In every clinical encounter, there's the outward interaction with the patient in which the therapist speaks in everyday language, and also there's the inward thinking process in which the therapist translates everything into clinical language. One final aspect of this complex process involves the therapist observing his or her internal experiences and using those as informative data about the clinical situation.

Here's an example: You are interviewing an 82-year-old woman. She seems to be a kindly lady; she looks like everyone's archetypical grandmother, including support hose. After a short time you notice that you feel a bit angry with the patient. That's strange. You wonder why you would be experiencing this irritation. Perhaps it's a reaction to something about the patient, but what might that be? Then you realize that you're struggling with the interview. It should be easy, but it's not. You can't seem to get the information you need. At this point you turn your attention to figuring out exactly what is going on. And, bam! You see it. Although the patient is entirely cooperative, sweet, and smiling, her sentences are empty. They have the form of sentences with nouns and verbs and prepositions, but there is no substantial content.

"What brings you here, Mrs. Penny?"

"Oh, I just haven't been feeling so good."

"And for how long has this been going on?"

"Oh, awhile."

"How long do you think? A day? A week? A month? Longer?"

"Oh, dear, I don't really know. Awhile."

"And in what way do you feel not so good?"

"Oh, you know, just not good."

When Mrs. Penny was asked about current events she said, "Oh, there's a lot going on with politicians." And when asked where she was she said, "in your office, in a building."

This sort of discourse is found in many individuals who have a dementia of some kind. It is as though their language has been emptied of content other than generalities and polite habitual phrases. It is as though their language has been emptied of individual thought and swept clean of any complexity. As a therapist, it is impossible to get answers to your questions from these individuals, simply because they don't have the information.

In other situations, the patient's language might be entirely fluid and seem normal on first glance, but the sentences might be altogether lacking in nouns, for example. These individuals might have a disturbance of language itself (an aphasia) that interferes with communication. In other words, the problem you are having in conducting this interview, the frustration you are experiencing, is an important clue to the patient's diagnosis.

In order to utilize this kind of clue, a therapist needs to be self-observant, noting the feelings and fantasies that flit through consciousness, noticing how he or she is interacting with the patient. In addition, it is imperative for the therapist to translate all of this complexity, all of this private information into clinical terms. Then, the next step is careful problem solving, bringing scientific and diagnostic thinking to bear.

Throughout any clinical interaction, the interior experience of the therapist drives the questions that are asked. That internal process involves observing one's self, processing complex information, and thinking carefully about what might be the matter with the patient, generating hypotheses based on knowledge as well as prior experience, and asking questions to try to ascertain whether those hypotheses are accurate or not.

Chapter 6

The History of the Present Illness

Introduction

Taking an effective history of an individual's present illness sounds easier than it generally turns out to be in real clinical situations. Let's look at what is involved. In order to trace the course of the patient's current condition, it is first necessary to have a sense of what factors you are following. This always begins with clarifying what the patient and the patient's family members perceive to be the problems. In other words, what are the chief complaints?

Also of crucial importance is the question of timing. Why has the patient come to the attention of health-care practitioners *at this particular moment in time*? Once you believe you understand the dynamics of the present situation, only then is it possible to turn the focus of your history-taking to the past, gathering information about when and how the current problems first began.

In looking for an organic condition, it is helpful to be on alert for several possible patterns. First, have there been fundamental changes in the patient, and what exactly are those changes? Second, does the individual have episodes or periods of time during which he or she is different from usual? Third, does this patient have lifelong difficulties, vulnerabilities, or disabilities?

A Straightforward Case

In many instances, information gathering about the present situation and the history of the present illness will be straightforward, then the diagnosis and treatment options will be clear. In other situations, therapists will face numerous challenges to figuring out what is going on now and what has happened in the past. Here are a series of examples in which clinicians encountered obstacles to obtaining a clear narrative history. Let's begin with a straightforward case.

> *Tony is an honors high school student who stops in to see his guidance counselor because he has been having trouble with schoolwork for a few weeks. Tony says that he can't seem to concentrate on his work and that this is uncharacteristic for him. He hasn't been able to finish his history paper on protest songs of the 60s, and he actually failed a math test.*
>
> *The counselor inquires as to when this all began. Tony "knows for sure" that he started to have trouble after he was "slammed in the head" during volleyball practice three weeks earlier. He hadn't lost consciousness, so at first he had thought that this incident would have no significance, even though he "did see stars" and felt "stunned and a bit nauseous" at the time. "But, I haven't been my old self since," he states.*

Tony was able to relate the entire story. He remembers being fine; then he was hit in the head, and he was no longer okay. Tony was aware of the crucial factors in the history, and he sought out his guidance counselor for help once he noticed that his schoolwork was being affected. The guidance counselor thinks it's likely that Tony had a concussion three weeks prior and that his symptoms are a consequence of a post-concussion syndrome. The counselor recommends that Tony have a medical workup to confirm the diagnosis.

A Clear History, But the Patient Is Unaware of an Underlying Problem

Here's another example in which the patient is *aware* of her symptoms but *unaware* that her symptoms might display a crucial diagnostic pattern.

> *Ebony is a 38-year-old, married woman with two children who comes in complaining about fights with her husband. On the one hand, she feels certain that she "is right" to be mad at him. "He never helps," she says. "He leaves the hateful chores to me—emptying the dishwasher, vacuuming, dealing with the trash." But on the other hand, she also believes that there are times when she "loses all sense of proportion" and is just "too upset." And Ebony doesn't like herself when she's like that.*
>
> *She especially did not like herself two weeks earlier when she got so angry with her husband after he "left his dirty dishes for me to clean up"*

that she threw a dish against the wall. The dish shattered, and she burst into tears. She had never done anything like that before. This was what led Ebony to make a therapy appointment.

"In the big scheme of things, the issues that we fight about are trivial," she says. "Really, my husband is a great guy. I know this. He works hard at his job and brings home a good salary. He loves me."

The therapist inquires as to whether the patient has any theories about what makes the difference between those times when she "can hold onto the big picture" and those times when she "loses all sense of proportion."

Thus begins the history-taking. This is the beginning of exploring with Ebony whether there is a pattern to the ups and downs of her anger at her husband and whether there is a pattern to the changes in her perspective about her feelings over time. Could it be that Ebony gets angry about the household chores when other demands are overwhelming her? Is it possible that she gets angry about the household chores when actually she is angry at her husband about other, perhaps deeper matters or issues that are more difficult to bring up? Or could there be some association between the intensity of her anger and how well she has slept the night before? Or the phases of her menstrual cycle?

As you are taking a history, one of the most important factors to keep in mind is that patients and their families may only be cognizant of the downstream effects or the fallout from a more fundamental problem of which they are unaware. In Ebony's case, the timing of her fights with her husband did fit the pattern of a premenstrual disorder. It turned out that neither Ebony nor her husband had considered this explanation. They hadn't noticed the pattern until Ebony's astute therapist suggested this as a possibility.

A Confusing History

An even greater challenge to the clinician is the patient who presents with vague or confusing symptoms and a lack of clarity about the history.

A college student named Aadi made an appointment at the counseling center. During his first appointment, he complained of feeling anxious and irritable. Then, he added that he was failing academically. He said that his family was driving him crazy because they were "worried" and "embarrassed" that he might have to take a leave of absence from school.

The therapist wondered what Aadi's fundamental problems might be and asked him a few really important questions. Aadi was vague in his answers.

What had prompted him to come in now? Aadi thought that perhaps he had come in for help now because of the imminent possibility of his failing school, but he wondered whether it was really because his parents had insisted.

When did he last feel like everything was okay? Well, he wasn't sure about that either. "Things changed kind of gradually." He felt okay in high school, he thought.

And did he have any ideas about what might be the matter? Well, not really, he just didn't like school, and his "parents were bugging him."

Aadi is very different from Ebony. Although Ebony hadn't perceived the underlying pattern of her symptoms, she was able to give a clear and detailed chief complaint and history. Aadi's chief complaint is vague and nonspecific. Also, with Aadi it's difficult to flesh out a clear history. Nonetheless, something is clearly the matter. Aadi is having symptoms; he is anxious and irritable. And he is not functioning well; he is failing in school.

Aadi's college counselor knew that there were a lot of diagnostic possibilities that might explain this presentation, including organic conditions that could be covert causative factors. She had seen it all! She'd seen a freshman with the same clinical picture—that student had been having trouble adjusting to school and had borrowed a few too many stimulant medications from roommates. She'd seen a college sophomore with a brain tumor. She also had once counseled a junior with early signs of Huntington's disease and a senior who had turned out to have central nervous system Lyme disease. All of these students had come in with somewhat vague histories and a set of chief complaints that were similar to Aadi's, namely, anxiety, irritability, and trouble with school.

In cases like this, it takes a clinician's careful inquiry to elicit more details about the chief complaint and the current circumstances. It requires the practitioner to think through what might be going on that the patient is either unaware of or not reporting, perhaps using the following questions:

- Are you using drugs? Which ones? How often? When did you first begin?
- Do you ever wake up with headaches in the morning? Do you have any other new physical sensations or difficulties?
- Tell me about your family history of medical and psychiatric problems, especially any disorders in which increased risk is conferred genetically.
- Have you spent time outdoors in grassy areas where Lyme disease is found? Have you ever been bitten by a tick? Have you ever had a target-like rash?

These are just a sampling of the kinds of questions that might be part of a searching inquiry.

The Patient Does Not Perceive the Problem

It is even more difficult to figure out whether an individual has an underlying organic diagnosis when changes in the individual are not perceived by anyone to be problems at all. A few examples include increasing preoccupation with spiritual concerns or religious conversions that may accompany temporal lobe epilepsy; the energizing experience of hypomania that one may get from corticosteroid medications; the easy weight loss caused by increased metabolism with hyperthyroidism; a more passive, compliant personality that may result from a brain tumor involving the frontal lobes. In these situations, the key to eliciting this history is for the clinician to inquire about whether the patient has or has not changed, in negative or especially in ways that might be perceived as positive by the patient or the patient's family.

Another challenge to history-taking is when disorders are relatively stable over a lifetime; think of an autistic spectrum disorder, attention deficit hyperactivity disorder, or a learning disability. In these situations, the patient might come to the attention of health-care personnel only after the individual's life circumstances have changed in such a way as to overwhelm his or her earlier adaptations to any deficits. The problem is that the patient and the family members may never have realized that the patient had any deficits; thus, they focus entirely on the situation that has tipped the balance.

The Patient and/or the Circumstances

In any patient's story, there will always be an interplay between external circumstances and the individual. It may not be easy to ascertain whether the patient has appeared in your office because of a psychological reaction to a stressful circumstance or because he or she has undergone some fundamental change that has led to an altered way of reacting. Here is one example that demonstrates that kind of confusion.

> *Faith was let go from her job as an assistant manager at a small automobile-supply company. The family had depended on Faith's income, because her husband had lost his job the previous year. The patient sought counseling. She told her therapist that she felt "devastated," "depressed," and "discombobulated."*

> *At first, the therapist assumed that the patient had lost her job because of the nationwide recession. Once he inquired, he learned that Faith was the only worker the company had laid off. In addition, apparently Faith had been having difficulties at work for more than a year before this. She had been coming home with stories about how her boss was being "demanding" and "trying to get more and more work out of me." She had been "called on the carpet" for making repeated mistakes on invoices and for taking too many personal phone calls on the company's time. It began to sound as though Faith was let go for reasons that had more to do with Faith herself and less to do with the economy. What exactly had happened to Faith?*

Thus begins the process of wondering, of hypothesizing about what might have happened and then inquiring further to see if your theory might be correct. Is it possible that Faith had a lifelong problem such as ADHD that was well compensated until her boss began to demand more of her?

Perhaps Faith became depressed and this affected her work. Certainly she might have felt the stress of supporting her family without her husband's salary. Plus one might wonder about how the dynamics of her marriage may have shifted once her husband was out of work. Had something like that caused her to become depressed?

If you open your thinking to the possibility that there might have been a change in Faith rather than primarily a change in Faith's circumstances, there are other diagnoses to consider. Is Faith showing the signs of an early dementia with diminished cognitive abilities? Could she have developed a sleep disorder such as restless legs syndrome or sleep apnea that led her to exhibit irritability, mental inefficiency, and trouble with concentration? Is that why she was having trouble at work?

If you theorize that your patient has changed, it is also important to carefully define exactly how the patient is different from the person he or she used to be. Then go on to evaluate these changes. Are they simply part of personal growth and learning? Or are the changes a consequence of having been influenced by or overwhelmed by some important life experience? Are you hearing about changes that are part of normal aging or that are expressions of an underlying disease process? These questions are important to pursue as you try to unmask any covert somatic disease, but the answers may not be easy to work out. Extensive inquiry, family involvement, neuropsychological testing and the utilization of consultants may be required.

Chapter 7

Specific Physical Signs and Symptoms

Introduction to Signs and Symptoms

Although the terms *sign* and *symptom* are often used interchangeably in common parlance, the formal distinction between them is useful to know. Signs are findings that can be observed, whether in the physical realm or in the arena of mind and behavior. There are innumerable examples: flat affect, delusional thinking, bruises, a hacking cough, bulging eyes, a drooping eyelid, chipped fingernails, grandiosity, yellow jaundiced skin. Patients may be entirely unaware that they exhibit these signs. If they have noticed them, they are often oblivious to their diagnostic significance. Some physical signs might be discovered only through a physical examination, such as overly brisk or asymmetrical reflexes, a heart murmur, scarred eardrums, abnormalities in the retina of the eye. These findings will not be discussed; this book focuses on observations that can be made from across the room during an interview.

Symptoms, as distinct from signs, are experiences that are reported by the patient and for which there may be no objective evidence. The patient always knows about his or her symptoms because, by their very nature, symptoms are subjective: dizziness, headache, stiffness, panic, weakness or fatigue, thirst, nausea, itching, double vision, feeling hopeless, trouble swallowing, déjà vu sensations, pain of all kinds.

Some signs and symptoms fall squarely in the physical realm: *signs* such as a rash, black eye, swollen wrist, pill-rolling tremor, and *symptoms* like a sore throat, blurred vision, chest pain upon inhaling, or itching. Other signs and symptoms would be considered by most clinicians to fall squarely in the psychological realm, including *signs* such as loose associations, hyperactivity, paranoia, or concrete thinking, and *symptoms* such as anxiety, depression, or trouble falling asleep.

However, we know that the soma and psyche, the physical and mental, are not distinct and separate. Straddling the line are signs and symptoms in the vegetative realm: energy level, appetite and weight, sleep, libido. Also, it is not surprising that a single underlying disease process may generate a mixture of signs and symptoms in both the physical and the mental spheres. Even signs and symptoms that are solely in the mental sphere may be generated by covert organic disorders.

This chapter begins with a discussion of physical signs and then moves on to describing an approach to physical symptoms, including those in the vegetative realm.

Physical Signs

You may be the first clinician to observe physical signs that signal the presence of organic disease. Even from across the room it is possible to notice crucial physical signs, such as a hoarse voice, coughing, a rash, swelling, emaciation, physical or functional asymmetry of the body, bulges in the neck, yellowing or bronzing of skin, a limp or unsteady gait, clumsiness, tremors, rigidity, diminished small movements of the face, protruding eyes, severe acne, extreme short stature, abnormal facial hair, and so on. All physical signs should be evaluated by a physician in order to diagnose and treat any medical ailments your patient might have. In addition, keep in mind that physical signs might be indicative of an organic condition that could be complicating or even causing the mental state for which the patient is seeking your help.

It would be impossible to discuss the medical implications of all the possible physical signs a clinician might observe even if that discussion could be confined only to those physical signs that are associated with diseases presenting as mental disorders. However, it is possible to present some fundamental notions that can guide your approach to thinking about physical signs and enhance your effectiveness in detecting them. This section is organized around the following elemental ideas.

1. *A single sign in the physical realm may be a crucial clue and can shift and broaden one's clinical diagnostic thinking.* For example, a reddish, butterfly-shaped facial rash is characteristic of systemic lupus erythematosis, an autoimmune disorder that also may cause anxiety, depression, or even psychosis.

2. *It is easy to overlook, dismiss, or misattribute the etiology of a physical sign, even if it is conspicuous.* The common mechanisms by which this happens are (a) thinking that a physical sign is unrelated to the patient's mental status findings or (b) believing that the physical sign results from a conversion disorder.

3. *Some physical signs have far-reaching significance; it is useful to observe these signs and to be aware that they may have serious implications.* One example would be recently developed abnormal eye movements, a finding that is not only significant for organic disease but that also provides specific information to knowledgeable professionals about what exactly that condition might be.

A Physical Sign—Perhaps a Crucial Clue

A single physical sign, carefully noted and understood, has the power to broaden one's diagnostic thinking. Here is an example.

> *During community meetings each morning at the day hospital, I began to notice that 50-year-old Mrs. Elderwood had a very slight, though persistent, slurring of speech. She did not have any history of alcohol abuse, and her medications did not seem to be causing the problem, so I decided to refer her to a neurologist. This subtle difficulty that the patient had with articulation turned out to be a sign that she had amyotrophic lateral sclerosis (ALS), also called Lou Gehrig's disease, a degenerative neurological disease that may be associated with a loss of emotional control. Her emotional lability had been much in evidence in her recent history and had been an important precipitant for her day hospitalization. In this instance, that single physical sign was the most important clue to a crucial, underlying, organic condition, with significant implications for prognosis and treatment.*

Ways a Physical Sign May Be Dismissed

There are many ways that clinicians may inadvertently dismiss, fail to notice, or overlook the significance of an important physical sign in a patient's presentation. Theoretically, one would think that physical signs, such as Mrs. Elderwood's slurred speech, would be very apparent. Yet the reader can appreciate how easy it is, in real clinical situations, to dismiss signs like slurred speech or extraneous motor movements or protruding eyes or any of a myriad of other possible signs. In mental health settings, this is most likely to occur when the signs are subtle, if one has an alternative explanation for them, when a practitioner doesn't know that the finding might have crucial significance, or when the clinician assumes that the sign has little or nothing to do with the mental life of the patient.

It was easy for the day hospital staff to overlook Mrs. Elderwood's slurred speech, even though difficulty with speech articulation is always caused by physical factors. The slurred speech was subtle. Also, it could be explained away quite readily (either consciously or with barely a thought) using theories about how the patient might possibly have been overmedicated, missing her dentures, or drinking too much (since many of the day hospital patients had problems with alcohol abuse). Although some of these theories would have implications for how to provide better care for the patient, none of them would actually make the link between the patient's slurred speech and the reason for her being in the day hospital in the first place. Once a clinician comes up with a plausible explanation for a physical sign, whether consciously or unconsciously, whether accurate or flawed, the tendency is to stop thinking about it any further. The physical clue moves to the background of our attention and doesn't figure as significantly as it ought to in one's diagnostic thinking.

If you do notice a physical sign in one of your patients, whether it is old or new, you want to be sure that you fully understand its cause and significance. It is crucial to be sure that a competent physician has evaluated the finding within a reasonable time frame, given the evolution of the sign. Also, you will want to talk with that physician or obtain the medical records of the evaluation. You are looking for answers to the following questions: What is the etiology of the physical finding? Do the physical sign and the psychological presentation have anything to do with one another? And if they are related, how are they related? Are they both being caused by one underlying disorder? Is one causing the other? Or are two somewhat independent processes interacting in a complex way?

When trying to sort out this issue of causality, there is the danger of being drawn too quickly to one of two poles. At one pole lies the danger of assuming that the physical sign has nothing to do with the psychological presentation. At the other pole is the danger of assuming that the psychological problem is the sole cause of the physical sign via a psychosomatic process, stress, a masked depression, the consequences of the person's lifestyle, or something of that sort. All practitioners, including primary care physicians, specialists, and psychotherapists, are vulnerable to these errors, especially when they are dealing with a patient who has a history of psychiatric hospitalization or in some other way looks like a "mental patient."

ASSUMING A PHYSICAL SIGN IS NOT RELEVANT TO THE MENTAL PRESENTATION

Here is an example of a case in which an obvious physical sign was assumed to be unrelated to the psychological problems the patient was experiencing. In fact, the physical sign was a clue to an underlying medical disease that also was generating a mood disorder.

A middle-aged attorney consulted a therapist because he had been feeling depressed for the first time in his life. The patient had a chronic "smoker's" cough, but the therapist assumed that this physical sign was insignificant and certainly unrelated to the patient's presenting psychological problems. A medical workup, initiated by the patient, revealed a malignant lung tumor.

Certain types of lung cancer, as well as cancer of the testes or ovary, are capable of secreting hormonal substances or setting off immune reactions (paraneoplastic syndrome) that can cause profound changes in mental status. An alteration in mood or even a full-blown psychosis may presage the overt appearance of the cancer. Cancer of the pancreas not uncommonly presents with symptoms of major depression that are prominent in the clinical picture, while other manifestations of the pancreatic malignancy, such as subtle gastrointestinal complaints, slip into the background.

There are many other physical signs whose possible bearing on the psychological problem at hand might be overlooked, even though they may be readily visible to a therapist from across the consulting room. For instance, bulging eyes (in which the entire circumference of the iris is visible) may be a sign of Graves' disease, a variant of hyperthyroidism, a disease associated with numerous psychological symptoms, including anxiety and depression. Tremors may be the physical manifestation of a myriad of possible diseases, including Parkinson's disease, liver failure, hyperthyroidism, or mercury poisoning, each of which might also cause important changes in mental status.

ASSUMING A PHYSICAL SIGN RESULTS FROM A PSYCHOSOCIAL SITUATION OR PSYCHOSOMATIC PROCESS

It is also important to guard against dismissing the significance of a physical sign by attributing it solely to an underlying psychological problem or psychosocial situation. An excellent example of this situation was recently related to me by an internist/friend. Here's what he remembered:

Many years ago he was doing his medical student psychiatric rotation at a big city hospital. He was assigned to a newly admitted hospital patient who had a long history of serious alcohol abuse and was now flagrantly psychotic. The psychiatric staff focused on treating the patient's psychotic symptoms with psychotropic medications. Paradoxically, day after day, the patient's psychosis worsened.

Having just finished his time on the medical wards, the student was primed to notice that the patient's skin was red on the sun-exposed areas of his body. In particular, on his neck there was a crusty rash in the shape of a necklace. The patient also had diarrhea. The psychiatric staff hadn't focused on these physical findings; they vaguely attributed them to the patient's alcoholism and to his homeless life on the street. They dismissed the medical student's suggestion that the patient might have a serious, covert medical etiology for these physical signs.

Despite this opposition to his ideas, the medical student went ahead and ordered nicotinic acid supplements for the patient, believing that the patient actually might be suffering from pellagra, a nicotinic acid deficiency disease. In a matter of days, the patient's condition improved dramatically.

The medical student, now my colleague, had been able to see that the rash on the neck of this psychotic inpatient represented a "medical pearl," referred to as Casal's necklace. The hospital staff was used to seeing psychotic patients who drank too much and lived on the street; these patients had poor nutrition and even worse hygiene. The staff members were mentally blind to the rash and the diarrhea; these were dismissed as the inevitable consequences of the patient's lifestyle. If the staff had wondered about the rash and ordered a consultation, it is highly likely that a dermatologist would have pointed out the significance of this crusty red necklace as a sign of pellagra.

Ironically, in one sense, the hospital personnel were correct; the patient's symptoms *were* a consequence of life on the street. The rash and the diarrhea, as well as the patient's psychosis, were linked by a fundamental cause, namely a deficiency of dietary niacin. This patient had a deficiency disease that was causing his mental symptoms, and that deficiency disease was caused by his lifestyle.

The inpatient staff members at this busy psychiatric hospital were very familiar with the potential consequences of thiamine deficiency in patients with chronic alcohol abuse, namely Wernicke's encephalopathy (a life-threatening syndrome characterized by confusion, difficulty with gait, and impaired eye movement, especially difficulty looking sideways) and Korsakoff's syndrome (an irreversible, profound disturbance in the ability to form new memories, often initially accompanied by confabulation). Thiamine deficiency in this population is so common and so serious that it has become routine to give thiamine supplements to any patient with alcohol problems who so much as walks into a hospital. But pellagra, deficiency of nicotinic acid intake, is much less common.

Another instructive clinical vignette begins with a familiar clinical picture, a young woman who is getting thinner and thinner. This case illustrates the complexity that may lie hidden in what seems like a most common presentation. Here's the story as told to me by Brooke after all the diagnostic mysteries had been sorted out.

Brooke told me that she had "had trouble adjusting" during her first year at college. In high school she had been a superb athlete and had excelled academically, but during her first year away from home at a top-ranked university, she had lost her appetite and begun to experience fatigue and mild feelings of depression for the first time in her life. She also had experienced some vomiting and had lost about 20 pounds.

Brooke said that her friends had always thought of her as the kind of person who would "tough things out when the going got rough," but this time Brooke felt that she simply couldn't manage; she decided to take a leave of absence from school. She told me that she had been "sure there was something physically wrong." A medical workup revealed that Brooke had Graves' disease, a disorder affecting the thyroid gland. Thankfully, medical treatment alleviated most of her symptoms, her depression lifted, and she regained her energy.

But Brooke was still quite thin and continued to experience nausea and occasional vomiting. And despite nutritional advice and encouragement, she did not gain weight. Now Brooke had a diagnosis—Graves' disease; she was better, but she wasn't back to normal. She was "frustrated and confused" and "not sure what was going on." All of this was getting her down.

At this point, Brooke's primary care physician and her thyroid specialist wanted her to see a psychotherapist. Her doctors were beginning to think that, in addition to thyroid disease, Brooke also had an eating disorder. The therapist Brooke consulted with agreed with them, but months of psychotherapy had no impact on Brooke's weight.

The tide turned only after one of Brooke's friends, a social work student, noted that something was amiss: Brooke didn't really fit the picture of someone with anorexia nervosa or bulimia nervosa. Unlike the typical individual with an eating disorder, Brooke was distressed about losing weight. And Brooke didn't think that she was fat, she thought she was too thin.

It wasn't until this friend insisted that Brooke get a second medical opinion that the true source of her continued gastrointestinal symptoms was identified. In addition to Graves' disease, Brooke also had a significant infection with Helicobacter pylori, a common, easily treatable, chronic, gastrointestinal condition. Often referred to as simply H. pylori, this bacterium has adapted to survive the hostile acidic environment of the stomach. It is associated with a wide range of gastrointestinal symptoms from chronic indigestion to ulcers. (It does not cause mental status changes.)

Brooke had a full recovery and successful return to college after a course of antibiotic treatment. The mystery of why Brooke had such difficulty during her first year in college had been a very difficult one to solve, because she had two medical diagnoses (Graves' disease and H. pylori), both probably contributing to her weight loss. Her H. pylori infection was difficult to diagnose because it was a common illness, but it had presented in an uncommon way.

Significant weight loss, a clear physical sign, may bring to a therapist's mind a differential diagnosis list that begins with anorexia nervosa or severe depression. These are the most common causes of weight loss for those patients who find their way into the offices of psychotherapists. It behooves us to keep in mind that anorexia and depression are diagnoses that are made on the basis of specific criteria. They are not fallback explanations, diagnoses of exclusion to be made when there is no other clear explanation for the findings.

Keep in mind that there are numerous possible causes of weight loss. This significant physical sign may be seen in patients who are suffering from nutritional deprivation as a consequence of poverty, addiction, or disorganizing illnesses such as a psychosis or dementia. In addition, there are a multitude of organic causes of significant weight loss. Those that are most important for mental health practitioners to have in mind are physical conditions that may also cause disturbances of mood and/ or cognition. These especially need to be included on every therapist's mental list of possible causes of weight loss: thyroid disease, pancreatic carcinoma, infection with the human immunodeficiency virus (HIV), metastatic cancers (that may spread to the brain), or a variety of disorders that may impair the absorption of essential nutrients from the gut.

PHYSICAL SIGNS WITH GREAT SIGNIFICANCE

Some types of physical signs are especially significant because they are readily observable and convey important information about the brain.

Neurological Soft Signs   Subtle neurological signs can be the evidence of early disruptive factors in the shaping of the brain; these are referred to as neurological soft signs. Lifelong, congenital mild body asymmetry fits into this category—slight facial asymmetry or the presence of a substantial difference in the size of one thumb in comparison to the other. Other neurological soft signs that therapists may hear about from their patients, especially when exploring childhood experiences, include clumsiness involving large muscle groups such as awkward running, difficulty with fine motor coordination as when cutting out small shapes with scissors, trouble with rapid alternating hand movements as in the child's game "rock, paper, scissors," problems with articulating tongue twisters, and pathological slowness in completing the tasks of daily life, or having "only one speed." Another neurological soft sign is called *synkinesia*; this is the tendency for an individual who is concentrating on a fine motor task with one hand to inadvertently mirror it, albeit awkwardly, with the other.

These findings are not specific to any one disorder and are not associated with injury to one particular brain region; however, they do constitute evidence of some mild, early impact on the brain. Soft neurologic signs are found more commonly in individuals with learning disabilities, autism spectrum disorders, and schizophrenia, among other disorders.

> *Teresa is very bright and an engineer who sees me for psychotherapy. Recently she decided to cut her work back to 20 hours per week. She told me that she wanted more time to herself after years of working at a 40-hour-per-week job. Further exploration revealed that her 40-hour-per-week job had taken her about 60 hours per week to accomplish. She regularly would stay late at the office and also return to her workplace on weekends in order to complete her assignments.*
>
> *At first I thought that Teresa's workload was too great, but it turned out that the problem was Teresa's pace. She is someone who works slowly and methodically and can't seem to speed up even when a task requires it. She is detail-oriented and has high standards, but her inability to work faster is not simply because of perfectionist tendencies, nor does she have obsessive-compulsive disorder.*
>
> *Whenever I greet Teresa in the waiting room, she is sitting comfortably on the couch, generally reading her* New York Times. *Once she sees me in the doorway, she slowly begins to fold the newspaper back along its natural creases. With attention to detail, she carefully forms the paper into a neat packet and then proceeds to slide it with great deliberateness into the tote bag she has placed on the floor beside her. Only then does she rise and walk down the hall and into my office.*

Each time I observe this sequence of movements, I try to figure out what makes Teresa so remarkably and disablingly slow. Here is what I have concluded. She does not anticipate my arrival; she does not begin to put her things in order upon hearing my last patient leave; she doesn't fold the newspaper while simultaneously rising from the couch; she doesn't compromise on the neatness of her folding or on how snugly she fits the newspaper into her tote bag. Each of these choice points adds extra seconds to the task of leaving the waiting room and, in the course of a day, this must be how extra minutes add up to the extra hours needed to complete her work. Teresa tells me that she was always a terrible athlete and an awkward runner; she has mild facial asymmetry; she is not dexterous. She has neurological soft signs, and this has had a substantial effect on her life.

Asymmetry of Structure and/or Function   Most people use one hand more than the other. And humans also favor one leg over the other, though in any individual, the dominant arm and leg are not necessarily on the same side. The result of this is some degree of asymmetry of muscle mass. This is easy to observe in individuals who vigorously use their dominant side. Just compare the right and left forearms of any tennis pro. Other than this effect of dominance, asymmetries of structure or function are signs of some underlying physical problem. Those physical problems may be at the periphery of the body or, of special significance here, the problems may lie in the central nervous system.

An example of an asymmetry of structure or function that reflects a problem at the periphery of the body would be an asymmetrical gait, limping, that might be caused by arthritis in a knee or foot. Muscle wasting and weakness of certain muscles of one hand might be caused by long-standing carpal tunnel syndrome on that side, a compression of the median nerve as it runs through the wrist into the hand. Keep in mind that asymmetries such as these that are not caused by problems in the brain but by a disturbance at the periphery of the body could be signs of a more generalized disease process that is having a secondary effect on the brain. For instance, peripheral nerve compression syndromes such as carpal tunnel syndrome may occur when an individual has hypothyroidism as a result of the swelling of soft tissues, although in that condition the nerve compression is *usually* on both sides. And hypothyroidism is capable of causing mental changes from depression to psychosis as a consequence of diminished circulating thyroid hormone. As for that limp from arthritis in the knee, it could be the consequence of an old football injury or possibly a symptom of late Lyme disease. Lyme disease is an infection that can involve the brain and cause mental status changes, most frequently fatigue, depressed mood, and difficulties with concentration. Arthritis could also be a symptom of systemic lupus erythematosis, sarcoidosis, or lead poisoning, each capable of affecting multiple systems of the body, including the joints as well as the brain.

But asymmetries of structure or function may at times be a consequence of pathology in specific regions of the brain; this is of particular interest because the underlying disease process in the central nervous system also might be causing mental status or behavioral changes. This notion that an asymmetry of structure or function might be caused by a problem in the brain is worth discussing a bit more fully, because it introduces the concept of focal findings, a fundamental and crucial concept in thinking about clues to hidden disorders.

With some brain functions such as the various aspects of language, one hemisphere is dominant, although both hemispheres of the brain participate and cooperate. In contrast, many other brain functions are lateralized. Lateralized means that only one hemisphere controls that function for a particular part of the body. For example, the sensations of touch, temperature, pain, and position sense on the right side of the body are controlled by brain regions in the left hemisphere and vice versa. This information reflects the wiring diagram of the brain and the nervous system. If you know the wiring diagram, then you can reason backward. If someone has an asymmetrical loss of certain types of sensation one can reason backward to figure out where the problem lies.

Asymmetry that is based on the lateralization of brain functions is considered to be a focal finding. Focal findings are like fingerprints at a crime scene. They are extremely informative. They not only tell you that the problem is *in* the brain, but they also tell you *where* the problem is in the brain. The important takeaway message for therapists is the concept that focal findings are highly significant.

Asymmetries of facial movement that have developed in adulthood may be particularly informative. Therapists are already focused on the face as a source of nuanced emotional information. In addition it is important to observe whether there are asymmetries of facial features at rest, smiling (conscious or automatic), eyebrow raising, eyelid movement, pupil size (difficult to see from across the room), and so on. Drooling may be an indication of subtle muscle weakness and/or diminished sensation on one side of the mouth. The nerves that would be involved in producing such asymmetries are cranial nerves, meaning that they have their origins in the brain; consequently, if there is facial asymmetry of some kind, this may be an excellent indicator of lesion location in the brain.

> *Just last month one of my patients, Judith, mentioned that her right eyelid occasionally obscured her upper field of vision on that side, just slightly. From where I sat I could perceive a slight asymmetry, a slight drooping of her right eyelid. Judith told me that her optometrist had suggested that she consider having plastic surgery to address the problem.*
>
> *The optometrist must not have been aware of the possible medical significance of one drooping eyelid, called unilateral ptosis. Although Judith is a very intelligent and sophisticated individual who trusted my medical judgment, she felt kind of awkward about seeing a neurologist; it was difficult for her to get over the feeling that this was such a minor, even "silly" problem, one that was hardly worth bringing to a specialist.*

One drooping eyelid, even one slightly drooping eyelid, could be a significant sign of pathology in the central nervous system, perhaps a tumor impinging on a cranial nerve or a stroke. Or perhaps she had something called Horner's syndrome, in which a tumor at the apex of the lung affects nerves that travel to the eye. She also could have had myasthenia gravis, a disorder in which the neurotransmitter acetylcholine is blocked from signaling muscle contraction by an autoimmune process. Or, this may have been an unusual presentation of a thyroid disorder.

The point here is two-fold: First, every one of these possible diseases could be associated with mental status changes. Lung cancers can cause depression; myasthenia gravis can present as a conversion disorder, especially because emotions worsen the symptoms; thyroid disorders are capable of causing a myriad of mental changes from anxiety to psychosis. Second, it is competent clinical practice for therapists to facilitate the full investigation of all physical signs for the health of their patients. Judith was relieved when she reported to me that the neurologist had spent an entire hour with her, had ordered a chest x-ray and numerous laboratory studies, and emphasized that he felt her symptom had merited serious investigation. She and I were both relieved that all of the findings were normal.

Abnormal Eye Movements   Abnormal eye movements are always associated with organic disease, though these may or may not be associated with current changes in mental status or behavior. Many disturbances of eye movement (e.g., strabismus or "lazy eye") are congenital and likely bear no etiological relationship to current difficulties beyond the important psychological meanings these eye problems might have for the patient. However, *new onset* of abnormal eye movements is highly significant.

Smooth, precise, and coordinated movement of the eyes is accomplished by a complex system, involving six muscles that move each eye globe, three cranial nerves that innervate those muscles after emerging directly from the brain, and a backroom operating system involving a multitude of brain regions acting in coordination. Abnormal eye movements may result from even subtle pathology anywhere in this system.

Some disturbances of eye movement may be difficult to discern in an interview setting, especially if one is not specifically looking for this sort of finding. That said, it is useful to observe whether a patient has diminished range of motion of the eyes (up or down, right or left); deviation of the eyes to one side; jerky motions back and forth or up and down, or rotary motion. It is crucial to keep in mind that subtle disturbances of eye motion may not be visible to the clinician but may cause the patient to experience and complain of double vision or blurred or hazy vision. These complaints should be taken extremely seriously. Diseases that may present with disturbances of eye movement include brain tumors, stroke, thiamine deficiency (Wernicke's encephalitis), progressive supranuclear palsy (a degenerative brain disease), multiple sclerosis, and poisoning with thallium or manganese.

Two other aspects of eye movement that are worthy of our attention are eye blinking and eye contact. An increased eye blink rate may be associated with Tourette's syndrome, tardive dyskinesia (which is a long-term side effect of certain medications), absence seizures, or dry eyes (which may be associated with an underlying autoimmune disorder or use of certain medications). On the other hand, diminished eye blinking may be seen in patients with Parkinson's disease or conditions in which the facial nerve is paralyzed, such as Moebius syndrome.

Abnormalities of eye contact are generally quite obvious to therapists, because eye contact is so basic to forming relationships. People gather crucial social information about the emotions and intentions of others by looking at the faces, and especially the eyes, of others. Individuals with autism spectrum disorders are more likely to have poor eye contact.

Disturbances in Body Movement   Human beings are so good at smooth, efficient, effective movement through the obstacle course of the real world that it is rare for an adult to trip, fall, or drop something. Multiple brain systems work together to make this possible by generating balance, coordination, muscle strength, and the capacity to navigate through space. When pathology affects any of the systems involved, disturbances may show up in the realm of body movement. Thus, unnecessary, extraneous movements or problems with smooth, coordinated bodily movement through space or in manipulating objects is an excellent marker of the presence of some organic condition.

Disturbances of gait are especially important and easy to observe. The police take advantage of this in asking drivers who are suspected of being inebriated to attempt to walk a straight line, heel to toe. Neurologists call this tandem walking. It is not only alcohol that can lead an individual to have problems with walking and turning. Numerous problems that have an impact on the nervous system can lead to difficulties in this arena, making gait disturbances of all kinds important signals of organic pathology.

Clearly, some difficulties with mobility may be the result of a temporary problem that is essentially irrelevant to the individual's mental status, such as a broken foot or acute viral afflictions of the inner ear's balancing apparatus. On the other hand, what might appear to be a peripheral problem may be a marker of a generalized disease that could be having an impact on the central nervous system, as when severe vitamin B12 deficiency leads to sensory deficits that interfere with being able to locate one's feet in space without visual cues.

At other times, a gait disturbance may be caused by a disorder of the central nervous system that is also producing changes in mental status.

Here are just two examples. Normal pressure hydrocephalus (NPH) is a treatable dementia that often presents with apathy and is associated with an abnormal gait; sometimes the gait disturbance takes the form of a magnetic gait, in which the individual's feet seem to stick to the ground. Parkinson's disease and related disorders are characterized by a reduction in normal spontaneous movement, including a diminished arm swing while walking. In addition, these patients may exhibit a shuffling gait and a tendency to lean forward. When patients with Parkinson's disease have their center of gravity too far forward, they may walk faster and faster in order to keep from falling forward.

Falling, without loss of consciousness, is another significant finding that may be associated with disorders that also affect mental status. Patients with Lewy body dementia may have unexplained episodes of falling as part of their presentation. Some individuals with narcolepsy, a sleep disorder, will have cataplexy as part of the symptomatic picture. Cataplexy is a sudden, brief loss of muscle tone. It might present as a dramatic attack of falling without loss of consciousness, or it might simply involve the momentary slacking of tone in a small group of muscles and perhaps dropping something.

Extraneous movements are easy to observe and are often associated with organic disorders that have a direct effect on an individual's mental status and behavior. Some examples include the following:

- Tics could be signs of Tourette's syndrome.
- Lip smacking, lip pursing, and other involuntary mouth movements might signal the presence of a seizure disorder.
- Picking movements may also be seen in seizure disorders, or they may be caused by atropine toxicity from combinations of medications when several have atropine-like side effects.
- Tremors are so varied and significant that they constitute a specialty area of neurology; tremors of different kinds may be associated with disorders ranging from thyroid dysfunction to multiple sclerosis, from tumors of the cerebellum to arsenic poisoning.
- Writhing or flicking movements, possibly disguised as normal gestures or mannerisms, could be signs of Huntington's disease or Wilson's disease, each genetically transmitted.
- Muscle jerking along with a rapidly progressing dementia is seen in Creutzfeld-Jakob disease, a disease of humans that is related to mad cow disease of cattle.
- Stereotypical movements, waxy flexibility, grimacing, and posturing are associated with catatonia, a syndrome that is often associated with underlying organic brain pathology.

Physical Symptoms

By their very nature, symptoms are subjective. It is crucial to take seriously all of the patient's reported symptoms; these may be the most important clues one gathers in attempting to track down whether the patient has an organic diagnosis and just what that diagnosis might be. All explicitly physical complaints should be evaluated medically. Signs and symptoms taken together can lead a knowledgeable clinician to hone in on which specific organ systems might be affected and help the practitioner to develop a list of disorders that could be generating the patient's physical and, possibly, mental problems. This is called the differential diagnosis.

The subjectivity of symptoms presents special challenges for practitioners. Though a clinician may fail to attend to a physical *sign* or misinterpret its significance, once perceived, its existence cannot be denied, because there is something objective to see, hear, smell, or even measure—the cough and sputum production, the protruding eyes, the swollen thyroid gland distending the neck, the yellowed whites of the eyes, the alcohol on the breath. But in the realm of symptoms, a clinician generally must rely solely on a patient's report of his or her subjective experiences.

We know that the patient's experiences and symptom descriptions are affected by a myriad of factors. In their accounts, patients may be more or less articulate, more or less knowledgeable about their body's functioning, more or less emotional, more or less secretive, and more or less able to separate language that is simply descriptive of the symptom experience from lay, diagnostic language that is ambiguous in its meaning. "My intestinal yeast infection has kicked up again." "My arthritis is killing me." "It's something I ate. I guess I have food allergies."

In addition, symptoms are influenced by what the patient is like as an individual as well as by the cultural, environmental, and psychosocial circumstances. The pain from a leg broken in a ski accident is often experienced and reported quite differently from that sustained in an automobile accident, even if the x-rays look remarkably similar. And if the fracture happened in a workplace accident, especially if there is the possibility of the individual receiving workers' compensation, the patient's experience of the pain may be enhanced and the pace of recovery slowed, sometimes by a conscious process, sometimes unconsciously.

The knowledge that symptoms are thus influenced has led to the understandable concern that when patients present with somatic chief complaints, the practitioner must be careful about the possibility of missing a stressful home or work situation, undisclosed family abuse, a covert depression, or other psychological problem. A startling percentage of visits to primary care offices are driven primarily by underlying psychological difficulties or precipitants. This raises serious concern about how to avoid reinforcing the rewards of the sick role while also attending to important, underlying psychosocial issues. This is a common problem and a serious one, as is the worry about the costs of pursuing a medical workup if the underlying problem is situational or the symptoms are psychologically driven.

However, the converse is also a significant matter that needs to be addressed. The knowledge that so many environmental and psychological factors influence a patient's symptom presentation makes it possible for clinicians to listen to a patient's reality through a filter that minimizes, misinterprets, or even dismisses altogether the individual's physical complaints. Therapists may lean too far in the direction of interpreting physical symptoms as having purely psychological roots without a sufficient investigation. This is an especially common error when the patient has either a history of mental health problems or obvious mental status or behavioral changes that pull for a psychological diagnosis.

Other factors also influence the tendency to prematurely close out the exploration of a possible organic etiology, such as the difficulty that therapists may have with remaining in a state of uncertainty about the cause of a patient's physical complaints or the pressures exerted by the patient to know what is the matter. Often what is needed is the ability to keep an open mind, be a patient advocate, seek out appropriate second opinions, and engage in watchful waiting as a patient's symptoms unfold over time. This is especially useful if the patient has a diagnosis that is difficult to make, as when the patient's disorder is rare or when a common disorder has an atypical presentation.

It would be impossible for this book to discuss all of the possible physical symptoms that patients might experience and discuss with their therapists. Physical symptoms need to be evaluated by medical professionals, and common sense should guide the clinician in deciding just which medical professional would be appropriate for a patient's particular complaint.

One group of symptoms, however, will be discussed here in some detail. The vegetative symptoms lie in an uncertain realm between the clearly physical and clearly psychological. It is important for therapists to be familiar with these symptoms, as they are frequently consulted about them.

VEGETATIVE SYMPTOMS

The so-called vegetative symptoms are in the realm of sleep, appetite, energy level, and/or sexual desire. Disturbances in these areas are commonly associated with psychological disorders, and therefore most therapists feel they are in relatively familiar territory when these symptoms are presented. Therapists are trained to inquire about sleep, appetite, zest for life, and libido when faced with a patient who is depressed or in mourning, for instance. Changes in an individual's vegetative state are common and often debilitating, and they are frequently associated with psychological conditions, but they also accompany many organic diseases. Thus, it is always important to consider the possibility that vegetative symptoms may have an underlying physical cause.

Sleep Trouble with sleep is a very common complaint in the general population and also in the offices of all clinicians. To introduce this topic and its complexity, this chapter begins with a story about Andy, whose chief complaint was trouble with sleep. Andy had consulted with one of my supervisees, and this discussion describes how she approached figuring out the causes of Andy's sleep problem.

> *Andy's chief complaint was that he had been having trouble with sleep for about 10 years. This was remarkable because he was only 24 years old. What exactly was the trouble that Andy had been having? He said that his pattern was to get about 6 hours of sleep each night, but he complained that his sleep was restless. He said that he was able to function quite well if he could take multiple short naps during the day. This strategy worked for him until he finished college and entered his current job. Now high-level performance was being demanded of him from 9 a.m. until 5 p.m., and Andy was exhausted and having trouble concentrating at work. Worst of all, his job was in jeopardy because of poor performance.*
>
> *My supervisee had taken her patient's subjective complaint of trouble with sleep quite seriously. The problem was that she assumed these sleep problems were being generated by an underlying depression. This led to her prescribing a variety of antidepressants for the patient. Andy tried one after another, each of which he found to be "intolerable"; one caused him to feel "spacey," another left him feeling "dizzy." Fundamentally, he was rejecting altogether the notion that depression was the real problem. He was trying to communicate to the psychiatrist that his experience was that sleep was his primary problem, and, moreover, that this had been his problem for many years.*
>
> *This young psychiatrist began to redirect her thinking and to ponder other diagnostic possibilities, especially the primary sleep disorders. Did Andy have sleep apnea, in which there is either a central nervous system problem with control of breathing during sleep (not associated with snoring) or obstruction of the airways when muscles relax as the individual enters*

deep stages of sleep? Did he have restless legs syndrome or nocturnal myoclonus in which nighttime disruptions of deep sleep are accompanied by various types of leg movements?

This doctor had never seen a patient with narcolepsy, but Andy's story was consistent with that diagnosis: light, restless nighttime sleep; short daytime naps that are refreshing; early age of onset; years passing before the correct diagnosis is made. There are other subjective experiences that someone with narcolepsy might experience, but these are often only revealed when a therapist specifically inquires: hallucinations upon falling asleep or awakening (these are intrusions of REM sleep into wakefulness); sleep paralysis (a brief inability to move upon awakening from sleep); and cataplexy in which individuals experience a sudden loss of muscle tone, often precipitated by strong emotion, and leading to symptoms like dropping things or falling to the ground without any disturbance in consciousness. Andy did not have any of these symptoms.

After much discussion, Andy agreed to have a sleep consultation and overnight sleep study plus neuropsychological testing. These evaluations revealed that Andy had two problems that were interacting with one another. He had mild to moderate attention deficit hyperactivity disorder (ADHD), and he had a disorder of circadian rhythm, specifically a delayed sleep phase disorder.

Andy would not feel tired until midnight. Then he had to drag himself out of bed when his alarm rang at 6 a.m. in order to get to work on time. This was not enough sleep for him, so he would be tired all day unless he could take a nap. This disorder of circadian rhythm would make his ADHD more symptomatic, hence his problems with concentration and poor work performance. When Andy tried to solve this problem by turning in early, he would just lie awake for hours because his biological sleep cycle was set for sleep much later in the night.

The solution was multipronged: a very gradual, planned shift in his sleep schedule, bright light exposure in the mornings, stimulant medication for his ADHD, and individual psychotherapy. The therapy was crucial in helping Andy deal with his problems at work and with the effects that his circadian rhythm disorder and distractibility were having on his life. This successful plan would not have been possible without the clarity of an accurate diagnosis of Andy's chief complaint, trouble with sleep.

A myriad of psychological disorders and transient psychosocial stresses may interfere with sleep onset or with the maintenance of sleep throughout the night: depression, posttraumatic stress disorder, anxiety disorders, and so on. In addition, a myriad of organic problems may lie at the heart of an individual's difficulties with sleep: the primary sleep disorders, pain of all kinds, systemic infections, autoimmune diseases, medication side effects, drug or alcohol use, and caffeine intake are just a few.

Sorting out the etiology of a patient's problems with sleep begins with taking a careful sleep history, including clarification as to whether the individual sleeps too little or too much. Does he or she have difficulties with sleep onset, sleep maintenance, or early awakening? Does the individual have disturbances during the night, such as nightmares, sleepwalking, snoring, leg movements, eating during sleep, or acting on dreams while asleep? Often the patient's bed partner will be an important source of information about nighttime behaviors of which the patient might not be aware. How difficult is it for the patient to wake up in the morning? Is he or she refreshed upon awakening? How tired is the individual during the day? How likely is it that the patient will fall asleep under various circumstances, such as while watching television or stopped at a traffic light?

Energy Level   Evaluating patients' complaints in the arena of low energy or fatigue is also a complex matter. Consider these chief complaints: "I'm tired all the time." "I have no energy." "I've lost my motivation." "I feel weak." "I'm simply exhausted." "I'm sleepy all the time." "Where has my stamina gone?" We understand that these various terms have different shades of meaning and imply different underlying problems, but clinicians should not assume that their patients are using the terms precisely.

Start by trying to clarify exactly what the patient is experiencing. Differentiate the following, one from another: actual muscle weakness, muscles that fatigue easily, a general lack of stamina with exercise, mental fatigue, excessive daytime sleepiness, not feeling rested upon awakening from sleep, feeling sick as with a flu, feeling a lack of motivation or drive, having trouble initiating activities, apathy, feeling depressed. After careful scrutiny, what begins as a symptom that rings as psychological may begin to sound more like a medical problem. Problems with energy level may turn out to be the presenting chief complaint for patients who have systemic infections (e.g., HIV, hepatitis) or cardiac problems, muscle diseases or dementias affecting the frontal lobes, sleep disorders or kidney failure, vitamin deficiency states or diabetes, and of course depression or malingering.

The following clinical example illustrates the challenge of evaluating this kind of symptom in a patient who has multiple medical and psychological factors that might be contributing to the problem. Linda's fatigue emerged in the context of a long psychotherapy. This narrative explains the context.

I was fresh out of residency training when 24-year-old Linda first consulted me in my private practice. She told me that her marriage was "in shambles" and that she felt "like a failure." But, during the second session, I realized that an even more fundamental worry had propelled her into my office. Some months before seeing me, Linda had noticed a lump in her neck. She had already consulted with an ear, nose, and throat (ENT) specialist, who had reassured her that this was simply a benign lymph node. "Not to worry!" But, this lump was getting bigger, and Linda found that she couldn't keep herself from worrying. In that second session, my first therapeutic intervention had been to insist that Linda get a second medical opinion.

It was not a benign node. I saw Linda on a weekly basis for psychotherapy until she died from this malignant fibrosarcoma, 20 years later. Soon after she received her grim diagnosis, and just before she had extensive surgery and radiation to her neck, Linda's husband abruptly fled the marriage. Linda believed that he had experienced her cancer as shameful and that he had not wanted to be burdened by her physical needs.

Over time, Linda's life became dominated by the appearance of metastatic tumors and the subsequent ups and downs of numerous surgeries followed by arduous climbs to recovery. First the doctors would tell her she was cancer-free, but soon she would find herself back in the hospital. Hope alternated with terror. "I'm on a roller coaster ride that is out of control, and I'm in a seat all alone, just hanging on for survival," she would say.

She had lost the life she had known and the future she had expected. Linda's career as an art therapist was so often interrupted by medical leaves that eventually she left work and lived on disability payments. She lost her health, her youth, her physical beauty, her marriage, and her chances of having children. The end of her life was perpetually in mind. "There's no one I can leave family pictures to," she often said.

It was in this context, following another round of surgery and radiation therapy that Linda complained of feeling particularly fatigued. Well, that was not a surprise! She had many reasons to feel fatigued: postsurgical pain and recuperation, radiation therapy that can cause profound exhaustion, stress and worry about the future, the undermining of motivation for any long-term endeavors, angry feelings about her fate, depressive feelings about her now-disfigured body.

I learned a lot from Linda. She was a better clinician than I. Her experience was that this fatigue had a "different quality" or was "out of proportion" to what she would have expected, even under these extreme circumstances. And she had integrated this thinking with certain changes she had noticed in her body but hadn't mentioned to me. Gradually, she had begun to use more and more skin moisturizer; her skin was dryer. And she had been "living on prunes" because she was constipated. Linda did some reading and came up with the idea that perhaps she had developed an underactive thyroid.

She wanted to know what I thought of this idea. Bingo! Once she suggested this diagnostic possibility, it was obvious. Not only were her symptoms consistent with hypothyroidism, but I also knew that radiation to the neck frequently affects the thyroid gland, located just below the Adam's apple. It all made sense. Laboratory tests confirmed this diagnosis, and treatment led to an improvement in Linda's energy level, her constipation, drying skin, and, by the way, her mood.

Appetite and Weight   Therapists see many patients who have difficulties with appetite and weight. Often individuals have lifelong struggles in this arena and may even be in therapy primarily because of problems with this aspect of their lives. As therapists, we are especially cognizant of the complex issues that may be active in this arena: body image, social image, cultural norms, body integrity, relationship boundaries, autonomy, nutrition, physical health, and so on. With the widespread use of psychopharmacologic treatments, we are also aware that the side effects of weight gain and alterations in body metabolism are common and may present serious health risks to our patients.

   The story of my patient Leticia is one example of the kinds of problems with appetite and weight that are commonly seen in the offices of therapists.

Leticia first consulted me because she was troubled by conflict with her two teenage sons. One son wanted to drop out of college to marry his ski instructor. The other was "always angry." The latest blowup had been when Leticia gave him a pair of slippers for Christmas. "They're what Dad would have wanted! I hate them," he had said.

A few months into the treatment, Leticia began to lose her appetite. She could only manage to eat "tea and toast" because of an "uncomfortable, anxious" feeling in her "belly." After a short time, Leticia's mood became overtly depressive. She then agreed to try antidepressant medication.

Leticia's depression resolved dramatically, but understandably, she didn't like the idea of being on medication if it wasn't necessary. So after feeling back to her normal self for a year, we decided to taper the drug and then stop it altogether. Leticia did well for another year and a half without medication, but then she became depressed again. This repeated several times. With each episode of depression, Leticia's very first symptom was exactly the same, a loss of appetite.

Leticia no longer has recurrent depressive episodes, because now she takes an antidepressant every morning and has for years. However, over this time her weight has risen by 40 pounds. Many factors have contributed:

antidepressant medication, lack of consistent exercise, enjoying the fruits of an active social life that often centers on food, and a genetic predisposition. Leticia doesn't like the way she looks, and she worries that this extra weight will be bad for her long-term health. She struggles to maintain a reasonable diet and exercise schedule, but the truth is that she loves to eat and hates to exercise. Fundamentally, Leticia has made a choice to live with the extra pounds rather than to live with being depressed.

Leticia's difficulties with appetite and weight emerged from a complex interaction of biological, psychological, and social factors. Problems with appetite and weight commonly accompany mental disturbances other than depression. Loss of interest in food is common with mourning. In mania there may be "no time to eat." During the "hibernation season" with seasonal affective disorder, patients report an increased caloric intake that is often high in carbohydrate content. Along with other criteria, anorexia nervosa presents with weight loss, a disturbed sense of satiety, and a fear of gaining weight.

Once again, caution is advised in coming to a diagnostic conclusion in patients who present with problems in this arena. It is crucial to take a careful and complete history, because appetite and weight are affected by and regulated by many biological factors. A large variety of organic diseases and physical factors can affect an individual's appetite and/or weight. I will never forget the 37-year-old woman I saw when I was a medical student on the consultation-liaison service.

The patient had been hospitalized on the medical unit because she was experiencing vague gastrointestinal symptoms and had had a dramatic loss of weight. She was profoundly depressed, with despairing mood and prominent psychomotor retardation. The medical team hypothesized that the patient's depression had led her to focus on her bowels and to worry inordinately about normal, abdominal sensations that everyone experiences. They thought that her weight loss was secondary to her deep depression, but they did do a thorough medical workup, because they knew there were other diagnostic possibilities. Two days later we all learned the truth: The patient had pancreatic cancer.

Given this patient's presentation, it was understandable that she and her family thought she had major depression. Many patients come to us with diagnostic impressions and dynamic interpretations of their eating behaviors already worked out. "I'm feeding my inner child." "I feel that I have to be perfectly thin in order to meet my mother's expectations." It is certainly possible that individuals who have lost or gained a significant amount of weight and who are also depressed or anxious or have other mental status changes may have developed a loss of appetite or increased intake of food because of the dynamics and/or the biology of their psychological conditions, but there are other possibilities.

Here are a few: As-yet-undiscovered cancers, such as pancreatic or lung cancer, may present with prominent depression and weight loss. Thyroid disease commonly causes depression and/or anxiety as well as changes in metabolism and food absorption from the gastrointestinal tract. An early dementia may present with apathy that might be difficult to distinguish from depression; these patients may lose weight simply because they have become uninterested in or ineffective at organizing nutritious meals. Addiction to amphetamines will lead to dramatic weight loss. Disorders such as celiac disease, irritable bowel syndrome, inflammatory bowel disease, or parasitic infections may affect weight and/or appetite that might be misinterpreted as stress-related or psychosomatic. Frontotemporal dementia can cause unusual changes in eating behavior, including obsessive interest in food, disinhibited eating, or a craving for sweets.

When taking a history, it is very important to keep in mind that anorexia nervosa and bulimia nervosa are diagnoses that are made on the basis of clear behavioral and psychological patterns and not on the basis of weight loss alone. Individuals who are very thin, who know they are thin, and who *don't like being thin* do not have anorexia nervosa. Individuals who eat well and do not purge but who have lost weight nonetheless do not have anorexia nervosa. Individuals who report vomiting that is not self-induced do not have bulimia nervosa.

Also, keep in mind the downstream consequences of significant weight gain or weight loss, including the complex psychosocial costs as well as the risks to health. Weight gain is a risk factor for numerous medical disorders, including cardiovascular disease and diabetes. Weight loss, when it is extreme, can lead to physiologic alterations that can be lethal.

Libido Sexual interest and sexual behavior are frequent topics of discussion in therapists' offices, and most therapists are comfortable engaging in exploration of these important aspects of their patients' lives. A patient or couple may be motivated to embark on treatment because of a change in sexual drive or desire, distress about sexual performance, or concerns about gender identity. These issues rightfully take center stage. Sexual engagement is a potential source of pleasure as well as a crucial component of deep bonding within a relationship. This is also an arena in which individuals may feel extraordinarily vulnerable, both physically and emotionally. An individual's sense of desirability, lovability, competence, and fundamental identity are at stake here.

In the arena of sexuality, psychological forces are profoundly intertwined with the biological. Think of the potentially dampening effect that marital discord can have on sexual interest, the dulling of libido that may accompany a major depression, or the profound sense of distrust and fear that might result from a history of sexual trauma. Then consider the chilling effect that physical pain has on sexual interest, the waning of libido that may accompany any chronic disease, or the sense of anxiety that may result when intercourse is sometimes painful (e.g., from endometriosis). Endometriosis is a common medical condition in which cells like those that line the uterus (endometrial cells) are found outside of the uterus (e.g., on the walls of the abdomen). These cells bleed and cause pain.

While being sensitive to the complex and meaningful psychological components of the patient's sexual experiences, it is important to keep in mind the possibility that underlying medical factors might be contributing to the situation.

A 65-year-old lawyer and his 60-year-old artist wife were seeing me for couples therapy. Their relationship had begun as an affair 20 years prior, and it had been torrid, captivating, and satisfying for both of them. Now their sex life had waned. He felt that she no longer paid attention to him; he believed that she no longer cared whether they continued to have sexual relations or not. She couldn't stand that he stooped when he walked, that he had aging spots on his face, and that he was impatient. He had begun to remind her of her father.

In rare moments when the husband exposed his vulnerability, he acknowledged that he sometimes had difficulty maintaining an erection and that this led him to "feel unmanly." In rare moments when the wife exposed her vulnerability, she revealed that her husband's inability to sustain an erection made her "feel undesirable." Beneath her sometimes-scathing anger was a deep layer of hurt and despair. If she couldn't have intercourse, "what was the point?"

He pointed out that she never initiated sex anymore, never tried to seduce him, and that he was the one who felt undesired. "Why do you care about the spots on my face? Under these circumstances, of course I can't maintain an erection!" Naturally, he also wondered about her early relationship with her father. Had anything "untoward" happened between them? She had no specific recollections of "anything like that."

She was distant; that made him angry. He was angry; that drove her further away. This was how things had been for more than two years, and this is how it continued to go, for months of therapy. It was a psychological whirlpool.

On the biological front, a complete history and a medical workup uncovered that the husband was taking a medication for high blood pressure that not infrequently interferes with sexual performance. I talked with the husband's primary care physician and worked out a change in antihypertension medication. Unfortunately, this did not lead to any change in erectile functioning.

A referral to a urologist who specialized in sexual dysfunction revealed that the husband had some compromise of vascular supply to the penis secondary to atherosclerosis, and that this might be contributing to the husband's difficulties with maintaining an erection. This did not erase the psychological complexities of the situation, but it did put them into a new context. The wife felt more sympathetic and less angry with her husband. The husband was distressed to learn that he actually did have a problem with sexual performance, but over time he came to see that this was not a "personal failing," nor was it all his "wife's fault."

Both members of the couple now saw that it was possible to take some measures that might improve the situation. The husband tried medication for erectile dysfunction. Knowing the biological facts of the situation allowed this couple to adjust their expectations and to gradually address misunderstandings and hurt feelings that had built up over the years. Addressing the multitude of factors that were contributing to this couple's difficulties did allow them over time to regain the satisfactions of sexual intimacy.

Changes in sexual behavior, sexual desire, arousal, or ability to attain orgasm may signal the presence of an underlying physical problem, and a medical workup under those circumstances is wise. In this book it is not possible to present all of the medical problems that could potentially have an impact on sexual behavior. It is important to have some of the most common ones in mind. At the top of the list would be medications and drugs of all sorts, including many antidepressants, alcohol, pain (or the anticipation of pain), diabetes and other endocrine disorders, atherosclerosis, and/or chronic illnesses. The adult onset of significant changes in sexual behavior also may signal brain pathology such as a tumor or dementia; watch for inappropriate, disinhibited, sexual behavior in social situations or dramatic shifts in sexual preferences such as the onset of voyeurism, pedophilia, exhibitionism, or fetishism.

Other Physical Symptoms   In thinking about how to respond to the myriad of other physical symptoms that patients might bring to your attention, it is helpful to be aware that different symptoms tend to elicit different responses. Some symptoms will prompt an immediate referral to a medical practitioner (excruciating pain), whereas others will barely register on a therapist's radar (indigestion). Yet any physical symptom may be significant as a clue to a masked organic disorder.

Here are some guidelines to keep in mind when evaluating physical symptoms beyond the vegetative symptoms that already have been discussed.

1. Take the report of any symptom seriously, and inquire carefully about specifics in order to know what the patient is *actually* experiencing.

2. Try to obtain objective measures of the impact that the symptoms are having on the patient's life. For instance, are the patient's symptoms interfering with work? Are usual, day-to-day activities affected? Ask specifically about driving, cooking, shopping, reading, socializing, paying bills, hobbies, exercising, and other endeavors that have been part of the individual's regular life. How much pain is he or she experiencing, on a scale from 1 to 10? How much time is spent in bed? Speaking with family members, friends, or neighbors may be invaluable.

3. Be sure to get a timeline history of the patient's complaints, including associated life events, illnesses, travel, toxic exposures, dietary changes, and how the patient's symptoms have evolved or changed. What treatments has the patient already tried for the problem, including alternative treatments and over-the-counter preparations? Does anything worsen or improve the symptoms?

4. As always, do a broader inquiry, asking about any other signs or symptoms that the patient may not have considered to be relevant.

5. Seriously consider referring the patient for a medical workup.

Chapter 8

Classical Presentations— Focal Signs, Dementia, and Delirium

Introduction

The classical presentation of any disorder is a recognizable pattern, somewhat like the modus operandi or "M.O." of a criminal. If you're familiar with the pattern, then once you find it, you pretty much know "who's done it."

The classical presentations of both psychological and organic disorders consist of constellations or clusters of signs and symptoms that emerge within a characteristic time frame and often under certain conditions or with particular precipitating factors. Throughout this book are descriptions of the classical presentations of numerous organic disorders, from normal pressure hydrocephalus (apathy that may look like depression or dementia, a gait disturbance, and possibly urinary incontinence) to pellagra (dementia, diarrhea, dermatitis—a rash on the sun-exposed areas of skin), from obstructive sleep apnea (excessive daytime fatigue, nighttime snoring, difficulty with concentration and possible depression) to hyperthyroidism (anxiety, racing pulse, loss of weight, heat intolerance).

As you read and familiarize yourself with these classical presentations, keep one caveat in mind: Diseases do not invariably present with a classical symptom picture; in fact, the classical presentation may not even be the most common form that the disorder takes. Disorders have many different ways of emerging and declaring themselves, although often their presentations are variations on a characteristic form. You are undoubtedly familiar with this concept as applied to the typical picture of major depression: a depressive mood, and feelings of hopelessness, helplessness, and worthlessness with possible suicidal ideation, and so on. Yet often one does not see this classical picture but rather a variation on this theme. For example, a patient with major depression might have prominent somatic preoccupations, irritability, hand-wringing agitation, or delusions that center on depressive themes such as guilt and punishment.

This chapter introduces three important topics that involve constellations of signs and symptoms. The first is the correlation between certain clusters of signs and symptoms and disturbances in particular brain regions. The second subject of this chapter is dementia, a complex and important type of presentation. Dementias commonly present as psychological mimics. The third topic is the concept of a delirium. Delirium is arguably the most common form that organic disorders take in the arena of mental phenomena.

Focal Signs of Brain Pathology

In contrast to pathology in many body organs, when it comes to the brain and nervous system it matters precisely where an injury or dysfunction has occurred. Distances of less than a centimeter can matter. There are few ideas more fundamental than the notion that injury to particular parts of the nervous system will predictably disrupt specific body functions and/or cognitive operations. In other words, focal sites of nervous system injury or dysfunction can be correlated with specific signs and symptoms.

This fact allows neurologists and other knowledgeable clinicians to think in reverse. Starting with a patient's physical and neuropsychological signs and symptoms and their alterations in function, it is possible to deduce whether the individual has brain pathology and which regions of the brain have been affected. Consider, for a moment, the familiar example of a right-handed man who rapidly develops both partial paralysis of his right arm and difficulty with language functioning (i.e., with the production of actual words in grammatically proper sentences). There is no obvious reason for why these two entirely different types of problems should have occurred simultaneously, one involving arm movement and the other affecting language. Was this individual coincidentally struck by two afflictions at the same time, one involving the arm and the other affecting the brain? Any mystery here is resolved by understanding that the right hand is controlled by the left hemisphere motor areas of the brain and that crucial linguistic circuitry lives in the same hemispheric neighborhood. It also helps to know that in this man one crucial artery supplied these areas of his brain. There was only one disease event, a stroke that compromised this artery and resulted in brain injury to an area of his left hemisphere, thus producing multiple, seemingly unrelated symptoms.

There are numerous clusters of sign and symptom such as the ones in the previous example. These are called focal signs or localizing signs. When present, these are extremely important in implicating the brain as the site of the disturbance (not the arm!) as well as in localizing the probable region or regions of brain involvement. Many different diseases can affect discrete areas of the brain and produce focal signs: strokes and transient ischemic attacks (TIAs), brain tumors (primary or metastatic), brain abscesses or cysts, multiple sclerosis, focal seizures, blood vessel malformations in the brain, and head trauma.

What is of particular importance to mental health practitioners is that not only physical signs and symptoms but also certain neuropsychological signs and symptoms or clusters of these may be localizing. In other words, certain mental signs and symptoms are highly correlated with organic disturbance in the central nervous system and will provide a knowledgeable practitioner with clues as to where in the brain the problem resides. Here is an example:

Patricia was a single mom with a daughter who was a star student at a local, prestigious private school. During one memorable therapy session, Patricia mentioned that she was "kind of concerned" about her daughter who had been complaining about having frequent, "weird" déjà vu feelings.

This information worried me. I didn't want to alarm Patricia, but I did want her to take immediate action. I explained that déjà vu experiences can be entirely normal but that they are sometimes associated with seizures involving the temporal lobes of the brain. I encouraged Patricia to call her daughter's pediatrician promptly, but I did not mention my worry that a temporal lobe brain tumor could be the cause of such seizures.

Not surprisingly, Patricia took quick action. By the next week, her daughter had been scheduled for surgery to remove what turned out to be a benign tumor. Patricia's daughter did well. She graduated in the top of her high school class and attended a first-rate university. She is now working and living with a boyfriend. She has had a few episodes of mild depression, but it isn't clear that these are related to her brain tumor and history of surgery; there is a history of depression on her father's side of the family.

The recommendations I made to Patricia were based on the knowledge that frequent déjà vu experiences may be correlated with pathology in the temporal lobe of the brain. Many correlations of this sort are now known.

Explicating the association between all of the possible neuropsychological symptom clusters and sites of brain damage is beyond the scope of this book, but it is important to be aware that this kind of correlation is often possible. Although neuropsychiatric capabilities emerge from widespread networks of interconnected nerve cells, nonetheless localizing signs and symptoms are frequently possible. In part, this is because these neuronal networks have major hubs, the sites of which are known or currently being mapped. As with airline systems, a problem that shuts down a hub city airport is more likely to cause major symptomatic disruptions to the system than are difficulties with any side-route between just two or three cities.

Emotional and cognitive abilities emerge from five major widely dispersed, interconnected networks in the brain: the networks for (1) attention and spatial orientation; (2) emotion and memory; (3) language—two important hubs within the complex system for language were identified early in the history of neurology and are called Broca's area and Wernicke's area; (4) executive functions and comportment; and (5) face and object recognition (Mesulam, 2000).

It is particularly important for therapists to recognize the signs of pathology that affect frontal lobe functioning. In this book you will find examples of two classical types of frontal lobe syndromes: (1) apathy, loss of initiative, lack of interest and curiosity; and (2) impulsivity, disinhibition, loss of insight and judgment.

LOOKING FOR FOCAL NEUROLOGICAL SIGNS

In order to effectively identify focal neuropsychological signs, here are some fundamentals to keep in mind. First and foremost, the development of any new cognitive disturbance in adulthood should always raise the question of brain involvement, whether it is a problem with memory, language, finding one's way around town, trouble with handwriting, balancing the checkbook, or a myriad of other possibilities.

Also, it may help to recall that some brain activities are so fundamental that we generally don't think of them as falling into the realm of cognition or as having a brain basis at all. Take, for instance, the capacity to recognize an object for what it is, to know that a pen is a pen and that a chair is a chair. Consider the ability to recognize a face, to perform learned motor routines such as brushing one's teeth, to know that our body parts belong to us and where those body parts are in space. What would you think if a patient was capable of writing but unable to read, able to speak and comprehend but unable to repeat after you, or unable to name only certain categories of objects such as tools? Truth is often stranger than fiction. Each of these disturbances constitutes clear evidence of organic disease. These individuals have disruptions of fundamental neuropsychological capacities and need to be referred for a neurological workup. It would be a mistake to assume that disturbances in these or other areas of fundamental functioning are psychogenic simply because they seem nonsensical and bizarre or appear to be motivated.

FOCAL VERSUS DIFFUSE BRAIN INVOLVEMENT

In contrast to these focal disturbances, a multitude of disease processes will affect the brain in a diffuse, widespread manner: toxicity from alcohol or other substances, diffuse infections of the brain, metabolic diseases such as kidney failure, and so on. These conditions will produce a constellation of mental signs and symptoms that are different from focal findings. Nonfocal, nonlocalizing signs include findings such as a change in the level of consciousness, distractibility, irritability, agitation, disorientation, and/or confusion.

Some disease processes will produce a combination of localizing and nonlocalizing signs and symptoms; for instance, initially, when an individual suffers from a stroke, there is not only damage to a specific area of the brain, but there is also widespread swelling of the brain. When the swelling subsides, the nonlocalizing signs and symptoms (e.g., change in level of consciousness, headache, confusion) abate, but focal signs frequently persist.

Introduction to Dementia and Delirium

Dementia and delirium are two very important constellations of signs and symptoms, each signaling the presence of some underlying medical condition. The syndromes of dementia and delirium are not like fingerprints at a crime scene, but more like finding evidence of breaking and entering along with some missing jewelry. Clearly a crime has been committed, but the clues do not implicate a particular culprit. In other words, the syndromes of dementia and delirium are not specifically correlated with particular disorders or with definite regions of the brain, but finding a delirium or a dementia is evidence that an underlying physical condition of some kind is present.

Delirium and dementia are also significant for being extremely common modes of presentation for physical disorders in any clinical setting. Numerous different disease states may present as a dementia, including Alzheimer's disease, Lewy body dementia, vascular dementia, frontotemporal dementia, alcohol dementia, HIV, normal pressure hydrocephalus, and the list goes on (Cummings, 1985). *Many more* conditions may present as a delirium, including toxic states, withdrawal states, disturbances in metabolism, many of the endocrine disorders, nutritional deficiencies, any systemic infection, heatstroke, sleep deprivation, post-surgery confusion, any central nervous system infection, traumatic injury, seizure, or bleeding, and on and on (Cummings, 1985).

Looking for the syndromes of delirium and dementia is like casting a wide net. You will catch a lot of different varieties of fish, a lot of different disease states. Once you identify delirium or a dementia in one of your patients, you will turn to a medical consultant to help figure out which specific underlying physical condition or conditions are causative. Then findings from physical examinations, x-rays, or laboratory tests may be useful in getting to a definitive diagnosis. However, keep in mind this crucial fact. First you have to cast the net into the water. Only observation by an experienced clinician, aided perhaps by simple bedside neuropsychological testing, will help in recognizing which individuals have a delirium or dementia in the first place. Both of these syndromes are identified solely by clinical examination. The practitioner relies on (a) careful observation of the patient's behavior, (b) findings from interviews and the mental status examination, and (c) discussions with family members and friends of the patient, who often have information that the afflicted individual is unable to provide.

Delirium and dementia are frequently challenging to identify, even though they are common and at times dramatically unmistakable. Both are complex clinical states that are highly variable in their expression. Even the precise definitions of the terms *dementia* and *delirium* are disputed. In addition, each may be very subtle in its presentation or camouflaged by a coexisting conspicuous psychological disorder, making it difficult to perceive. The following discussions of dementia and delirium will help you in identifying these common and important clinical states.

Dementia

Dementia is not a diagnosis. Dementia is a syndrome that may be caused by many possible, underlying disorders. Dementia is the category in which these various disorders are placed because they share certain characteristics, although they also differ in their underlying physiology and the specifics of their clinical presentations.

In other words, the term *dementia* is similar to a term like *pneumonia*. Pneumonias are all infections of the lung; but some are viral, some are bacterial, some are fungal, and some are parasitic in origin, with many possible specific organisms involved within each of these groups. Just as with the category of dementia, all of the pneumonias share certain characteristics, but they also differ in their modes of presentation and their clinical course.

THE CHARACTERISTICS OF THE DEMENTIAS

The characteristics that the dementias share are the following: (a) a gradually developing and persistent deficit in more than one area of cognition; (b) these deficits must interfere with the individual's previous level of functioning; (c) the onset is most often in adulthood; and (d) the cognitive deficits are not accompanied by impairment of or clouding of consciousness. In trying to more fully grasp what a dementia is, it also may help to understand what a dementia is not. Cognitive deficits that are lifelong are not considered to be dementia, because the definition includes decline from a previous higher level of cognitive functioning. Inborn developmental disorders are not dementias. Cognitive deficits that result from an acute incident (such as an infection, stroke, or head trauma) are also not dementias, because the decline must be progressive in order to be considered a dementia.

If the documented cognitive deficits are not severe enough to interfere with the individual's functioning, the patient is also not considered to have a dementia. Under these circumstances the individual is said to have mild cognitive impairment (MCI). It is understood that some individuals with MCI will remain stable or improve over time, whereas most will worsen and go on to be diagnosed with some form of dementia. Lastly, a dementia occurs with clarity of consciousness. This is extremely important. A clouding of consciousness is the hallmark of a delirium but is not present in dementia.

CLINICAL PRESENTATIONS—THE MANY FACES OF DEMENTIA

The various forms of dementia have different clinical presentations depending largely on which parts of the brain are affected. Here are two case examples to help in picturing the many possible forms a dementia may take. My 47-year-old patient Rita has an accepting and almost poetic perspective on life. She told me this story about her father, who had recently moved to an assisted living facility in another city.

> *"I called my Dad after my flute recital last week. It was sweet. I told him that I had done a passable job but that, really, some of the 12-year-olds played much better than I did. And they had harder pieces! Dad was very wonderful. That's Dad. He said, 'Well, Reet, you did it. You know, it's hard to take up something new as an adult. I'm proud of you.'"*

> *"Then, 20 minutes later my phone rang, and it was Dad calling. He said, 'Hi Reet. How are you doing?' I told him that I had just had my flute recital, and he asked me how it had gone. I went through the whole thing with him again. Again he was sweet and had some new things to say, but he had no memory whatsoever that I had already told him about the recital. He had no idea that we had just had that conversation. And yet, in the moment you'd never know there was anything wrong with him. He's as related, mature, kind, and thoughtful as he ever was."*

Rita's dad had a significant memory deficit. He also had some trouble with spatial orientation. His doctors said that he had Alzheimer's disease as well as vascular dementia.

Now here is an example of an entirely different form that dementia may take.

> *One of my patients gave a party at his home and invited his old college room-mate, Mark. The two friends hadn't seen one another for several years. Upon arriving at the party and before even saying hello, Mark launched into an aggressive diatribe about a certain mutual friend having been included on the invitation list by my patient.*
>
> *"How could you have?! He is despicable."*
>
> *This had felt totally out of the blue to my patient who was entirely unaware of the nature of Mark's personal dispute with the other guest. And besides, Mark's behavior was obviously inappropriate. It was my patient's party after all.*
>
> *Mark drank too much at the party, and he ate too much as well, helping himself to too many shrimp and artichokes from the buffet table. My patient remarked to me that Mark had never been like this before, even in the old days at frat parties. Now Mark seemed oblivious to social rules.*

Mark's behavior displayed a lack of self-monitoring; he was oblivious to the reactions of others. He was impulsive and lacked the private censoring of inappropriate behavior that is the basis of comportment and socially attuned conduct. Not long after the party, my patient learned that Mark had been diagnosed with frontal dementia. Mark's disinhibited behavior at the party had resulted from his impairment in executive functioning and comportment.

On the surface, these two cases could hardly seem more distinct, yet Rita's Dad and Mark both had dementia. Rita's dad had a mix of Alzheimer's disease and vascular dementia; Mark had a type of frontal dementia. These individuals had progressive, persistent cognitive deficits that interfered with functioning, and they did not have any clouding of consciousness.

COGNITION AND DEMENTIA

Because cognitive deficits are the core feature of a dementia, it would be useful to clarify which mental capacities are generally subsumed under the category of cognition. Here is a quick listing: memory, orientation (to time, place, person), visuospatial skills, language abilities, attention, concentration, calculation, constructional capability, the ability to recognize objects, the capacity to carry out planned motor movements (praxis), fund of knowledge, abstract thinking, judgment, and insight. Also considered aspects of cognition are the executive functions, including initiating, planning, sequencing, problem solving, self-monitoring, comportment (social manner or conduct), and appropriately maintaining and shifting set.

Although it is agreed that cognitive deficits are essential to the definition of a dementia, there has been considerable disagreement about which areas of cognition are central. Some definitions of *dementia* require memory impairment (difficulty with retaining new information) in addition to at least one other cognitive deficit. However, some authorities would consider a significant, progressive decline in any area of cognition to qualify as a dementia. For instance, some patients may present with only a gradually developing deficit in the use of language, called a *semantic dementia*. (The sudden development of language impairment, as might be caused by a stroke, would be called *aphasia*.)

Other clinicians find it is helpful to think of the dementias as falling into three broad classes, depending on which cognitive functions are initially most affected: (1) cortical dementia with prominent disturbances of memory and/or language functioning, (2) cortical dementia of the frontal lobe type in which executive functions are disrupted and behavior is apathetic or disinhibited, and (3) *subcortical dementia*, in which motivation, psychomotor activity, mood, and affect are primarily affected (Cummings, 1985). The term *subcortical* is useful in characterizing those individuals who present with progressive emotional difficulties, lack of initiative, and psychomotor retardation with slowed mental processing. This is the kind of clinical picture that one sees with normal pressure hydrocephalus, Parkinson's dementia, dementia with Lewy bodies, vascular dementia, or with the dementia associated with HIV infection of the brain. The individuals who present with either a subcortical dementia or cortical dementia of the frontal lobe type are most readily misdiagnosed as having a psychological problem.

Variations in the clinical picture of dementia are determined by many factors. As is always the case, each individual is different in terms of genetic makeup, life experience, education, personality, fundamental physical health, and socioeconomic situation. However, the most important factors determining the presentation are which parts of the brain are afflicted and the order in which they are affected over time as the particular neurological disease progresses.

The different underlying diseases in the dementia category have classical patterns of presentation, but there is considerable variation for each disease entity. For instance, Alzheimer's disease most often begins with memory deficits, but it may first present with language deficits. There also may be considerable overlap in the presentation of different types of dementia; Alzheimer's disease may predominantly affect the frontal brain and initially look like fronto-temporal dementia.

To complicate things even further, many individuals have more than one type of dementia. A commonly seen combination is Alzheimer's disease plus vascular dementia. Vascular dementia, or multi-infarct dementia, results from blood vessel pathology that leads to spotty patches of brain injury that accumulate over years. High blood pressure and atherosclerosis predispose individuals to develop vascular dementia. But in addition, Alzheimer's disease may be associated with blood vessel wall fragility and lead to vascular dementia.

Pitfalls in Identifying the Dementias

In order to facilitate recognition of a dementia in clinical situations, it is useful to be aware of the ways that clinicians may be fooled into overlooking this syndrome or thinking that the diagnosis is a mental disorder.

The Dementia May Be Hidden   When cognitive deficits are mild, some patients will make a conscious effort to conceal them. Others may unconsciously deny that they are having difficulties at all. If the onset of the dementia is gradual, patients may imperceptibly adapt to their declining capabilities over time by gradually dropping out of activities that are too cognitively demanding; they might retire from work, withdraw from social engagements, and start watching TV rather than reading.

When an individual leads a fairly habitual life that is devoid of taxing mental tasks, a dementia may not become apparent for some time. But if that individual is required by circumstances to accommodate to something new, such as the closing of a neighborhood grocery, the loss of a spouse, or a move to assisted living, he or she may become suddenly overwhelmed or depressed. Adapting to change requires the mental flexibility and cognitive capacities this person no longer has. Mental collapse in the face of change may first be interpreted to be entirely psychological, while the covert withering of that individual's cognitive capacities is overlooked.

The Dementia May Look Like a Variety of Psychological Disorders If the patient with dementia has a coexisting depression, the depression may mask the dementia. It is often difficult to tell whether a depressed individual who also has cognitive difficulties has a true dementia or a major depression that looks like dementia. This latter situation is sometimes called a pseudo-dementia, though there is nothing pseudo about the significant cognitive impairments that accompany severe depression: difficulty with concentration, slowed mental processing and motor behavior, decreased motivation.

In addition to mimicking depression, dementias may present with features of other psychological disorders. Family members and clinicians may focus on managing these behaviors and miss the underlying dementia. Patients with frontal dementias may look like they are angry, acting out, or impulsive. They display disinhibited behaviors, such as making insensitive remarks in social situations, telling tactless jokes, engaging in argumentative or hostile behavior, urinating in public places, making inappropriate sexual overtures, or eating gluttonously. It is easy to interpret these behaviors as purely driven by psychological dynamics.

Declining cognitive abilities also may present with psychotic features, paranoia, hallucinations, or delusions. For example, patients with disturbances of memory may develop paranoid ideas when they cannot find something they have misplaced. Patients with Lewy body dementia are known to experience visual hallucinations with benign content, such as these:

"Jerry, did you feed the cats?" (There were no cats!)

"Oh, look in the yard! How sweet the children are. Should we invite them to come in for lunch?" (There were no children.)

Lewy body dementia is a form of dementia that is associated with more day-to-day fluctuations in functional ability than Alzheimer's disease. It also is associated with mild Parkinson's disease–like symptoms affecting movement.

Delusions of duplication or substitution are commonly associated with dementia. A classical example of this sort of delusion is Capgras syndrome, in which an individual believes that someone who is extremely familiar to them has been substituted with a look-alike. In other words, the patient believes that his wife is an imposter; she looks like his wife, talks like his wife, behaves just like his wife, but he knows that she isn't the real wife.

Dementia Is Not Just a Disease of Old Age The dementias are not just diseases of old age; they may present in middle age or even young adulthood. Yet, when young adults or middle-aged individuals experience newly developing difficulties with cognition, practitioners do not tend to think of the dementias as diagnostic possibilities. It is crucial to keep in mind that although the majority of patients who are diagnosed with Alzheimer's dementia are elderly, in some families Alzheimer's disease will present clinically when patients are in their thirties, forties, or fifties. Lewy body dementia tends to begin earlier than Alzheimer's disease and is commonly seen in late middle age and sometimes in early adulthood. The fronto-temporal dementias also have an earlier onset than Alzheimer's disease, as does alcohol-related dementia. Cerebral autosomal dominant arteriopathy with subcortical infarcts and leukoencephalopathy (CADASIL) is a genetic disorder that causes a mixed picture, a frontal/subcortical dementia. It often presents in mid-adulthood with a mood disorder or change in personality and migraines.

Declining Cognition Is Not Simply Due to Aging   Clinicians also tend to make another kind of error, conceptualizing an elderly patient's declining cognitive capacities as just an inevitable result of aging. Unfortunately, there is widespread belief that the aging brain is simply an increasingly senile brain, that dementia is the equivalent of aging. Patients, families, and too many clinicians are apt to dismiss the signs and symptoms of a dementia in this way. The dementias are caused by disease processes that produce pathological changes in the brain. These pathological states are common in the elderly, but they are not inevitable with aging.

> *One of my patients has a 94-year-old mother who told her that "something unusual" had begun to happen to her. On several occasions she simply could not remember the name of something—an acquaintance, a book, the street on which her daughter lived. What she found most remarkable was that hours later, when she was thinking about something else, suddenly the name that had escaped her would just pop into her mind. My patient asked her mother when these experiences had first started. "Oh, just a few months ago," she said. Of course my patient was astounded since this kind of experience is commonplace for virtually everyone beginning sometime in midlife.*

This 94-year-old woman did not have dementia but simply delayed normal aging. She was describing a problem with access to memory— memory retrieval not memory storage. Names are frequently most difficult for people to recall. This is thought to be because names have relatively few associative neurological links. While you may have many associations to the actual person, book, or street, the *name* itself is essentially arbitrary.

The widespread belief that dementia is inevitable with aging is very unfortunate. Also unfortunate is the notion that it doesn't matter whether you diagnose the precise type of dementia that an individual has because "there's nothing you can do about it anyway." In fact, treatable illnesses may present as dementia, and medications may help cognition and behavior for some time, even in the dementias that lead inevitably to death.

Early identification and treatment of the dementias is important. The pseudo-dementia of depression is entirely treatable. Identifying and attending to the underlying medical causes for other types of dementia (such as severe vitamin B12 deficiency or normal pressure hydrocephalus) may prevent further cognitive deterioration. In addition, it is important to recognize the value of having a diagnosis. Patients and families want to know what is the matter and what to expect in the future. They need time to process this information and to plan together. The following case is a good example.

Sophie spent her winters in Florida, but each summer she would return to her home in the Boston area to have time with her children and grandchildren. During one of these summers, Sophie consulted me for psychotherapy because she "had some things on her mind." Those things had mostly to do with the unfinished mourning of her husband and facing the prospect of aging as a widow.

Sophie was 73. She was financially secure. She was in good health. She exercised. Her life was busy with friends, church, volunteering to read aloud in the local elementary school, and keeping up with her large extended family. Every summer for 7 years we met for a few sessions, just to talk about the things that were on her mind. Toward the end of that time, I watched her develop the symptoms of Alzheimer's disease.

At first, things that had been easy for her became more difficult; she would feel overwhelmed at the prospect of driving to new places or speaking at church meetings. She began to misplace things—her keys, shawl, or umbrella. She had trouble finding her car in the parking lot; she lost track of doctors' appointments. Then her children noticed that she was having problems with financial forms and that she was bouncing checks. Sophie noticed that people no longer invited her to serve on church committees. After getting her sleeping pills "all mixed up," she began to feel increasingly anxious. "It's frightening that I can't trust my own mind," she said.

Sophie's children let me know that they were worried. They wanted their mother to get more help with keeping her appointments and with bill paying. And they did not want her to drive. As is frequently the case with patients who are aging, Sophie was adamant about not wanting to give up the keys to her car.

"They are the keys to my autonomy," she declared. "I need a vote of confidence from my children. I don't need their worries. They just undermine my sense of trust in myself."

It helped to get some objective data from the memory clinic. Neuropsychological testing revealed that Sophie had early Alzheimer's disease. This information was not entirely unexpected by anyone in the family, including Sophie. Nonetheless, it was deeply disturbing. But the diagnosis also helped the children to rally around their mother and to make plans for the future.

We had a series of family meetings in which Sophie was a full participant. Everyone agreed that two of the children would take over Sophie's financial matters, that the house in Florida would be rented, the Boston apartment would be sold, and that Sophie would move to an assisted living facility where she already knew several residents. Anticipating the future, the family also unanimously decided on a particular assisted living facility because it had a "memory unit" that could provide more intensive care for Sophie in the future.

But everyone did not agree on whether Sophie should continue to drive. This issue brought out the family's emotions—tears and anger, sadness, frustration, and love. The open expression of such powerful feelings led Sophie to feel "cared about," but she also felt "treated like a child." As a concession to her children, she agreed to never drive at night, but she refused to "give up." She would keep her car keys!

Sophie moved to the assisted living facility, where she made a good adjustment. Her social skills helped a lot. Family members anticipated and provided the kind of assistance that Sophie would need in order to make a smooth transition: reminders about activities, companions accompanying her to dinner, frequent visits by the grandchildren.

After not having heard from Sophie for some time, I called to see how she was doing. She was glad to hear from me and said that she was doing well and had some good friends at the new place. But I noticed that she was different; she no longer had much on her mind. And just before we said good-bye, Sophie let me know that she wasn't driving anymore and that it was okay with her now. The children had sold her car.

Delirium or Acute Confusional State

Delirium is the most common mental presentation of an underlying organic condition, particularly in a hospital setting. The constellation of signs and symptoms that characterize a delirium may result from any of a vast multitude of different organic conditions, many of which are life threatening if not appropriately treated. For this reason, being able to identify a delirium is a core capability that every clinician should learn.

This discussion has an extremely important take-away message. Any rapid deterioration in a patient's mental status should be assumed to be a delirium. Because the underlying cause of a delirium may be life threatening, any delirium should be considered a medical emergency.

You may have heard delirium called by other names: acute confusional state, toxic or metabolic encephalopathy, acute organic brain syndrome, toxic psychosis, or organic psychosis. These various terms reflect an effort to conceptualize in a sound bite just what a delirium is. Ironically, although a delirious state is difficult to define precisely, it is actually familiar to just about everyone, especially in its milder forms. For instance, one may become delirious from running a high fever, emerging from general anesthesia, being drunk, or taking a medication that makes you feel "out of it."

A delirium is caused by physical factors or conditions with broad systemic effects, including an impact on brain functioning. A delirium is usually fully reversible, because the underlying physical cause is often transient, self-limited, or treatable. Though a delirium is not caused by actual structural damage to the brain, acute incidents within the brain that may also lead to structural damage, such as a central nervous system infection, initially may produce a delirium along with other manifestations.

The mental status findings that comprise a delirium will be elaborated in more detail as follows, but here is a brief outline. The main feature of a delirium is considered to be (a) clouding of consciousness or, according to some authorities, (b) disturbance of attention. In addition, there is (c) disturbance of arousal, either in the direction of anxiety and agitation or lethargy and apathy. A delirium also produces (d) global impairment of cognition. While a dementia produces a decline in particular cognitive abilities, such as memory or spatial orientation, a delirium leads to widespread impairment in ordinary mental functions. With patients who are delirious, not only do their narratives not make psychodynamic sense; often they simply don't make *any* sense.

In comparison to a dementia, a delirium also (e) develops fairly rapidly (over hours to days) and characteristically (f) fluctuates over time (hours to days), so that a patient might be lucid in the morning but confused and drowsy by the afternoon. In addition, there may be (g) altered speech production, (h) perceptual disturbances, (i) instability of sleep/awake cycles, (j) lability of affect, and (k) psychotic symptoms.

The multitude of possible combinations of these features makes a delirium an extremely variable syndrome. This contributes to the clinical challenge of identifying its presence. Delirium is notoriously underdiagnosed, even though this condition signals the presence of a definite physical condition, which may even be life threatening. What does a patient with a delirium actually look like? Several examples follow, starting with a first-hand account from the patient's point of view, looking back after her recovery.

I knew Debbie very well, having treated her in psychotherapy for more than five years. Now we were meeting only once a month. Debbie suffered with chronic posttraumatic stress disorder and had a history of major depression; she also had long-standing chronic obstructive pulmonary disease (COPD). Debbie would plan to arrive early for her appointments in order to have time to catch her breath after climbing the two flights of stairs to my office. Debbie and her various physicians were aware that the COPD made her vulnerable to developing respiratory infections. Everyone kept a lookout for this.

One day I received a phone message from an exhausted-sounding Debbie. She was in a hospital and wouldn't make it to her appointment. When we did meet again, this is what she told me had happened.

"I hadn't felt at all ill, though I had been more tired than usual. Then late one morning my partner drove me to a meeting, and she must have noticed that something was the matter. Apparently, I wasn't making sense. And I guess people at the meeting noticed that I didn't seem like myself. So later, when Renee picked me up, she told me that I really needed to go to the hospital."

But Debbie had had no awareness that she wasn't making sense or that anything might be seriously awry. All she felt was sleepy.

"I think I'll feel better if I just take a nap," she told her partner.

Initially Renee went along with this plan, but after a few hours of Debbie's napping, apparently Renee noticed that there was a "rattling" sound coming from Debbie's chest when she breathed. Renee was frightened and decided to wake Debbie and insist on taking her to the emergency room. Debbie only vaguely remembers the trip to the ER.

"There were random things just floating by. I saw a little toy train, a bottle, some pastry. They floated by, just out of reach. It was kind of nice. I was feeling safe. In the emergency room, they put things on my face to 'help me breathe,' but I wasn't concerned about my breathing. And, I didn't like how the hard plastic felt on my face. I just didn't like it. So, when the nurse stepped out of the room, I took the thing apart and played with the little pieces. I didn't feel any sense of danger. I felt just fine."

When Debbie arrived in the emergency room, her blood oxygen saturation level had been dangerously low at 67%. Apparently she had developed covert pneumonia, and because of her already compromised lung function, this infection was threatening her life. Upon reflection after recovery, Debbie was shaken by her remarkable lack of good judgment. Her mind had been untrustworthy. It was frightening for her to think of how delirious she had been. It was terrifying to realize how close to death she had come. And it moved her deeply to think of how her partner had saved her.

Here's another example of someone who was delirious, this time from the observer's point of view:

> *Gretta's mother was 85 years old and lived in an assisted living facility. One summer, her mother became delirious. The weather was hot, and she gradually became dehydrated. She also had a urinary tract infection. This might not have been a terribly big problem, but Gretta's mother already had moderately severe dementia, probably of the Alzheimer's type, and this made her more vulnerable.*
>
> *What Gretta noticed was that her mother had a "glazed look in her eyes and was kind of out of it." She also was agitated and "wasn't making any sense." When they arrived at the local hospital, this white-haired, gnarled-fingered octogenarian told the triage nurse that she was there "to have her ninth baby." She then proceeded to talk about how she wanted to name the baby Alicia but that she "already had an Alice."*
>
> *Gretta's mother also remarked on how much new building development there had been in the hospital area. Because this was simply not true, my patient asked her mother where she thought she was. Gretta's mother thought she was in Germany, where she had spent most of her life, thousands of miles from this local hospital.*

Gretta's mother's disorientation is a good example of mistaking the unfamiliar for the familiar, commonly seen in organic disorders. Here is yet another example of delirium:

> *John was quite disturbed by a visit to see his beloved 30-year-old sister just after her surgery in the ICU. "She was crazy! She thought the nurses were torturing her. I mean, really torturing her. She thought they were out to do terrible things to her. And this wasn't just an idea. She was terrified. One minute she would be all riled up and try to pull out her IVs, and the next minute she'd be asleep." By the next day, John's sister was no longer delirious. "I was really paranoid, wasn't I?" she said to him.*

THE PRESENTING FEATURES OF DELIRIUM

Now, with a clearer picture of what delirium can look like, here is a review of the salient features:

- *Clouding of consciousness.* Most authorities believe that the central feature of a delirium is a clouding of consciousness. The fact that "clouding of consciousness" is itself difficult to define does complicate matters. Other phrases that attempt to capture this same idea are "dulled awareness" or "impaired clarity of mind." Note that the presence of clouding of consciousness is one feature that distinguishes a delirium from a dementia. In a dementia there is full clarity of consciousness.

- *Impaired attention.* Another key feature of a delirium is an impairment of attention. In fact, some researchers believe that attentional difficulties are the primary feature of a delirium and certainly the most prominent ones in the early stages of a delirium when the signs and symptoms are mild.

  What does trouble with attention look like in a clinical situation? Individuals may have trouble maintaining a conversation or a coherent stream of thought. They may complain that thinking requires great effort. Attentional disturbances also may include easy distractibility, difficulty maintaining focus or goal orientation, impersistence in any endeavor, responding to irrelevant environmental stimuli such as noises or people walking by in the corridor, or difficulty appropriately shifting focus from one thing to the next.

- *Altered state of arousal.* The clouding of consciousness and attentional difficulties generally occur along with hyperarousal, hypoarousal, or a mixed state of arousal. Hyperarousal is at one end of the spectrum and involves psychomotor restlessness, agitation, irritability, or even hostile combativeness. At the opposite end of the spectrum is hypoarousal, with psychomotor retardation, lethargy, somnolence, or stupor. A mixed state of arousal has features of both hypoarousal and hyperarousal (as an individual who is only half-awake might also be restless and agitated).

- *Global impairment of cognition.* Patients with a delirium also exhibit a global impairment of cognitive functioning. Confusion, disorientation, and disorganized thinking are common. Memory, especially working memory, and constructional ability are disturbed, as are calculation, writing, insight, and judgment. Mild difficulty with naming may occur.

- *Altered speech.* Incoherent, disorganized speech, slurred speech, or mutism may be seen.

- *Perceptual disturbances.* Hallucinations and illusions are common, generally either visual or tactile. Sometimes picking behaviors (picking at the bed sheets, pajamas, or one's body) will go along with the tactile and/or the visual hallucinations of bugs crawling on one's skin, referred to as *formication* after the Latin root for "ant."

- *Disturbances of the sleep-awake cycle.* This is common.
- *Lability of affect.* Fluctuating affect including fear, anxiety, depression, anger, apathy, or euphoria are common.
- *Psychotic symptoms.* Delusions, ideas of reference, misidentification syndromes, and paranoia also commonly occur.

WHO GETS A DELIRIUM?

Anyone may develop a delirium, but the following factors increase the risk:

- Multiple medications (e.g., prescription, over-the-counter, herbals, or illicit drugs). It is possible for a delirium to develop in a situation in which none of the medications is excessive, yet the combination of drugs may lead to a delirium.
- Sensory deprivation, including failing sight or hearing, being in a hospital, especially an ICU with limited orienting signals
- Dehydration
- Dementia
- Aging
- Sleep deprivation

When someone does develop a delirium, often multiple factors are contributing. As an example, this scenario is common: An elderly individual (diminished cognitive capacity) with failing sight (sensory deprivation) who is in the hospital (unfamiliar surroundings, sensory deprivation, psychological stress) also develops a urinary tract infection or pneumonia (physiologic stress). Individuals such as this might become particularly confused and agitated in the evening, perhaps as a result of biological changes that occur cyclically during a day, perhaps as a consequence of further sensory deprivation that comes with darkness. This is a common occurrence called *sundowning.*

Something else to keep in mind is that individuals with dementia are more prone to develop a superimposed delirium when they are afflicted with acute medical conditions or have drug reactions. This creates a complex diagnostic picture in which the delirium may be more prominent than the dementia.

WHAT MAKES A DELIRIUM DIFFICULT TO IDENTIFY?

It is also useful to keep in mind the many factors that make a delirium difficult to recognize, such as the following:

- The signs and symptoms of a delirium may be very mild and subtle.
- The signs and symptoms wax and wane; at times, the patient may be entirely lucid.
- A delirium may look like a purely functional or psychological problem. This is especially true when the individual has psychomotor retardation, perceptual disturbances, delusions, paranoia, ideas of reference, or prominent symptoms in the affective sphere, such as irritability or hostility, emotional lability.
- In a medical setting especially, symptoms of delirium are often interpreted to be psychological reactions to being sick, learning of a bad prognosis, being away from the comforts of home, and so on.
- A state of hyperarousal may be misdiagnosed as mania or an agitated depression.
- Patients who are elderly are at higher risk for developing a delirium as well as dementia. These two may be confused during a clinical exam; both may be present.
- Patients with a dementia are prone to develop a delirium, even with a relatively minor medical problem such as a urinary tract infection. The resulting clinical picture (dementia with a superimposed delirium) may be extremely complex and difficult to diagnose. The delirium may be missed entirely. Any rapid worsening of mental status in a demented individual should be assumed to be a delirium.

Chapter 9

Specific Mental Signs and Symptoms

Introduction

This chapter is structured along the lines of an expanded mental status examination, focusing on signs and symptoms in the mental realm that may point to the presence of an organic disorder. The chapter does not aim to be comprehensive but rather to introduce *how to think* about findings when you are making a diagnostic assessment.

The discussions begin with findings that are commonly seen in the offices of therapists; later topics might seem to belong more fittingly in the world of neurologists—difficulties with language, impairments in consciousness, disturbances of memory. These abnormalities are included for several reasons: (a) They may be confused with findings that are psychologically motivated; (b) they constitute clear evidence for organic disease; and (c) the emergence of these findings in patients with previously unclear diagnoses will help clarify the nature of their problems.

With the development and investigational use of real-time brain imaging, there has been a growing understanding of the neurological basis of mental status findings, normal as well as aberrant. We now know, for instance, that brain regions involved in processing of sound are active while individuals are experiencing auditory hallucinations, and brain regions involved in the processing of visual stimuli are active while individuals are having visual hallucinations. This kind of information offers a fascinating window into the biological basis of mental status findings and also illuminates the deep biology–psychology link. This area of scientific inquiry informs the following discussions.

Mood, Affect, and Emotion

Introduction

Let's begin by defining how these terms will be used in this book. *Mood* is what people report they are feeling; mood is a symptom. *Affect* is a sign; it is observable; it includes tone of voice, facial expression, gesture, and body language. *Emotions* are the whole package—conscious feeling states, affective expression of feeling states, and any accompanying physiologic changes such as elevated heart rate, sweaty palms, loss of appetite, flushing, blushing, and so on. Patients who seek help from mental health practitioners frequently have difficulties with affect, mood, and/ or emotion. This realm of human behavior is generally considered to be psychology-central. Yet organic disorders also may manifest themselves in this arena, mimicking psychological disorders.

In May 1999, *The New England Journal of Medicine* published the case report of a 65-year-old woman with Parkinson's disease who had no personal or family history of mood disorders. The authors initiated a therapeutic intervention, namely deep brain stimulation, in an attempt to lessen the patient's parkinsonian tremors. Within seconds the patient's emotional state was transformed by the treatment. Here is what the journal reported:

> . . . the patient . . . started to cry, and verbally communicated feelings of sadness, guilt, uselessness, and hopelessness . . . such as "I'm falling down in my head, I no longer wish to live, to see anything, hear anything, feel anything. . . . " When asked why she was crying and if she felt pain, she responded: "No, I'm fed up with life, I've had enough. . . . I don't want to live any more, I'm disgusted with life. . . . Everything is useless, always feeling worthless, I'm scared in this world." When asked why she was sad, she replied: "I'm tired. I want to hide in a corner. . . . I'm crying over myself, of course. . . . I'm hopeless, why am I bothering you . . . " (Bejjani, 1999, p. 1476)

Within 90 seconds of stopping the therapeutic intervention, the patient's depressive frame of mind disappeared. "She recalled the entire episode" (Bejjani, 1999, p. 1476).

This profound depressive emotional state did not arise from unresolved intrapsychic conflict, nor did it emerge in response to the patient's external life circumstances. In short, it did not develop as a consequence of personal meaning. Instead, it came upon her when a technician turned on the electricity in one prong of an electrode that had been implanted in the middle of the *substantia nigra* of her brain. Other electrode contact points that were sited a mere 2 millimeters from the first produced the desired therapeutic effect, namely a marked diminution in the patient's debilitating tremors without any changes in the patient's mood (Bejjani, 1999).

This clinical example raises a multitude of questions, all of them interesting. The most salient point is that emotion is not always generated by personal meaning. Our daily work as therapists is based on a fundamental assumption that patients' moods and affective expressions are caused by conscious and/or unconscious meanings in the context of their personal experiences, thoughts, and memories. Yet this is not always the route by which they arise. There are situations in which affect or feelings and the associated physical manifestations of emotions will emerge as a result of underlying physical factors, such as random autonomous brain activity (seizures), medication side effects, withdrawal reactions, or diseases of the thyroid, parathyroid, adrenal, or pituitary glands.

It may not be possible to identify an underlying organic disorder on the basis of affect, mood, or emotions alone; medical conditions may present with what looks like garden-variety depression or anxiety. But certain features of emotional life are clues to the presence of organic disease. Let's first look at these clues in the realm of affect. Then the discussion will turn to mood and emotion.

AFFECT—THE OUTWARD EXPRESSION

Introduction Patients who come to the mental health system frequently have trouble with affect, be it the expression of impulsive anger, a feeling of overwhelming sadness, affective lability, or isolation of affect. Crucial to our thinking as therapists is the notion that affect is always linked to inwardly felt emotion and that a psychological dynamic drives the relationship between the two.

The principle feature that one observes when organic disorders express themselves in the arena of affect is a loss of congruence between the person's affect and his or her mood. When the internal and external do not match, think carefully about why this is the case.

Numerous organic conditions may manifest with affect that is incongruent. This incongruence has two forms. On the one hand, patients may have entirely normal ups and downs of mood, while their outward emotional expression is blunted; on the other hand, patients may display extremes of affect that do not represent what they are feeling on the inside.

Blunting of Affect Parkinson's disease produces a blunting of facial and gestural expression. Individuals with Parkinson's disease have a loss of the small, natural muscle movements that are involved in the minute-to-minute micro-expressions that convey emotional information. Their faces are often described as being masklike, their movements are slowed, and their voices may be low in volume. They will also display other characteristic features, including a pill-rolling tremor.

Individuals with Parkinson's disease often look depressed, but if you ask them how they feel, some will tell you that they are perfectly happy, whereas others will report that they are depressed. In other words, one cannot rely on the subtle nonverbal cues of facial expression, gesture, and modulation of voice volume that are usually so telling and reliable. One must listen to what the patient reports in order to assess the individual's internal emotional state in cases of Parkinson's disease or other disorders with parkinsonian features, such as Lewy body disorder, the second most common form of dementia, and progressive supranuclear palsy, another movement disorder that resembles Parkinson's disease and is associated with dementia.

In autism spectrum disorders, one also may see flattened or bland affect. And a lack of congruence between affect and mood is found in Moebius syndrome, a congenital paralysis of the facial muscles. Individuals with this rare disorder are unable to produce the facial expressions that communicate emotional states.

The most common disorder seen by therapists in which there is a lack of congruence between affect and emotion, typified by flat affect and inappropriate laughter, is schizophrenia. Schizophrenia is a disease that is brain-based and associated with many neuropsychological abnormalities, though it is not a focus of this book.

Noncongruent Extremes of Affect   Episodes of crying or laughing that are not congruent with what the patient is feeling may also signal the presence of an underlying organic condition. The current term for this syndrome is involuntary emotional expression disorder (IEED), though in the past it was referred to as pseudo-bulbar affect. Patients with IEED will display bursts of crying and/or laughing that appear uncontrollable. The episodes are either out of proportion to any external precipitating circumstances, or they come on out of the blue. Most important, patients report that their outbursts are either an extreme form of what they feel inside or that the affective expression is entirely unrelated to what they feel. Moreover, patients often find these episodes to be disturbing.

As an example, Joshua D. Grill and Jeffrey L. Cummings reported the following scenario in the March 2008 issue of *Current Psychiatry*. The patient they describe has had a significant head injury. Her mood is normal, and there is no mention of symptoms of posttraumatic stress disorder.

Mrs. R, a 68-year-old retired teacher, is referred to you for suspected mania after a closed head injury from a car accident. The referring physician reports that Mrs. R experienced mild anterograde amnesia [loss of memory for what happened just before her head injury] that has resolved, but she continues to suffer from "persistent mood swings as evidenced by substantial inappropriate laughter."

Mrs. R is not manic. Her mood is normal, with a relatively euthymic affect. When asked about her accident or injury, however, she breaks into bouts of laughter that appear to be uncontrollable and last up to several minutes. These episodes include respiratory changes that make her laughter nearly indistinguishable from crying. Mrs. R explains that the episodes occur every time she discusses the accident—regardless of her efforts to prevent them—and complains that they are extremely frustrating and embarrassing. She avoids situations that might trigger the episodes. (Grill & Cummings, 2008, p. 101)

IEED may be mistaken for a mood disorder, especially when the individual is also depressed. Although the signs of IEED may occur in the setting of depression, they are not indicative of depression. Rather, this behavior signifies an underlying organic condition, in this case traumatic brain injury. Other conditions that may be associated with this kind of presentation are some cases of amyotrophic lateral sclerosis (Lou Gehrig's disease), multiple sclerosis, strokes, and Parkinson's disease.

Short bursts of uncontrollable laughter or crying may also be seizure events. Gelastic seizures, as these are called, are a relatively uncommon type of seizure. Nonetheless, it is important to identify them, because effective treatments approaches are available. In addition, the new onset of seizures of any type may be triggered by serious, underlying conditions such as brain tumors, Alzheimer's disease, or infections.

MOOD AND EMOTION—THE INNER EXPERIENCE

Introduction   It may be difficult to identify moods and emotional states that are generated by underlying organic conditions. This is partly because psychological forces always come into play and interact with the biological, making any physical component challenging to decipher. For example, patients readily imbue their feeling states with secondary personal meaning. Yet any patient's interpretation of his or her symptoms may be an after-the-fact explanation and have nothing to do with the timing or the fundamental cause of the emotional state. In addition, moods and emotions that are produced by physical factors or medical disorders may then influence an individual's behavior and lead to downstream consequences. Here is an example.

Your patient is a mother of two teenagers. Her chief complaint is that she gets very irritable at times. She believes that her irritability arises whenever her children try "to test her limits." She wants to find a way to control being short-tempered, recognizing that her behavior tends to escalate the conflicts with her children.

In therapy, your patient discovers that her children are always testing limits, but only sometimes does it "get under her skin." She is irritable only on days after she has been on-call at the hospital and up all night.

Only when she is sleep-deprived does she respond to her children with anger and rigidity. But it is also likely that the children sense when their mother is in a "bad mood" and approach her in a different way—perhaps with a covert annoyance that the patient detects. When the patient is not exhausted, she and her teenagers get along quite well.

The psychological and the biological, the meaningful and the arbitrary, become inexorably intertwined. Despite this complexity, some features can help in identifying when organic factors are contributing to emotional states. Each will be discussed in turn: (a) emotions with unusual intensity for the individual, including catastrophic reactions; (b) emotions that come "out of the blue"; (c) extreme fear or anxiety; (d) elation; and (e) factors from the patient's history.

Emotions with Unusual Intensity for the Individual   A psychologically meaningful precipitant is the most common cause for emotions that are unusually intense for a given individual's characteristic emotional repertoire. Disappointment, loss, emotional trauma, narcissistic injury, the list is endless. Especially strong emotions also occur in the context of mental illnesses, mood disorders, personality disorders, or psychotic disorders. In addition, emotions with unusual intensity for the individual may be an indication that organic factors are playing a part.

My patient remembers her father as a kindly storekeeper who was well respected in the small community in which she grew up. But each night after dinner, he would turn into "an angry tyrant." My patient would cling to her mother at those times, feeling frightened and confused. It wasn't until she was older that she fully grasped what accounted for this daily transformation in her father. Father didn't seem to drink in excess, but that glass of wine he had with dinner on top of the scotch he downed upon arriving home from work were enough to do it. Now she understood.

Drugs and alcohol are frequently associated with alterations in emotional state and often with the intensification of emotions. Just about any sort of emotion may result from the side effects of medications, or from intoxication or withdrawal involving substances or drugs: anger, irritability, anxiety, panic, depression, sullenness, euphoria.

In addition, a variety of medical diseases are capable of producing emotional disturbances with signs and symptoms from this same repertoire of intense emotional states. The consequences of traumatic head injuries can vary widely depending on the nature of the trauma and which parts of the brain were affected. In the realm of emotions, the short-term and often the long-term consequences of head injury may be an alteration in the individual's emotional resilience and flexibility. It is common to find irritability and the propensity to anger quickly, or in some cases even to become violently enraged. Be on the alert for any history of significant or repetitive head injuries in your patients.

Many other medical conditions may lead to an alteration or intensification in an individual's usual range of emotions: disorders of any of the endocrine glands (including diabetes or thyroid, parathyroid, adrenal, pituitary, or ovarian disorders), metabolic disturbances such as liver or kidney diseases, autoimmune diseases such as lupus erythematosis, poisoning, nutritional deficiencies, and the list goes on. Many sleep disorders will present with considerable irritability and/or depression. Seizure disorders deserve special mention because they are common and are frequently associated with intense emotion.

The following case illustrates a camouflaged physical factor that led to periods of emotional irrationality in one of my patients.

Everyone called her BJ as if they knew her well. She was one of those lucky individuals with unusual social skills, the kind of person who was president of her college class—and not at a tiny New England college, but at a mammoth state school in the Midwest. At the same time, she was a private person. In weekly therapy I came to know her well. She approached life with a piercing realism that was mixed with generosity, acceptance, fair-mindedness, and a loving spirit. She also possessed an unusual ability to stay level-headed, but sometimes she would lose perspective and feel wholly irrational and driven by raw emotion. She hated herself at those times, and this is principally why she came into therapy.

BJ would lose perspective most often in relation to her husband. She described him to me with her usual balanced perspective and deep understanding of inner dynamics. He was a good person, and she trusted him. But, despite her complex understanding of him and her love for him, she "couldn't help it." There were things about his behavior that she did not like. He was messy. Sometimes he would leave crumbs on the counter when he buttered his toast in the morning. He would forget to pick up his dirty socks from the floor of the TV room before going up to bed at night. He was frequently late in coming home for dinner, though usually only by 10 or

15 minutes. At times he would "tune out" during conversations. He was obsessed with buying collectibles on eBay. Occasionally he would lose his keys, throwing the household into a tizzy as everyone was recruited to help in the always-urgent search.

BJ knew that her husband had attention deficit hyperactivity disorder. She knew that he was trying hard. But sometimes, only sometimes, none of that mattered. Sometimes she just "couldn't stand it." At those times, she would try to keep her rage to herself. She would find herself withdrawing, preoccupied with an inner debate. On the one hand, she thought it was understandable to be angry about the accumulating eBay purchases that she considered to be a waste of money; she thought it was understandable that she was furious to always be the one who cleared the sink drain of accumulated food. On the other hand, she felt that her reaction was entirely "over the top." Most of the time she realized that these matters were a very trivial part of the big and quite wonderful life that she and her husband shared. So why now was she so mad?

Why indeed? We began to explore just why BJ would get particularly upset at some times and not at others. We explored the possibility that her ire was displaced. Maybe she would get angry about these trivial things when she was really angry with her husband about more important matters. Or perhaps BJ would only lose perspective when she felt stressed at work or worried about money or only after having had a fight with the children. But only one theory held up to scientific scrutiny, and having once realized it, BJ felt much relieved. Virtually every instance of intense anger occurred in the week before BJ's menstrual period. It was a bit humbling to realize how this pattern, now so clear, could have been camouflaged for so long.

BJ began to take medication to ameliorate her premenstrual reactions. But equally important was the shift in meaning that took place with this new understanding of BJ's episodes of intense negative emotion toward her husband. BJ and her husband now talk of BJ being "hit by monthly emotional storms," and they have new strategies for dealing with the situation. Most important, BJ's intense negative emotions no longer lead her to dislike herself.

Another variety of intense emotional outburst, called a catastrophic reaction, has been associated with certain organic disorders. A catastrophic reaction is a dramatic emotional collapse that comes on when an individual's coping skills are overwhelmed. It is often triggered by what observers believe is a minor event, but for the individual with a physical or cognitive deficit, the so-called minor event is threatening because it requires performance in the arena of disability.

The catastrophic reaction may take the form of crying, anger, expressions of hopelessness and resignation, displacement of responsibility, and/or defensive denial. Although these emotional expressions may make psychological sense in the context of the individual's potential sense of shame and anxiety about his or her deficits, the outbursts are entirely out of proportion to the precipitating events; frequently they are socially inappropriate and represent a change from the individual's usual coping style. Catastrophic reactions have been best described in patients who have expressive aphasia, a disorder of language production. Catastrophic reactions may also occur in individuals with traumatic brain injuries.

Emotions That Episodically Come "Out of the Blue" When emotional states arise and subside for no apparent reason, it is our propensity as therapists to think that repression is playing a leading role. We hypothesize that the underlying content is unconscious, leaving its associated physiologic and feeling state behind. There are, however, important organic disorders that can present in just this fashion, with emotions—often very intense emotions—that patients describe as coming "out of the blue," having "a life of their own," or possessing "an on-off quality."

There are two rare disorders in which random episodic secretions of hormones from tumors produce transient symptoms that are readily misinterpreted as psychological. Pheochromocytomas are tumors of adrenal gland tissue that may secrete bursts of epinephrine-like hormones that cause intense anxiety, usually accompanied by headaches and elevated blood pressure. Carcinoid tumors, usually found in the gastrointestinal tract, secrete serotonin, causing flushing of the face along with possible diarrhea and an increased heart rate. Given the episodic nature of these syndromes, they are easily misinterpreted as anxiety or panic attacks.

Focal seizure disorders also can present with intense emotions that have a life of their own. Focal seizure disorders are common and frequently masquerade as psychological disturbances. This type of seizure results from organized localized electrical activity in the brain and often produces intense emotions, including fear, terror, impending doom, foreboding, dread, ecstasy, sexual excitement, a heightened feeling of awareness, or spiritual sensations.

These sorts of seizures may not involve any loss of consciousness or even clouding of consciousness. The actual seizure experience is only moments long, though the beginning of the seizure may be experienced as a recognizable aura or warning signal of what is to come. The individual also may be left with an aftermath of fatigue, anxiety, or difficulty concentrating. Focal seizures are generally stereotypical, unfolding pretty much the same way each time they occur for any particular patient, although one individual may have more than one type of pattern.

The following extended case report illustrates the intertwining of the psychological and biological in the presentation of emotions that come out of the blue.

Joseph came to see me for therapy after his prior psychiatrist had retired from practice. He was a smart man who came from a tough neighborhood and an unsupportive family. He worked as a manager at a computer firm.

In the first session, Joseph related a narrative that captured his approach to life's difficulties. It was not an unusual story. Each morning on his way to school, the young Joseph had had to walk past a gang of bullies who hung out by the candy store at the top of the hill. Each time he walked past, the gang of kids teased him. Joseph dreaded his daily walk up that hill, and he felt utterly humiliated each morning as he walked down the street on the other side of the hill to school. Anger grew inside him, until one day, as he reported it, he simply walked up to the leader of the gang and slugged him. "Everything changed after that."

Unfortunately, Joseph had followed that same pattern during his adult life whenever he faced difficult relationships in college, at home, at work, or at the gym. Anger would build inside him and he'd feel "ready to explode." Now he didn't actually "slug" anyone, but he had had two episodes of extreme rage, each occurring after he had seen a young person being treated badly. During these episodes he had actually "collared" and verbally threatened the offending individuals, terrifying them. He had also scared himself. He confessed to me that this anger inside felt alien and that it was so extreme that he worried he had the potential to "really hurt someone."

The adult Joseph had become more and more afraid of his potential volatility in the face of confrontation. This may have been an important component to his ineffectiveness at standing up for himself at work, where he was apparently underpaid and overworked in comparison to other employees. So Joseph found himself more and more passive, discontent, and angry. Often during the workday he would have short periods of extreme anxiety and then find that he simply could not concentrate. He looked forward to the end of each day, when he could go home to a six-pack of beer and a vigorous workout at the gym.

When I inquired carefully about Joseph's episodes of anxiety at work, it became clear that they had no specific precipitants. Joseph was living with chronic tension, discontent, and anger, but when I asked him to carefully observe his episodes of anxiety, he was certain that they just "came out of the blue." And they didn't last very long, only a minute or so, yet they would leave Joseph with difficulty in concentrating and a feeling of fatigue.

This got me to wondering whether Joseph was having partial seizures. Apparently Joseph's prior psychiatrist had wondered the same thing, because several years before she had sent him to a neurologist. He had had an EEG, a painless study that measures electrical activity in the brain using sensors placed on the scalp. No sign of seizures had been discovered at that time.

I explained to Joseph that one negative EEG does not necessarily rule out a seizure disorder, because seizures are episodic events and may not occur while one is being tested; in addition, it is difficult to record seizures that originate from deep structures in the brain. I tried to persuade Joseph to have a repeat EEG study. I explained that, if he had been having untreated seizures all these years, the problem actually could have worsened and might be detected more easily on an EEG at this time. Even though I warned Joseph that untreated partial seizures may go on to become generalized major motor epilepsy, he did not find my arguments compelling enough to convince him to go through testing again.

So the therapy continued with me encouraging Joseph to stop drinking and to stand up for himself more effectively. Nothing changed. Then, one autumn day Joseph came into therapy looking obviously shaken from an emotional experience he had a week before—it had lasted a mere minute, but it was still haunting him when he arrived in my office.

Joseph had been driving on the highway that ran past an old playground he had frequented as a child. The swings and slide were still in use, but the merry-go-round was in disrepair and had long ago been abandoned as unsafe. Joseph had driven this route countless times, but this time he was overcome by a sudden sense of "actually being back in that playground." The merry-go-round was creaking, and children's voices were laughing and calling to one another. "I was so overcome that I had to pull over to the side of the road. It took me over. I was terrified."

This intense and profoundly frightening experience had lasted for only a minute. It had come out of the blue and shaken Joseph to the core. These characteristics were typical for focal seizures. After this deeply disturbing episode Joseph agreed to see a neurologist. An EEG revealed a pattern of activity that was diagnostic for temporal lobe seizures.

Joseph started anticonvulsant medication and gradually began to feel better. He no longer had random episodes of anxiety. He felt "calmer inside." He felt less angry and less worried about "out-of-control-rage." Joseph had thought of his anger as self-protective and self-righteous. Anger had defined him as "tough" and "standing for justice." But this anger also had been an inner "monster" that Joseph had feared and worked hard to control, backing away from anything that might rouse it. Now that he was rid of the "monster," Joseph began to feel free to stand up for himself.

Gradually, Joseph began to defend himself against mistreatment in his office. He effectively approached his boss to ask for a raise; he stopped taking on the disagreeable work that others had been in the habit of leaving to him. He felt more pride in himself and more content.

In any specific individual, the signs and symptoms of a focal seizure will depend upon which parts of the brain are involved. This chapter section focuses on emotions that come out of the blue—typical for seizures. Other seizure signs and symptoms will be discussed later in this chapter.

Although seizures will occur at random times, a variety of conditions will increase the likelihood that someone with an underlying seizure disorder will have a seizure. These include stress, sleep deprivation, changing states of consciousness from awake to asleep or vice versa, alcohol withdrawal, and certain medications (including bupropion and the tricyclic antidepressants) that lower the threshold for having a seizure. In Joseph's case, it is possible that he would become particularly stressed when he would observe a young person being mistreated; it is also likely that his seizure threshold would drop along with his blood alcohol level after his nightly binges.

It is important for therapists to be aware that in unusual cases seizures can be triggered by specific experiences that are particular to the individual and as varied as the voice of a particular television announcer (Ramani, 1991), the sight of a safety pin (Hoenig, 1960), brushing one's teeth (Chuang, Lin, Lui, Chen, & Chang, 2004), or the sound of church bells (Foote-Smith, 1991). This is called *reflex epilepsy*. Without knowledge of this phenomenon, patient reports of these experiences would seem bizarre and their etiology would be extremely puzzling.

Extreme Fear or Anxiety   Covert organic disorders will differ in the types of emotions they produce. In assessing patients clinically, it is especially important to try to make the distinction between fear and anxiety, different but overlapping emotional states. Anxiety is more common. Fear involves a sense of immediacy and of a more serious threat, even if the nature of that threat is not clear.

In addition to clarifying the nature of the patient's emotions, it is important to ascertain what precipitates these feelings. Organic conditions are more likely to produce anxiety or fear that is not triggered by an external situation alone. These are patients who are fearful or anxious for reasons that the patient's psychodynamic narrative doesn't fully explain.

Anxiety is the hallmark of many mental disorders, but it also may be an important symptom of organic disease states, from hyperthyroidism to hypoparathyroidism, from lupus erythematosis to liver failure, from postseizure states to the autoimmune disease giant cell arteritis, from excess secretion of cortisol (Cushing's syndrome) to true hypoglycemia (possibly caused by a tumor of the pancreas called an insulinoma).

In contrast with anxiety, true fear is actually less common in mental illness. Patients may report feeling fearful in some cases of phobia, paranoia, panic attacks, or posttraumatic stress disorder, but when a patient describes daytime experiences of fear, terror, dread, or impending doom, especially without clarity as to what is feared, it is important for practitioners to consider that the patient may be having focal seizures. Fear is the most common emotion that is associated with seizures.

Here is Karen Armstrong describing an experience of fear during one of her seizures:

> I was gripped suddenly with a quite overwhelming fear. . . . The world had become uncanny and horrifying. . . . I was aware only of my extreme terror, a cold, sickening dread that made everything around me seem brown, rotten, and repulsive because it had no meaning. (Armstrong, 2004, p. 55)

The neurologist Steven C. Schachter has collected patient descriptions of their seizure experiences in a book called *Brainstorms—Epilepsy in Our Words* (Schachter, 2008). Here are some excerpts that describe the emotional component of these individuals' partial seizures:

> Patient 21: "During the seizure . . . I experience . . . a powerful sense of anguish, pain, loneliness or tension in the pit of my stomach, though it is not adequately described by those terms and cannot be related to any other experience." (p. 35)
> Patient 64: "I experience a combination of déjà vu with extreme fear. Nothing I do takes me out of the déjà vu—that is, everything that happens become a part of it, and so the general feeling is of being in front of an oncoming train with no way to escape. The seizures last a minute or two at their peak, but the aftereffect can be up to an hour, more frequently a half hour. I often feel quite tired afterward, especially if I have had a few seizures close together. The seizures are transparent to people around me—I can function in every way—walk, talk, dine." (p. 78)

Sleep-Related Fear   Many sleep-related experiences of fear have diagnostic significance. Nightmares are commonplace in normal individuals, and therapists are aware that frequent nightmares may be symptomatic of posttraumatic stress disorder, but there are other diagnoses to consider as well.

Seizures may manifest themselves as nightmares. Nocturnal seizures may or may not be associated with biting one's tongue or incontinence during sleep. If an individual reports awakening with feelings of fright, as though he or she has had a nightmare but without dream content, then the diagnosis of night terrors is likely. Night terrors occur in a different stage of sleep than nightmares and are amenable to treatment with medications.

REM sleep behavior disorder is a serious condition in which individuals experience fear and other intense emotions while dreaming and act on their dream content while still asleep. Normally, skeletal muscles lose their tone during REM sleep. But with REM sleep behavior disorder the expected loss of muscle tone does not occur; this leaves the sleeper free to move about. The individual with REM sleep behavior disorder may simply flail about during periods of REM sleep, but he or she may also yell, or actually run "from monsters," or try to "fight off enemy attackers" by grabbing the nearest object and assaulting the only other person in the room, namely the bed partner. The sleeper is not the only individual who is terrified and in actual danger under these circumstances. The partners of patients who have REM sleep behavior disorder frequently live in a state of fear about being punched or bitten or in other ways injured during sleep.

REM sleep behavior disorder is associated with Parkinson's disease and Parkinson's-related disorders, such as dementia with Lewy bodies. At times REM sleep behavior disorder may be a harbinger of these disorders, coming on years before other symptoms are apparent. REM sleep behavior disorder may also be correlated with the use of certain medications, including selective serotonin reuptake inhibitor antidepressants.

Feelings of Ecstasy   The feeling of ecstasy, an intensely positive emotion, is rather uncommon. When seen, it is most often part of a religious experience, a drug-induced feeling of elation, or a symptom of mania. Mania in turn is generally associated with bipolar disorder, but this is not always the case. A manic presentation also may be caused by physical disorders including brain tumors, multiple sclerosis, Huntington's disease, late-stage syphilis, steroid medications and numerous other drugs and substances.

Feelings of elation may also be symptomatic of a seizure disorder. Fyodor Dostoevsky had epilepsy. This is his description of the ecstatic feeling that would precede his seizures.

> I experience such happiness as is impossible under ordinary conditions, and of which other people can have no notion. I feel complete harmony in myself and in the world, and this feeling is so strong and sweet that for a several seconds of such bliss one would give 10 years of one's life, indeed perhaps one's whole life. (Hughes, 2005)

Factors from the Patient's History   In attempting to sort out whether a somatic disorder or physical factor might be contributing to your patient's emotional experiences, it is important to comb through the patient's history. Recall lessons learned from other sections of this book. Think about the time course of the emotional symptoms. Take a complete history.

> *Bob had always thought of himself as self-conscious and nervous, but he said that his anxiety hadn't always been "this bad." He described a constant level of background anxiety that he attributed to being newly divorced and living alone at age 47. "I wish I could relax," he told me.*
>
> *Bob couldn't even find respite in sleep. Every night as bedtime approached, he would worry about how the night would go; he had trouble falling asleep as well as staying asleep. "Sometimes I'll fall asleep and then just wake up an hour later. Every time I wake up, it's just another opportunity for insomnia!"*
>
> *Bob drank no coffee, only tea, and only in the morning. Then he told me (but only when I asked!) that he also drank Coke—all afternoon—"to stay sharp." He thought of Coke as being less problematic than afternoon coffee, underestimating the amount of caffeine that it contained.*

Bob believed that his insomnia was caused by his "anxious nature" and his recent divorce. He thought of his caffeine intake as a way to cope with the daytime fatigue that resulted from his insomnia. He was caught in a long-standing, self-perpetuating cycle that is common in clinical practices.

Bob gradually cut back on his Coke intake and confined himself to only one cup of caffeinated tea in the morning. After that, his insomnia improved dramatically, and his low level of constant anxiety lessened. Yes, he still worried, but if he spent half an hour before bedtime in quiet activity, he found that he was able to fall asleep easily most of the time, and he stayed asleep all night.

Bob's story demonstrates how important it is to be "reasonably suspicious" of any patient's explanations for his or her symptoms. It also shows how crucial it is to take a complete history, being alert to recent changes in the individual's emotional state and to any physical factors that might be causing those changes.

Change in Personality

A change in personality is likely to be a significant clue to the presence of an underlying somatic disorder. This phrase, a "change in personality," attempts to conceptualize a fundamental alteration in the person's nature. While most aspects of the mental status exam focus on behavioral changes in an individual who is fundamentally recognizable as the same person, the concept of a change in personality describes alternations that get to the essence of who that person is.

The most famous description of a change in personality, in this case associated with a brain injury, was the remarkable case of Phineas Gage.

> Phineas was a married, 25-year-old, well-respected and competent foreman who worked for the railroad. On September 13, 1848, he was working in Cavendish, Vermont, when a blasting accident occurred, sending a metal rod straight through Phinea Gage's left cheekbone and out through the top of his skull. This tamping rod was found 30 yards from the accident site covered in blood and brain. The rod weighed about thirteen pounds; it was 3 feet 8 inches long and 1¼ inch in diameter, tapering at one end. (Macmillan, 2000)
>
> This kind of detailed information is known about the incident because Dr. John Martin Harlow took care of Phineas Gage and then wrote about the case. The medical community was astounded to learn that Phineas Gage had fully recovered. He had survived the accident as well as an infection that followed. However, the story does not end here. In 1868, Dr. Harlow wrote about the case once again. This time he reported on the mental manifestations of Phineas Gage's traumatic brain injury. Here are his words:
>
>> His contractors, who regarded him as the most efficient and capable foreman in their employ previous to his injury, considered the change in his mind so marked that they could not give him his place again. The equilibrium or balance, so to speak, between his intellectual faculties and his animal propensities, seems to have been destroyed. He is fitful, irreverent, indulging at times in the grossest profanity (which was not previously his custom), manifesting but little deference for his fellows, impatient of restraint or advice when it conflicts with his desires, at times pertinaciously obstinate, yet capricious and vacillating, devising many plans of future operation, which are no sooner arranged than they are abandoned in turn for others appearing more feasible. A child in his intellectual capacity and manifestations, he has the animal passions of a strong man. Previous to his injury, although untrained in the schools, he possessed a well-balanced mind, and was looked upon by those who knew him as a shrewd, smart business man, very energetic and persistent in executing all his plans of operation. In this regard his mind was radically changed, so decidedly that his friends and acquaintances said he was "no longer Gage." (Macmillan, 2000)

"No longer Gage." That phrase sums up the notion of a change in personality. Family members especially know it when they see it. Phineas Gage exhibited one form that a change in personality may take: he was disinhibited, behaving in ways he would not have allowed of himself before his accident. Other forms that disinhibition may take include being disheveled, socially inappropriate, impulsive, sexually provocative, gorging on food, abandoning manners, or exhibiting poor judgment.

A different type of change in personality might involve individuals becoming slow, concrete, and apathetic; whereas in the past they cared deeply about the grandchildren, or baseball, or a favorite TV show, now they are disinterested.

A change in personality is fundamentally a biologically based alteration in the brain substrate of personality. It is important to differentiate this from the changes one sees when an individual has had a life-altering experience. You have likely heard patients say things like this:

> *"Back in Ireland when I was growing up, I remember my father being quiet and passive and always keeping to himself. But my mother used to tell me that he hadn't always been like that. She said that the war had changed him. He hadn't been wounded or anything. He had just seen too much. He went to war and was never the same again."*

Or this:

> *"Something happened to her while she was in the Peace Corps. Maybe it was the isolation in that village in the middle of nowhere and being exposed to a simpler way of life. She was kind of a lost soul when she went. She was looking for something. After she returned she didn't want to see us very often. She said our family was too materialistic."*

These are descriptions of people changing as a consequence of profound emotional experiences. The changes are dynamically understandable, although we may not be privy to the details.

Causes of a Change in Personality

The frontal and temporal lobes and their connections are the main sites of brain damage in patients who have had a change in personality, though the causes of that damage are wide-ranging. Tumors, strokes, dementia, infection, and trauma are commonly the underlying etiology. Patients with late syphilis, Huntington's disease, or Wilson's disease may display changes in personality.

Long-standing seizures involving the temporal lobe and limbic regions of the brain may also be associated with changes in personality over time. These personality features are not specific to seizure disorders, nor do they occur in everyone who has this condition; and furthermore there is dispute about exactly how to categorize the personality changes that are possible. Nonetheless, in some individuals it may be helpful to recognize these transformations as clues to their possible origin.

Bear and Fedio catalogued the interictal (between seizures) personality traits and hypothesized that what underlies all of the characteristic features is an intensification and personalization of emotional experience (Bear & Fedio, 1977). These individuals take life seriously. They feel strong emotions. They are concerned with moral, ethical, philosophical, and religious issues. These matters are of intense interest to them, not in an academic sense but in a deeply personal way. Their interest in religion is generally not traditional; they may have multiple religious conversions; they may even be atheists, but religion is on their minds.

The 18 behavioral features that Bear and Fedio included were the following: emotionality, mania, depression, guilt, humorlessness, altered sexual interest, aggression, anger and hostility, hypergraphia (excessive writing), religiosity, philosophical interest, sense of personal destiny, hypermoralism, dependency, paranoia, obsessionalism, circumstantiality, viscosity (Bear & Fedio, 1977). The term *viscosity* is an attempt to describe the difficulty of extricating oneself from conversations with these individuals who are relationally "sticky." As with the other personality characteristics, this trait is neither specific nor diagnostic; for instance, individuals with long-standing multiple sclerosis are also frequently described as being "sticky."

Individuals with long-standing epilepsy also may be circumstantial, contributing to this relational "stickiness." Their writings tend to be voluminous, often with relatively little content. It is not uncommon for these patients to come into the clinic with long lists or pages of diary entries for the therapist to read. It is hypothesized that this apparently powerful drive to write has been harnessed by some especially talented individuals with epilepsy (such as Dostoevsky) in the service of producing masterpieces of literature.

Apathy: Lack of Motivation, Loss of Initiation

Apathy is important to recognize, because it is a hallmark sign of disturbances that have a direct or indirect impact on the frontal lobes of the brain. Apathy is readily mistaken for depression, probably because the two states share certain characteristics, including a diminished motivation for action and loss of interest in activities the individual used to care about, but apathy is not a mood disorder. It is an abnormal motivational state, and it can be distinguished from depression.

Here are some things that family members say in describing what apathy looks like.

"She is eerily quiet."

"He speaks much less than he used to. And I just can't get him interested in anything."

"He used to love watching football. He'd get really involved. I remember. I'd be in the kitchen, and he'd be yelling and cursing at the TV. Now he just sits there. He doesn't yell anymore. He doesn't seem to care much about what happens."

"We were nervous about raising the subject of her giving up driving, but she just agreed to hand over her car keys. It was strange."

Individuals who are depressed frequently lose interest in their usual activities or even in life itself. Individuals who are depressed also may exhibit psychomotor retardation, a slowing of both physical and mental processes. But depressed patients feel dysphoric; they will say they feel "down" or "sad" or "hopeless." In contrast, individuals with apathy may not be distressed at all. With mild apathy, patients simply will lose interest in those things they used to find compelling; when the apathy is extreme, they will fail to initiate even the most basic activities, including moving about or talking. In addition, these individuals may lack insight about their change in behavior.

Apathy is most commonly seen with frontal dementia syndromes, some frontal lobe tumors, strokes, traumatic brain injuries, and normal pressure hydrocephalus. It is important to note that individuals with apathy may have impulsive emotional outbursts at times. This does not nullify the accuracy of describing these individuals as apathetic. Their lack of impulse control and their apathy both emerge from frontal lobe dysfunction.

Mutism

Mutism is often a psychologically motivated form of withholding, a passive-aggressive expression of anger. Hospitalized teenagers who do not speak but continue to send text messages to their friends clearly have a psychologically based mutism. But whenever you encounter a patient who is mute, there are causes beyond the psychological to consider. Is the patient severely apathetic? Catatonic? Does the individual have impairments in the ability to utilize language?

Mutism may be a manifestation of severe apathy in which the individual simply takes no initiative, even so far as uttering a word. The causes of apathy include brain tumors, traumatic injuries, and dementias that affect the frontal lobes of the brain. When the mutism is part of a catatonic presentation, it is crucial to keep in mind the myriad of organic disorders that frequently underlie catatonia. This topic is discussed in more depth in the next section on psychomotor activity.

Mutism also may stem from a problem with the production of language, a clear sign of a somatic disturbance. The difficulty may reside in the parts of the body that are used to produce speech sounds or in the brain, often as the consequence of a stroke or certain forms of dementia. This topic is discussed in the section on language.

Psychomotor Activity

Moving at a pace that is outside the range of normal is a significant finding, whether the individual is hyperactive or pathologically slow. Mental processing speed may vary, along with motor activity. This section will focus on global psychomotor activity. Specific movement disorders or disturbances of gait will only be mentioned briefly in this section; these should always trigger a medical workup.

Decreased Motor Activity

Slowed physical activity is most often seen in individuals who are depressed. Many somatic conditions may also be associated with decreased psychomotor activity, including Parkinson's disease, hypothyroidism, strokes, head injuries, and the dementia that may be associated with HIV.

Perhaps the most interesting, complex, and misunderstood presentation of profound slowing is catatonia. Many people mistakenly think that catatonia is always a form of schizophrenia. While schizophrenia may present with catatonic features, more frequently catatonia is the manifestation of a mood disorder or of a medical condition that may be serious enough to warrant emergency attention. A medical workup is imperative for patients with catatonia, because so many somatic conditions may underlie this presentation.

One life-threatening, catatonic-like condition is neuroleptic malignant syndrome, an idiosyncratic reaction to antipsychotic medication that presents with mental status changes and muscle rigidity; these patients also go on to develop a fever. If patients with neuroleptic malignant syndrome are mistakenly thought to have catatonic schizophrenia and treated with increasing doses of antipsychotic medications, this will increase their chances of dying.

An important disorder that is related to neuroleptic malignant syndrome was first described long before the advent of psychotropic medications. This syndrome is called malignant catatonia or lethal catatonia because of its high mortality rate when untreated. These patients present with catatonia and then go on to develop a fever, unstable blood pressure, rapid heart rate, and coma. This is the same illness course that one sees with neuroleptic malignant syndrome.

Patients with catatonic symptoms are unforgettable. They may be entirely immobile and rigid; they may assume bizarre positions. Here is a description of what is called a psychological pillow:

> *I recall the patient well. He was lying in his hospital bed with his head held just above the bed, at the angle one would expect had it been resting on a pillow. Only there was no pillow. The patient maintained this position for hours.*

Other patients display extreme negativity, grimacing, waxy flexibility (continuing to hold their limbs in whatever position you place them), or echopraxia (echoing the movements of others). Patients with catatonia often display symptoms in the verbal arena as well, including mutism or echolalia, repeating what others say.

INCREASED MOTOR ACTIVITY

Minimally increased motor activity is generally referred to as restlessness or fidgetiness, while the term *agitation* is reserved for more extreme levels of hyperactivity. Catatonic excitement is perhaps the most severe form. Increased psychomotor activity is common in mental disorders when patients are paranoid, anxious, or manic. Therapists are familiar with the schizophrenic patient who is frightened and pacing or the patient with an agitated depression who is worried and hand-wringing.

Somatic disorders also commonly produce increased psychomotor activity and should always be considered as a diagnostic possibility. Attention deficit hyperactivity disorder, the hyperactive type, is frequently seen in outpatient populations. Increased levels of motor activity also may indicate a delirium, the extremely common state of globally compromised mental functioning that may be caused by a myriad of possible underlying medical conditions and/or by drugs or medications, either as a consequence of idiosyncratic reactions or from states of toxicity or withdrawal. Two well-known drug-related syndromes that are associated with extreme agitation are delirium tremens, a life-threatening alcohol withdrawal syndrome, and amphetamine toxicity.

In some disorders, motor hyperactivity is actually driven by an underlying sensory experience; this is somewhat analogous to having an itch that is relieved by scratching. People who have restless legs syndrome describe unpleasant physical sensations, most often but not necessarily only in their legs. These feelings of "hot ants running up and down inside my calves" or "that jumpy electrical sensation" disappear when the person moves the part of the body that is affected. Akasthisia is a medication side effect that produces an extremely uncomfortable whole-body sensation of "having to move"; this may be the underlying driving force behind a patient's pacing or agitation. Individuals who have Tourette's syndrome also experience a sensation of building tension that is relieved by performing one of their unique tics, be it a motor movement or vocal expression. It is only through interviewing the patient that a clinician will learn whether motor behaviors are being driven by physical sensations. This information is crucial in making an accurate diagnosis.

SPECIFIC ABNORMAL MOTOR MOVEMENTS

Specific types of abnormal movements can provide crucial clues to a diagnosis. Expertise in this area constitutes a subspecialty of neurology. To the untrained eye, patients who have specific types of movement disorders (tremors of various kinds, chorea, athetosis, dystonia, myoclonic jerks) may leave the impression that they simply move around a lot or that they have unusual gestures or mannerisms. Keep in mind that patients often use gestures to try to disguise their involuntary movements.

Several important disorders that affect mental status are associated with abnormal involuntary movements. Parkinson's disease is characterized by a variety of movement abnormalities including a pill-rolling tremor. A substantial percentage of patients with Parkinson's disease will develop some cognitive impairments. Huntington's disease used to be called Huntington's chorea after characteristic flicking, dance-like movements. Huntington's disease presents with a picture of gradual psychological deterioration; often patients are correctly diagnosed only after the movement disorder emerges. Wilson's disease, a genetic disorder of copper metabolism, will lead to less specific disturbances in movement. Creutzfeld-Jakob disease, a rare dementia, presents with rapid mental deterioration and is frequently associated with abnormal jerking muscle movements.

Perhaps the most common abnormal motor movements seen by therapists are those that result from psychotropic medications. These are not associated with mental status changes but deserve mention here because they are so common. Most of these abnormal motor side effects are reversible, although tardive dyskinesia, a movement disorder that can result from the use of certain medications, especially the older antipsychotics, is generally not reversible. Tardive dyskinesia most often manifests as abnormal movements involving the tongue and mouth but also may cause abnormal involuntary movements of limbs, the torso, or even the diaphragm. It is important to *not* assume that long-standing movement disorders are secondary to medications. A medical evaluation is important.

Hallucinations and Illusions

INTRODUCTION

Hallucinations are sensory experiences that occur without a corresponding external stimulus. The patient sees little children dancing around the bedroom when actually no one is there. Illusions, on the other hand, are distortions of actual sensory experiences; a shadow is mistaken for an intruder. Hallucinations and illusions may occur in any sensory realm: auditory, visual, tactile, somaesthetic (body sensations), olfactory (smell), gustatory (taste). Many of these categories will be discussed in more depth below. Hallucinations or illusions are frequently caused by organic disease or physical factors and should be medically investigated.

It is a commonly held notion that hallucinating is synonymous with being psychotic. This is not true. Believing that the hallucinations are real is what signifies psychosis. Hallucinations and illusions are brain-derived events. Brain centers that are involved in the normal perception of visual stimuli, auditory stimuli, or tactile stimuli, for instance, are firing when the corresponding visual or auditory or tactile hallucinations occur. In order for individuals to believe that their hallucinations or illusions are real, there probably also needs to be brain dysfunction involving those higher cortical areas that assess whether an experience makes sense.

A 96-year-old woman told me about a hallucinatory experience she had had one evening. She was surprised to see that someone was sitting in her bedroom chair. It was Paula, an old friend. "Paula, I didn't know you were visiting!" she apparently said out loud. Very quickly she figured out that this didn't make any sense; she knew that Paula was at home in Florida, 500 miles away. Then she remembered that she had taken a synthetic narcotic medication for her back pain just an hour earlier and realized that this had caused her to hallucinate. When she looked back at the chair, it was empty.

This woman was not at all psychotic, but she had had a visual hallucination. Patients who are having hallucinations or illusions and who know that these are not real may be reluctant to talk about their experiences, fearing that they will be thought to be crazy. Patients who have hallucinations wrestle with how to understand them, and, especially if they do not know about the possibility of organic causes, they may arrive at explanations inspired by ideas that are available in the culture around them.

CAUSES OF HALLUCINATIONS

Mental health clinicians are used to thinking of hallucinations as symptoms of psychiatric illness. Indeed, auditory hallucinations and, less often, visual hallucinations are seen in many patients with schizophrenia, psychotic affective disorders, and conversion disorders. Hallucinations and/or illusions also may be found in normal individuals under certain conditions: in states of sleep deprivation, accompanying intense emotional experiences such as mourning, and upon falling asleep (hypnagogic hallucinations) or awakening (hypnopompic hallucinations).

Often however, hallucinations and/or illusions are signs of an underlying physical condition. Here are some of the possibilities, ranging from transient, benign, and treatable to life threatening. Hallucinations and illusions are described during states of sensory deprivation. Clinically, sensory deprivation is not rare. Significant impairments in hearing or vision will produce sensory deprivation, and individuals with these limitations may experience hallucinations in the compromised modality. In the visual realm, this nonpsychotic syndrome is called the Charles Bonnet syndrome.

> Ms. Xavier was only 64 years old when she experienced a devastating stroke that resulted in a loss of vision in the left half of her visual field in both eyes. She was referred to a psychiatrist for an evaluation because, despite a cheery surface demeanor, the nursing staff members felt that she was actually quite depressed.
>
> Only very sheepishly and reluctantly at the end of the hour-long psychiatric appointment did Ms. Xavier mention that she occasionally had "visitors." They were playful children who would appear out of the blue, but only in her left (blinded) visual field. Soon after her stroke, she said that the children visited her quite often, but now they rarely appeared, and she missed them.
>
> The psychiatrist's first thought was that Ms. Xavier had a psychotic depression. But, upon further inquiry, it became clear that Ms. Xavier was fully aware that her visitors were hallucinations. Though the psychiatrist found that Ms. Xavier was indeed depressed, he came to realize that her visual impairment was the substrate for the emergence of these hallucinatory experiences.

The syndrome of synesthesia is sometimes misunderstood to be hallucinatory or illusory. Synesthesia is a benign condition in which there is a stable, lifelong cross-association of sensory modalities. Experientially, for example, the individual will read a word and simultaneously see colors that vary according to the combination of letters making up the word, or the individual may hear music and see colors that correspond to different notes.

Migraines are another frequent cause of visual imagery, from the geometric patterns that are classical in this syndrome to more complex visions. Migraines and migraine variants are extremely common, often debilitating, and frequently misdiagnosed, especially when the headache component is absent. Migraines are now hypothesized to be the symptom of spreading alterations in brain signaling (first excitation and then inhibition), with secondary affects on blood vessels.

Another diagnosis to consider when a patient presents with hallucinations is narcolepsy. This is a sleep disorder in which aspects of REM sleep intrude into waking life, including the hallucinatory experience of dreaming. Individuals with narcolepsy frequently report hallucinations that are associated with sleep onset or awakening (hypnagogic and hypnopompic, respectively). Patients may sense that someone is standing next to the bed. They may experience themselves flying or levitating. Or they may have vivid visual hallucinations.

Of the more serious physical causes for hallucinations and illusions perhaps the most common are the effects of substances: poisons (lead thallium, manganese, mercury), innumerable medications, both prescribed as well as over-the-counter, herbal remedies, illegal substances, and alcohol. Hallucinations and illusions may be caused by the primary effects of the substance, as with LSD or mescaline, or the side effects, some of which are predictable whereas others are idiosyncratic.

In addition, one must consider potential toxicity caused by an excessively high blood level of the substance. A patient may have purposely overdosed or perhaps misunderstood the directions on the bottle and taken too much. In elderly individuals with slowed metabolism, even a low dose of a medication may cause a high blood level. In addition, drug-drug interactions, as when one medication changes the metabolism of another, may lead to hallucinations or illusions, even when the dose of each individual drug is reasonable.

There also are the consequences of drug withdrawal. For example, the condition known as delirium tremens (DTs) is one of several possible alcohol withdrawal syndromes. DTs may present up to 10 days after stopping drinking and is associated with hallucinations, frequently small animals—the ''pink elephants'' of popular culture. Even with modern-day treatment, the mortality rate of DTs remains substantial.

Hallucinations and/or illusions also may be symptoms of any delirium. In particular, individuals with compromised brain function (e.g., from prior strokes, trauma, early dementias) are prone to experience hallucinations under conditions of stress from any physical ailment (such as a urinary tract infection or pneumonia) even if that disease does not directly involve the brain. Often under these circumstances the acute physical condition is not obvious, in part because the patient's ability to give a history is compromised, but the hallucinations will resolve only after the urinary tract infection or pneumonia has been treated.

Hallucinations and illusions may be one symptom of a focal seizure or part of an aura that occurs in advance of a generalized (grand mal) seizure. Hallucinations that accompany seizures may be simple (the "ding ding" of a railroad crossing) or complex (the vivid experiencing of an entire scene). Often the hallucinations will occur on one side of the body or in one side of physical space, thus providing a clue as to where the seizure focus resides in the brain. Seizures may have a variety of possible underlying causes: prior head trauma, an underlying brain tumor, infections or parasitic cysts in the brain, or autoimmune diseases.

CLINICAL EVALUATION

In clinical situations, patients may not report that they are having hallucinations. Certain types of unusual behavior may lead a professional to infer that a patient is hallucinating: picking at clothing or skin as though removing bugs, paying a great deal of attention to an empty corner of the room, whispering to a nonexistent someone.

Many factors help a knowledgeable practitioner to sort out the possible causes of hallucinatory experiences. Be sure to inquire as to the precise nature and content of the hallucinatory experience, whether the individual thinks the experience is real, where on the body or where in physical space the phenomenon occurs, whether the experience is threatening or emotionally benign, when the hallucinations began, when they occur, how long they last, and any accompanying signs and symptoms in addition to the clinical context.

Generally speaking, the hallucinations that are most likely to be part of a mental condition are those that actively relate to the patient (e.g., voices that threaten or command the patient, visions that interact with the patient).

AUDITORY HALLUCINATIONS AND ILLUSIONS

In evaluating patients for auditory hallucinations, one must first be sure that the patient isn't describing noises that might have a physical origin within the ear or brain. Tinnitus is a ringing or buzzing sound in the ear. Tinnitus may be symptomatic of a variety of disorders from the presence of earwax, to the consequences of loud noise exposure, to aspirin toxicity, to a tumor in the brain involving the acoustic nerve. When patients report a repetitive pulsing or wooshing sound, consider that this might be coming from an abnormal blood vessel formation within the skull called an arteriovenous malformation. These symptoms require medical investigation.

Next it is important to clarify whether the individual hears sounds, voices, or music. Which side do they come from? How long do they last? If they are sounds, are they simple, repetitive, or complex? If they are voices, be sure to inquire about whether these voices come from inside or from the outside. Does the person think these voices might be his or her own thoughts? Are the voices recognizable? How many different voices are there? Are they threatening? What do they say? This information will help in thinking about the diagnostic possibilities.

> *Margie told me that she had grown up as a "poor girl in a wealthy suburb."* *"The other kids had new clothes every school year. I had two outfits, total. And I'd go home to cold-water showers." Also, Margie's father was an alcoholic and could be brutally punishing.*
>
> *The patient was reluctant to talk about her childhood in any detail. She had long since married and had children; she didn't believe that "looking backward would help any." So we focused in therapy on Margie's chief complaint: "I don't know what to do with my life." Part of the problem was that Margie had trouble being effective. "Sometimes I feel foggy," she stated. She had trouble sleeping through the night, and when she awakened she would frequently "hear music." Margie clarified that there wasn't a song "stuck in my head." She actually heard the music coming from somewhere outside. She was fully aware that there was no external source for this music, but it seemed entirely real. This was an auditory hallucination.*
>
> *I referred Margie to a neurologist, who ordered an EEG and found that Margie had focal seizures. She had probably been having seizures for years. When she was treated with anticonvulsant medications, the auditory hallucinations disappeared and her daytime fogginess improved. The source of her seizures may have been the repeated head trauma she was subjected to during her childhood. "Yeah, he would throw me against the wall when I was a kid."*

VISUAL HALLUCINATIONS AND ILLUSIONS

Visual hallucinations are so often associated with organic conditions that they should be assumed to have a physical basis and worked up vigorously. Visual hallucinations will take different forms depending on which parts of the visual system are affected. Patients may see colors, flashing lights, geometric patterns, or a persistence of visual images after they have shifted their visual frame. Patients may see complex visions of animals or people, imaginary scenes or events from the past. In addition, patients may see themselves from an outside perspective.

A myriad of organic disorders can cause visual hallucinations. Here is a sampling of some of the most common. Hallucinogens, alcohol and other drug experiences, and withdrawal syndromes are commonly associated with visual hallucinations. Narcolepsy is a sleep disorder in which the dream imagery of REM sleep may intrude into waking life. Dementia with Lewy bodies is associated with complex, benign visual hallucinations. The cardiac drug digitalis, as well as medications that are prescribed for erectile dysfunction, may cause disturbance in color vision such that the world seems tinted.

Migraines are commonly associated with visual hallucinations, which may take many different forms. Commonly, patients report seeing geometric patterns, but the visual hallucinations associated with migraines may be simple or complex. It is important to be aware that migraines are a brain disturbance and can occur without any actual headache. Migraines are medical mimics and may present looking like strokes, seizure disorders, or eye disease. In addition, migraines may be one of the presenting features of certain genetic diseases that have mental manifestations, including the mitochondrial diseases and cerebral autosomal dominant arteriopathy with subcortical infarcts and leukoencephalopathy (CADASIL), in which patients also have multiple strokes. It is imperative for clinicians to keep in mind that worsening migraines, the new onset of migraines, or patient reports of "the worst headache of my life" may signal conditions that require emergency care: strokes, brain hemorrhages or infections, or brain tumors, among others.

Visual illusions are readily interpreted as being psychological—a yellow fire hydrant is mistaken to be a little girl in a yellow raincoat; the visual world appears larger; or suddenly everything is small, like looking through the wrong end of binoculars; or perhaps one's body parts appear distorted. All of these illusions may be associated with organic pathology such as seizure disorders, brain tumors, and often a delirium.

A common toxic psychosis may ensue when too many medications with atropine-like effects are prescribed. A memorable saying from medical school describes atropine toxicity—dry as a bone, red as a beet, mad as a hatter. Hallucinations are commonly associated with this condition.

> *I looked in from the doorway of the hospital room. The patient was in bed, wrapped in rumpled sheets. He was in constant motion, picking wildly at the bed linens and at his pajamas. He was clearly terrified. "Bugs!" he said. "Get these things off me." Between the strings of intelligible speech were unintelligible mutterings. His lips were dry. His face was red. He was agitated and seemed confused.*

This patient had atropine psychosis, caused by a combination of medications he had received in the hospital: an antidepressant, a sleeping pill, and antipsychotic medication—all with significant atropine-like side effects. He was seeing bugs and also feeling bugs.

TACTILE OR SOMATIC HALLUCINATIONS

Examples of tactile or somatic hallucinations include the sensation of bugs crawling on or under the skin, feeling "electricity" coursing through one's limbs, or having a sense that one is levitating or flying. Patients may also experience their bodies as distorted in size or shape. These somatic hallucinations may be caused by organic conditions such as toxic or abnormal metabolic states, migraines, drug or alcohol withdrawal syndromes, or seizure disorders.

OLFACTORY OR GUSTATORY HALLUCINATIONS

Olfactory hallucinations generally involve the smell of unpleasant or even repugnant odors, such as "ammonia," "rotten eggs," or "burning rubber." Similarly, gustatory hallucinations are also frequently unpleasant ("it tasted like something dead") or metallic ("copper pennies"). These types of hallucinations are the least common. Frequently they are associated with seizure disorders.

One of my patients, Ms. Peterson, told me that she had had a curious experience.

> *"At first I was angry at Sarah." Sarah is Ms. Peterson's daughter. "My car reeked from cigarette smoke. Sarah had just borrowed the car, and she knows that I don't allow smoking in my car." But then Ms. Peterson realized that she smelled cigarette smoke elsewhere too. The smell would come and go. Eventually she realized that she was hallucinating. Ms. Peterson had been diagnosed with temporal lobe epilepsy not long before this. Her olfactory hallucinations were symptoms of her partial seizures.*

Here is a vivid description of an olfactory hallucination that routinely signaled the beginning of a seizure:

> It began with the smell. It was a sweet but sulfury aroma, reminiscent of bad eggs and giving off an aura of imminent menace. Like any odor, it was also intensely evocative. I recognized it immediately. This is how it always started. (Armstrong, 2004, p. 46)

Sense of Reality

This section addresses subjective experiences in which there is a subtle alteration in a person's sense of self or of the world. These states are referred to as depersonalization and derealization, respectively. Frequently the two occur together. Therapists often hear about these phenomena when patients describe states of extreme anxiety, as may occur during traumatic events or as part of posttraumatic stress disorder. Individuals with these diagnoses may report states of derealization in which the world seems altered and unreal, or they may describe out-of-body experiences (e.g., watching themselves from the ceiling while being raped).

In addition, mental health professionals may be familiar with patients who experience dissociative episodes or fugue states, extended periods of dissociation that can last from hours to many months. A dissociative episode may involve derealization, depersonalization, amnesia, and loss of identity. Not infrequently, therapists may actually observe what they believe to be a dissociative episode in their offices. The patient behaves in an altered fashion, momentarily seeming to be somewhere else or out of touch. Afterward, the patient may report having had an altered sense of time, self, or reality.

It is crucial to rule out brain disorders when patients present these kinds of symptoms, because disturbances of a sense of reality may arise from organic disorders involving the brain. For instance, partial seizures commonly involve experiences of depersonalization, derealization, a feeling that the world is "uncanny" or "bizarre," a feeling that one's body parts are distorted in size, seeing one's self from another vantage point, and other distortions of one's sense of self and the world.

Déjà vu and jamais vu episodes are two forms that a disturbance in one's experience of reality may take. These may be conceptualized as brief distortions of memory and time. Déjà vu (already seen) incidents involve feeling that one has previously experienced what is now happening while simultaneously knowing that this is not true. Jamais vu (never seen) may be thought of as the opposite of déjà vu.

During an episode of jamais vu, an individual feels that he or she has never been to a place that is actually familiar or has never seen something before, even though it is simultaneously known to be a familiar object. It is normal to occasionally have déjà vu experiences, but the presence of frequent déjà vu experiences or of jamais vu episodes raises other diagnostic possibilities.

> *Some years ago, a friend of mine e-mailed to say that she was having a terrible time with her 20-year-old daughter, Alina. Alina had just returned home after a long hospitalization for a viral brain infection. My friend was thrilled to have her daughter home again, but reentry was not going well. Here's part of the e-mail about Alina's first day home.*
>
> *"Alina opened her bedroom closet, looked in, and started to cry. Then she said . . . (You are not going to believe this!) She said, "These are not my clothes!"*
>
> *My friend was distraught; she interpreted this behavior to mean that her daughter was not happy to be home.*

In fact, this was an example of jamais vu. The daughter was having a seizure as a consequence of her viral encephalitis. One symptom of the seizure was this brief altered sense of reality. She did not recognize her own clothes as being familiar.

Delusions

Delusions are very common in the patient population served by mental health professionals. Delusions are unshakable false beliefs, and they come in many different forms; most of the common varieties are familiar to therapists: ideas of reference, paranoid, grandiose, and somatic delusions. Delusions of any kind may be associated with underlying organic disorders, but certain types of delusions are often associated with covert physical disorders.

CONTENT-SPECIFIC DELUSIONS

It is useful to be aware of the types of delusions that are frequently indicative of organic pathology. One way to conceptualize these delusions is to take the following approach: While patients with mental disorders will exhibit delusions that put an unusual spin on the familiar, patients with organic disease will often manifest delusions that transform the unfamiliar into the familiar. The early 20th-century neurologist John Hughlings Jackson said that this mistaking of the unfamiliar for the familiar was a good example of the reversion to more automatic or reflexive means of thought that occurs when higher levels of brain function are inhibited (Feinberg, 2002).

To make this clearer, here are some examples. An individual with schizophrenia may think that the mail carrier (familiar) is an agent of the CIA (unfamiliar); or he may believe that he is not just any medical student (familiar) but actually God's special messenger (unfamiliar) in the world of health care. On the other hand, a patient with organic disease may assert that she is not in an emergency room (unfamiliar to the patient) but rather in her own kitchen (very familiar)—"It's just that strangers have brought in some unusual equipment."

Other delusions that are highly correlated with organic disease involve misidentifications. These are variously referred to as misidentification syndromes or reduplicative syndromes. Capgras syndrome is the most well-known of these types of delusions. Patients with Capgras syndrome believe that the person who is with them may look exactly like their real husband, wife, daughter, or son, but that this individual is actually a look-alike imposter. The patient believes that the real relative or significant other is elsewhere. Here are two examples of Capgras syndrome that will give you some idea of how this presents clinically:

> A woman anxiously whispers to her husband, "You're going to have to leave because my husband is coming home soon."
>
> A man leans over and conspiratorially says to his wife, Karen, "You know that Karen, she is a bitch!"

We experience people as being familiar not only because of recognizing how they look, smile, walk, and talk, but also because we experience a set of feelings that accompany those perceptions. Theoreticians hypothesize that delusions of misidentification develop when underlying brain pathology disconnects the experience of perceiving the familiar person or place from the feelings that are associated with the familiar person or place in question.

There are many other types of misidentification syndromes, all of which may be associated with organic pathology. Here are a few: In Fregoli syndrome, the patient believes that a particular individual has the capacity to simultaneously take on the appearance of multiple different figures in the patient's life. Heutoscopy, also called doppelgänger, is a delusion in which the patient believes that he or she has a double, a twin, or an impostor. Reduplicative paramnesia involves the belief that a familiar place, such as one's home, is in fact not the real home; the individual believes that the real home exists somewhere else. With phantom border syndrome, the patient believes that there are unwanted guests in the house. For example, a frightened woman calls her son to say that there is a stranger in the house. The "stranger" is her husband.

Insight

Mental health professionals use the term *insight* when speaking of the ability to be self-reflective, to see one's self clearly, and to understand how one is perceived by others. A narrower use of the term involves the degree to which someone is aware of his or her illness, be it mental or physical. An individual's psychological makeup will influence how he or she responds to illness, but some brain impairments may destroy the capacity for psychological insight, in particular those disorders affecting the frontal lobes of the brain.

La belle indifference, lack of concern about an obvious physical disability, was classically thought to characterize hysteria. Patients with what we now call conversion disorders may display this indifference about their symptoms. However, one must never assume that lack of concern or denial of physical symptoms is based on a psychological process.

It is not at all uncommon to see even profound denial of obvious physical disabilities in patients who have neurological disorders. Neurologists refer to this as *anosognosia*. Patients who have had strokes may believe that their paralyzed limbs are fine or that they belong to someone else. There are patients with lesions in the parts of their brain that make it impossible for them *to know* that they can see; these individuals assert that they are blind, but they are able to negotiate an obstacle course with ease. Individuals with Wernicke's aphasia may be unaware that their verbal communications are incomprehensible to others. It would be a mistake to assume that any of these individuals are in psychological denial.

I recently heard a group of neurologists discussing how often patients who are disoriented for time on the basis of an organic brain disorder are not upset about it. "They might be off by 25 years, but they just don't seem to care."

Judgment

Judgment involves making decisions about taking action within a particular context. The classical way to test for judgment is to ask: What would you do if you were in a crowded theater and saw smoke? And what would you do if you found a sealed and stamped envelope on the sidewalk? The problem with this approach is that it doesn't test what people actually would do if they were in the situation, feeling the emotions of the predicament. It is possible to learn more about a patient's judgment from taking a careful history, especially if it is supplemented by information from family members and friends of the patient.

Many high-level mental capacities contribute to good judgment: the ability to size up a situation, inhibit impulsive responses, anticipate the consequences of an action, think through a sequence of actions, initiate action, monitor outcomes and course-correct if necessary, learn from mistakes, utilize experience, and know one's limitations. Impaired judgment may result from disturbances in any of these areas of functioning and is common in patients with mental disorders as well as in those who have organic conditions.

Individuals with disorders that interrupt frontal lobe circuitry may disregard social norms (e.g., urinating in the bushes outside the library, wearing slippers to work, or leaving dinner in the middle of the meal without a word). Distractibility may help to explain why someone would run a stop sign, whereas impulsivity might partly account for leaving the scene of an accident.

Patients in a delirium may exhibit behaviors that are semiautomatic, displaying an absence of higher levels of reasoning. Examples include emptying dirty dishes from the dishwasher into the cupboard, clearing the table and putting the dishes into the trash, leaving the front door of the house wide open, or driving the wrong way on a one-way street.

Poor judgment may also result when complex situations overwhelm an individual's mental capacity to problem-solve. Here are two examples. An elderly man with early dementia does not call his landlord to fix the broken air conditioner during a heat wave. A widow who is now back in her home after having had a stroke decides to rent rooms in her home to young students who have no money even though she is living on a limited, fixed income.

Impairments in Consciousness

Any disturbance in consciousness is a clear sign of a physical phenomenon and should be investigated medically without delay. Even brief or mild impairments in consciousness may signal a true medical emergency.

This section will focus on three manifestations of impairments in consciousness that therapists are most likely to encounter: (1) clouding of consciousness that lies at the mild end of the spectrum from full alertness to coma, (2) drowsiness or mild sleepiness in the spectrum from full wakefulness to sleep, and (3) absences or gaps in consciousness.

One might assume that impairments in consciousness would be virtually impossible to overlook. This is certainly true for lethargy, dulled awareness, or frank coma, but subtle or brief disturbances in consciousness are frequently missed or misinterpreted. It is not uncommon for clinicians to assume that brief disturbances of consciousness are episodes of inattention or dissociation. On the basis of clinical observation alone, it might be impossible to distinguish a dissociative episode or moment of inattention from a fleeting disturbance in consciousness caused by a seizure event, underlying brain tumor, episode of micro-sleep indicative of a sleep disorder, or some other important medical condition.

It is crucial for all clinicians to have a working knowledge of how impairments in consciousness actually look in clinical situations. There is perhaps no one sign that is more significant in indicating the presence of an organic condition. Disturbances of consciousness are extremely common. Consider the prevalence of drug or alcohol-induced, sleep-disordered, seizure-related, stroke-related, metabolic, infectious disease, and postoperative effects on consciousness.

CLOUDING OF CONSCIOUSNESS

Severe alterations in consciousness are easy to identify. Your patient's wife calls on the phone in a frantic state. It was time for her husband to leave for his therapy appointment, but she cannot arouse him from sleep. Perhaps your patient took an overdose of medications; perhaps he had a stroke or heart attack. You would call an ambulance without hesitation. It would be obvious that an organic process was in play. But at the mild end of the spectrum, a clouding of consciousness may be very difficult to identify accurately. Is the individual sleepy? Simply not paying attention? Not interested? Depressed? Although clouding of consciousness is extremely common and indicative of an organic phenomenon, paradoxically its definition is also elusive. To give you a feeling for this common mental state, here is an example from my own experience.

> *I was enjoying a cross-country road trip, except for one thing. I was allergic to the cottonwood trees that line the banks of western creeks. In an effort to stop sneezing and to relieve the itching of my eyes, I tried a single dose of the antihistamine chlorpheniramine. Soon I was feeling out of it. I was in a dreamy state that was not at all unpleasant, though I did have a sense that I couldn't trust my judgment while in this altered condition.*
>
> *I sat down on a bench, taking a break from window-shopping in a town that looked like the set for a Western film. I have no idea how long I sat there. It could have been an hour, or perhaps it was simply minutes. I might have dozed off. I don't really know. I thought about getting up and continuing my shopping, but I didn't manage to move. I was in a state of dulled awareness.*

If you had approached me while I was under the influence of this medication, you would have noted the characteristic picture of a clouding of consciousness. The individual is somewhat dulled and vague, passive, and more slowly responsive than usual. There is a diminished awareness of the environment. The person is easily distractible and readily loses the thread of a conversation. In fact, you couldn't count on the individual grasping or retaining any of the exchange. This alteration in consciousness, however vague, would affect performance on virtually any cognitive task. This is clouding of consciousness.

There are a multitude of possible causes for a clouding of consciousness, including medications of all kinds, illegal drugs, alcohol, head trauma, bleeding into the brain, brain tumors or infections, seizures and postseizure states, liver or kidney failure, the list is endless. Depending on the etiology, a clouding of consciousness also may fluctuate; the individual may at times appear perfectly normal and then, later in the day, the mental fog will roll in. Observant family members or hospital, assisted living, or nursing home personnel may be extremely helpful in reporting this kind of variability in alertness.

Identifying states of impaired consciousness is more difficult when levels of alertness fluctuate. If you happened to see a patient during his or her time of clarity, you may miss the situation completely. Disagreements among staff members about the patient's mental state may emerge when the various clinicians assume that everyone is seeing the same clinical picture but interpreting it differently. In fact, the patient is changing.

COMA

When patients are in light stages of coma or in a variety of unusual states of coma, their behaviors may be difficult to interpret accurately. Therapists are often in the position of counseling the family members of these patients, and therefore it is helpful to have a working understanding of the coma spectrum.

There is no mistaking a severe coma state in which patients are entirely unresponsive, even to painful stimuli. In a semi-coma or stupor, they will respond in a reflexive, automatic manner, but only to painful stimuli such as being pinched by the examiner. As one moves to the least severe end of the coma spectrum, the problem of sorting out organic situations from functional ones becomes more difficult, because reflexive responses begin to look more like behaviors that might be consciously directed. For instance, patients may open their eyes in response to their names being shouted. They may utter exclamations. They may speak whole sentences, though they will sound confused. It is possible for individuals who are not familiar with neurological disease to interpret reflexive behavioral responses as being filled with psychological meaning.

Coma vigil and persistent vegetative state are especially confusing. In these rare syndromes, signals from the brainstem that ordinarily function to keep the high-level cortex alert are interrupted. Patients in these states are lacking any awareness but may seem awake, and their eye movements may appear to be somewhat purposeful; patients may seem to "search" the room or briefly look at the examiner.

In contrast, in the locked-in syndrome, higher levels of the brain are intact and alert but cut off from being able to carry out movements other than eye blinking. This was apparently the state in which Jean-Dominique Bauby, the former editor of the French fashion magazine *Elle*, wrote *The Diving Bell and the Butterfly* (Bauby, 1997). He blinked out the letters of the text, one at a time.

Though psychogenic or hysterical states of unresponsiveness may occur, one ought never to assume that altered states of consciousness are being produced by a psychological mechanism. It is imperative that an urgent medical assessment be facilitated. Trained neurologists are capable of distinguishing various states of consciousness based on findings from a neurological examination that is designed to assess the comatose patient.

EXCESSIVE DAYTIME SLEEPINESS

Excessive daytime sleepiness may be an important clue to the presence of an underlying organic disorder. The question is, what is excessive? Daytime sleepiness would be entirely normal in response to life situations such as traveling across time zones, working on a changing shift schedule, pulling an all-nighter, or having a cold. Barring circumstances such as these, it makes sense to investigate further if you learn that patients are falling asleep at the table after dinner, nodding off during meetings, feeling compelled to close their eyes while stopped in traffic, regularly taking naps during the day, and so on.

Here are examples of two therapeutic sessions, one illustrating a benign situation and the other a serious condition.

At the end of the day each Thursday, I meet with two young physicians for marital therapy. During these sessions, it is not uncommon for the husband to nod off to sleep for a brief moment while his wife is actively engaged in telling me about one thing or another. It would be easy to interpret this as an expression of the husband's feeling left out, disconnected from his wife, or angry, but it turns out that the husband's specialty involves a demanding night schedule, and his falling asleep invariably occurs when he has been on call the previous night. Often by the time the husband sits down in my comfortable, quiet office, he has had no sleep for 36 hours.

In this case, drowsiness is a normal reaction to sleep deprivation. The husband tends to dip into sleep only when he is in the listening mode, because that is when he is less mentally stimulated. Anyone who is tired will be more prone to dozing off under certain circumstances: a warm room, dim lighting, rocking motion such as riding on a subway or in a car, diminished mental stimulation, being passive rather than active.

> *On the other hand, I see a 48-year-old artist for individual therapy at 4:30 p.m. on Tuesdays. Frequently during these sessions the patient's eyes begin to close, his breathing slows and deepens, his muscles relax, he sinks deeper into the chair, and then, if I remain silent and still, his head slumps forward, and he's asleep! This patient is overweight and has a very large neck size, a known risk factor for sleep apnea. Though he lives alone, he tells me that he knows that he snores, because there are times when his snoring is so loud that it wakes him up.*

I have sent this patient for a sleep evaluation, and he does have obstructive sleep apnea. This is a serious disorder in which the airway begins to collapse as an individual's muscles relax in the deeper stages of sleep. Snoring sounds are produced when air is forced through this partly collapsed airway. In addition, the sleeper moves into lighter stages of sleep in which breathing is easier. This may occur hundreds of times per night, disturbing the normal pattern of sleep stages during the night. This disruption of what is called sleep architecture causes nonrestorative sleep and daytime fatigue.

In addition, if sleep apnea is severe and effective breathing is seriously compromised, blood oxygen levels may drop during the night, possibly compromising the supply of oxygen to the brain. The heart responds by pumping more blood through the circulation; this is an additional workload for the heart during approximately one-third of every day. Untreated, chronic obstructive sleep apnea is not only associated with an increased incidence of automotive accidents, diminished work and school performance, impaired attention and concentration, impaired memory, and depression, but also with serious cardiovascular disease. This drowsiness is anything but benign.

In addition to sleep apnea, a variety of other primary sleep disorders present with excessive daytime sleepiness: narcolepsy, central sleep apnea without snoring, disorders of circadian rhythm, and periodic leg movements of sleep. One common sleep disorder is restless legs syndrome, in which an individual experiences uncomfortable, sometimes painful sensations primarily (but not exclusively) in his or her legs and mainly in the evening and early nighttime. These sensations disappear as soon as the person moves the legs but then reemerge when his or her limbs are again at rest. When the case is severe, the disruptions to falling asleep and to maintaining sleep can be extremely distressing; daytime exhaustion and difficulty with concentration are common.

Some sleep disorders are rare. One example is recurrent hypersomnia, also called Kleine-Levin syndrome. This is a disorder of unknown etiology that may be conceptualized as the opposite of anorexia nervosa: It is more common in adolescent males than in females; it manifests with increased eating and loss of sexual inhibition; and rather than exercising excessively, these individuals sleep up to 20 hours each day.

In short, excessive daytime drowsiness may signal the presence of a pathological situation. Beyond the primary sleep disorders, here are some of the other possibilities: medication side effects, illicit drug and alcohol use, infectious illness (such as hepatitis or mononucleosis), metabolic disturbances (kidney or liver failure), and endocrine diseases such as hypothyroidism, hypoparathyroidism, or Cushing's syndrome. Seizures are generally followed by periods of sleepiness, even seizures that last only a moment and do not impair consciousness. If the seizure is overlooked, the drowsiness may appear to come out of the blue. Drowsiness could also be the first clue to the presence of an expanding brain tumor or a chronic subdural hematoma, an accumulation of partly clotted blood under the dura, one of the membranes surrounding the brain.

One of my patients told me the following story after a visit to her hometown in Mississippi.

> *"They were lovely, these old friends of my family. They invited me over for dinner. Only it was a kind of tragic dinner. I ended up feeling awful. I had noticed that Simon was just not himself. But I didn't say anything. Simon couldn't remember what he had planted in his garden, and he's quite the vegetable gardener. And he kept nodding off during dinner. I guess I just thought he was getting old. He is 85. The next day Mary took him to the hospital, and they said he had a subdural."*

When I asked my patient what had caused Simon's subdural hematoma, she said that he had hit his head on the corner of a bookcase 1 month earlier. It had been an exceedingly minor incident, but the doctors thought "that might have done it." Subdural hematomas are usually a consequence of head trauma. In the case of a chronically accumulating subdural hematoma, the head trauma is often minor, and often the subdural hematoma presents with excessive sleepiness worsening to lethargy many weeks after the incident.

Gaps in Consciousness

Any lapse in consciousness, no matter how fleeting, is abnormal and needs to be taken seriously with a referral for a medical workup. Gaps in consciousness may present in several ways. An observer may notice that the individual is not responsive for a moment. Or the patient may have a sense of discontinuity in time, because no memories are laid down during the time when consciousness is disturbed. The patient might or might not volunteer this symptom.

It is common and easy for episodes of this sort to be misinterpreted or simply dismissed. When a patient who has a history of psychological trauma reports that he or she has gaps in memory, one might conceptualize these as emotionally driven dissociative episodes or fugue states. In patients who abuse alcohol, it would be reasonable to hypothesize that memory gaps are from blackouts. But keep in mind that individuals who have had psychological trauma may also have experienced blast injuries, torture, or physical abuse with lasting injuries to their brains. And individuals who drink are prone to falling and hitting their heads. Gaps in consciousness may be a symptom of a *complex* partial seizure; this is a focal seizure but one that is associated with some alteration in consciousness during which memories are not stored. Keep in mind that patients with a history of significant head injury are at increased risk for the development of seizures.

During my first year of training, a fellow resident psychiatrist had a new patient admitted to his care. The patient seemed entirely normal.

> Kolby was a middle-aged, married man who had been brought to the hospital by his wife. She reported that her husband had had an unusual angry outburst and had run into the street screaming, but Kolby had no memory of the incident at all. The situation remained a mystery until day two of the hospital stay. On that day, in the middle of an interview with my fellow resident, out of the blue, Kolby's face changed ever so slightly. He suddenly seemed out of touch. His eyes glazed over. And then Kolby licked his lips. Within 2 seconds, it was over. Kolby just went on with the conversation.

What had happened? Had anything happened? It would have been easy to misinterpret this incident as signifying nothing important, but that crucial gap in consciousness changed everything. A workup revealed that Kolby had been having complex partial seizures caused by a brain tumor.

Attention, Concentration, and Vigilance

Attention, concentration, and vigilance are complex phenomena that are influenced by many factors, including an individual's motivation, environmental circumstances, mood, and biological state of hunger, thirst, fatigue, pain, and so on. Enduring, recurring, or fluctuating disturbances of attention, concentration, or vigilance are strongly correlated with underlying biological factors and should be investigated.

First, here are definitions of the terms. *Attention* is, metaphorically speaking, the spotlight of the mind. Attention allows individuals to filter out distractions and focus on things in the outside world or in the interior world of the mind. Optimally, attention is flexible and adaptable to the individual's mental and biological states as well as to current circumstances. It is important to be able to shift focus away from cooking dinner when you hear the baby crying or to move back and forth from reading to taking notes.

Concentration is attention over time. Concentration involves the harnessing of attention toward a goal: understanding the argument someone is making, reading a book to its conclusion, solving a crossword puzzle.

Vigilance is a state of being on the lookout. Scanning of the environment is an important mental function that is heightened when someone is in an unfamiliar or potentially dangerous situation.

Disturbances of attention and concentration and/or vigilance are commonly seen in mental disorders. For instance, patients who are depressed often have problems with attention and concentration. Paranoid individuals or patients who have posttraumatic stress disorder frequently have heightened vigilance.

In addition, however, these areas of mental function are sensitive measures of a myriad of organic disorders that can have either a direct or indirect effect on the brain. Patients with a history of brain damage from strokes, bleeds, trauma, and so on may continue to have long-standing problems with managing complex demands on attention; this may manifest as feeling overwhelmed or becoming easily irritable when faced with multiple demands. Any substances or medical disorders that lead to a delirium with clouding of consciousness will affect attention, concentration, and/or one's level of awareness of the surrounding environment.

Attention deficit hyperactivity disorder is worthy of special note, because it is a common disorder that is frequently first identified in adulthood, although it is a developmental disorder. Patients with this disorder have difficulty controlling their attentional focus. They may be fully attentive when the stakes are high or the situation is novel; they also may focus intently on tasks that interest them, but generally they are easily distractible. Impulsivity and hyperactivity also may be part of the clinical picture.

Hemi-Neglect

Hemi-neglect is a dramatic disturbance in attention that is associated with parietal lobe brain damage. Although patients with hemi-neglect have intact sensory capabilities for hearing and sight, they do not attend to input from half of the visual space, usually the left half. The individual will respond to a visitor who enters the room from the right but not the left, will eat food from the right side of the plate but not the left, will drink coffee if it is placed on his right but not his left, and so on.

An elegant study by Bisiach and Luzzatti in 1978 demonstrated that this neglect is not only for the world outside but also applies in the mental world. In their study, they first asked patients with unilateral neglect to imagine themselves standing on the steps of a famous building, facing across the square. And what was it that they saw in their mind's eye? Each patient named the buildings that stood to the right of them, omitting altogether those buildings on the left.

Next, the researchers asked these same individuals to picture themselves standing and looking out at the square, but this time from a different building on the opposite side of the square. Now what did the patients see? This time the patients also only mentioned those buildings that lay to their right, and this time the buildings were the ones they had omitted earlier when, in their imagination, they were gazing out at the square from the original position (Bisiach & Luzzatti, 1978). Hemi-neglect is not a sensory problem; it is a problem with the distribution of attention in space.

Disorientation

Disorientation is significantly correlated with organic disease, and the new onset of disorientation may constitute a medical emergency. The term *disorientation* is actually used to refer to several fundamentally different problems: disorientation to time, place, or person; topographical disorientation, which is disorientation in physical space; and right-left disorientation. Each of these will be discussed separately as follows.

Disorientation to Time, Place, and Person

Accuracy of orientation requires memory. As individuals go through daily life they are continuously updating information as to where they are in space and time. Because time is always changing, orientation to time requires more minute-to-minute updating than does orientation to place. Individuals should know the year, the season, the month, and the date within a day or two.

When orienting to place, most individuals do not need to update very often the information about the city or state in which they are living. But when patients with memory difficulties visit your clinic or hospital they may become confused about where they are. They may not know the facility's address or even whether the building is a hospital, office building, or bank. And their disorientation may not be obvious. You have to ask.

> *The patient was dressed in a fashionable, rose-colored suit. She walked from the waiting room into the geriatric psychiatrist's office carrying her copy of the* New York Times *and a stylish purse that matched her shoes. She was a warm and personable, chatty 75-year-old.*
>
> *Now that the patient was sitting across from him, the psychiatrist thought back to his conversation with her daughter. He had responded quickly to the daughter's concerns about her mother and had made room in his schedule to see the mother while she was visiting from Florida. But now he figured that the daughter must have been overly concerned when she insisted that her mother needed an urgent dementia workup.*
>
> *Then he did a mental status exam. The patient did not know the year. She didn't know the month or even the season. She knew she was in a doctor's office in a hospital, but she couldn't recall the name of the hospital. Although the patient looked sophisticated and vibrant, she had a severe problem with memory storage, consistent with Alzheimer's disease.*

People not only update information about time and place, but they also keep tabs on family members, sports teams they follow, political events, natural disasters, and so on; knowledge of this sort is generally tested in the mental status exam under the category of fund of information. An individual's fund of information is a reflection of many interacting factors in addition to memory functions: level of education, cultural background, and personal interests. Disorientation to time and place is more purely a measure of the capacity for memory.

Disorientation to person means that the individual does not know who he or she is. Given that who one is does not change during a lifetime, disorientation to person is either a sign of obvious, severe brain deterioration virtually to the point of coma, or it is psychological.

> *I am reminded of a story Jose told me about one of his roommates, a disturbed young man who idolized Jose. One night it became clear that this roommate was becoming psychotic. Jose was the only person the roommate would trust to take him to an emergency room.*

In the ER the roommate was required to sign all the usual forms, which he did without protest, but he didn't sign his own name. He signed Jose's name. He thought he was Jose. This disorientation to person was entirely psychologically driven and resolved with treatment for the roommate's first schizophrenic episode.

TOPOGRAPHIC DISORIENTATION

This term refers to difficulty in navigating through space in the real world. Some individuals are born with difficulties finding their way to new places, reading maps, or translating from the abstract representation of a map into the real world. These are relative weaknesses in neuro-psychological functioning, and they do have a neurological basis. They are learning disabilities in a nonverbal realm.

Here we are especially concerned with topographic disorientation when it begins during adulthood. The new onset of topographic disorientation indicates brain dysfunction. Clinically, patients with topographic disorientation are "the wanderers." They are the patients who become lost while walking in their own neighborhoods. They are the individuals who don't know where they are if they happen to exit the elevator onto the wrong floor of their assisted living facility. One individual who had Alzheimer's disease left the room where he was having psychological testing in order to go to the bathroom. Fifteen minutes later he was nowhere to be found. A frantic search by hospital security personnel eventually located the patient on the hallway of a surgical floor.

RIGHT-LEFT DISORIENTATION

Right-left disorientation refers to the inability to distinguish right from left on one's self (my right versus my left hand) or in the environment (the interviewer's right versus left hand). The latter requires a mental rotation. Difficulty with these tasks may be present from birth or may develop in adulthood.

I began to see Mary for psychotherapy when her long-term marriage was falling apart. She was a very smart and highly successful business consultant who traveled frequently for her work and exuded an air of self-confidence. But one day she confessed to me that she often thought of herself as stupid.

After some exploration, it became clear that this notion had emerged while she was in school. She had done poorly in geometry and physics and human anatomy and hadn't understood why. The conclusion she had come to was—"I must be stupid." As with many individuals who have learning

disabilities of one kind or another, she had carried this notion about herself
and kept it a secret for years.

It turned out that this private experience was based partly on Mary's
inability to mentally rotate objects in space. She would get confused when
looking at anatomy charts in biology class. Was the liver on the right or the
left? In addition, she perceived two-dimensional representations of three-
dimensional objects as simply "a bunch of lines." She explained to me that
the drawing of a cube never "popped out of the page" for her.

A newly developed difficulty with right-left discrimination in an
individual who once had this ability is a significant finding and indicates the presence of a neurological problem. When testing for right-left
discrimination, a clinician must be sure that the individual does not
have a language problem that impedes understanding of the words
right and *left*.

Confusion

Confusion is a term that is often employed by clinicians, although it is
used to refer to a number of different problems. It may be utilized to
describe someone who is disoriented as to time, place, or person. Or it
may be used when referring to someone who has a delirium with clouding of consciousness and a lack of clarity of thought. Additionally, the
term confusion may refer to someone who uses grossly irrational thinking. Despite the lack of precision of this term, there is no confusion
about the fact that this finding in any of its forms is highly correlated
with organic conditions and may even constitute a medical emergency.

A psychologist who worked in a Boston hospital outpatient clinic informally presented the following mental status exam. The patient had
been referred by a primary care physician who believed the patient had
a psychological problem.

"I asked the patient where we were and he said, 'Philadelphia.'

"'And how much is 4 plus 4?' I asked him. He said, 'Blue.'

"'And tell me who the president is?' 'Frank Sinatra.'

"And then I held out my tie and asked the patient what I had in my
hand. 'A tie,' the patient responded.

"And then I pointed to my watch. 'What is this?' 'A watch,' the
patient said.

"The patient could name anything I pointed to, but the rest of his mental
status was ka-fluey! And he seemed 'out of it.' Sitting with him did not
feel like sitting with a patient who had a psychological disorder."

This middle-aged man was disoriented, had a lack of clarity of thought, and exhibited a mild clouding of consciousness. He was certainly confused. The psychologist sent this patient to the emergency room, where a neurological workup revealed that the patient was having continuous partial seizures, also referred to as "partial status." The is a relatively uncommon diagnosis that can be easily missed but readily treated if identified correctly.

Here is a quote from a patient who has two different varieties of seizures, each with elements of what he calls "confusion."

> I have two types of seizures. The first is a "confusion" spell and is exactly that. I get "confused" as I try to count out money at the cash register on my job as a cashier/counter clerk at a small restaurant. Or, as I am about to say something in conversation, I "forget" just what I was about to say. As I am working around the house, I am about to do something and "forget" just what I was about to do. There are no warnings before this happens. The confusion lasts for just a few minutes (maybe two or three) and then I'm okay and continue on with no after effects.
>
> The second type of seizure is more serious. I am functioning normally and just "black out" with no warning. I do not know it is happening and I am not aware of anything during this time. I am told, by those who have observed me, that I may act confused, or I may just stare and say nothing. I may fidget, or be still. I may try to talk, but I don't usually make sense. If people try to talk to me, I don't respond. They can last from 2–5 minutes. When it is over, I continue whatever I was doing. Most of the time I am aware I have had a "blackout." Sometime I feel a little confused at first, and I often feel tired for a while. (Schachter, 2008, p. 23)

Confused thinking without any clouding of consciousness is often associated with dementia. Here is an example.

Jenna, one of my patients, was helping her elderly parents to move from the family home. Jenna's father had vascular dementia, a common form of dementia that is often associated with long-term standing high blood pressure and atherosclerosis.

Jenna and her father were sorting things into two boxes, one box for giveaway items and one box for keepers. After a short time, Jenna noticed that her father was putting giveaway items as well as keepers into the same box. So, pointing to one of the boxes, she asked her father, "Dad, is this the stuff we're saving or the stuff we're throwing out?" Her father replied, "Well, it's both."

The idea that one box could be for *both* was a thoroughly un-reasonable concept. The whole notion of categorizing items, of keeping a goal in mind, seemed to elude her father. This kind of irrational, non-logical thinking is another meaning of the term confusion.

Memory

INTRODUCTION

Memory is fundamental to understanding any individual's past and central to the work of all mental health practitioners. Memory is also a crucial component in the construction of a self, family, community, and even a civilization. Given both the private nature of memory as well as its far-reaching cultural and philosophic significance, it is easy to lose sight of the fact that memories have a neurological substrate.

CURRENT IDEAS ABOUT MEMORY

Current research is elucidating the multifaceted, coordinated physiological workings of the brain that make the various aspects of memory possible. Understanding current ideas about memory will help in evaluating patients who may have memory problems. Memory disturbances are frequently correlated with organic disease, and the specific aspects of memory function that are disrupted will vary depending on the nature of the underlying physical problems.

Implicit and Explicit Memory   There are two fundamental types of memory. The first is referred to as *implicit* or *procedural memory*. Implicit memory does not require conscious recall; it is memory for actions, skills, and habits. Examples of this type of memory include knowing how to ride a bicycle or how to find one's way around the bedroom after dark. Individuals who have Alzheimer's disease may not have disruptions in implicit memory until late in the course of the disease. These patients may improve in skills over days of practicing, though they may not consciously remember having been exposed to a practice session.

Although people with Alzheimer's disease may not have trouble with implicit memory, they do have severe disturbances in a second type of memory called *explicit* or *declarative memory*. This form of memory requires conscious recall.

Explicit memory is further subdivided into episodic (or autobiographical) memory and semantic memory. *Episodic memory* involves remembering one's personal experiences in time and place, including the emotions. "I remember when my father brought home a puppy." "I blushed when you asked me to marry you." *Semantic memory* is a memory for information, facts, knowledge, and abstractions. "There are about 50 calories in a small egg." "The stock market crashed in 1929."

Working Memory   In order to understand what someone is saying, you need to keep the beginning of a sentence in mind until you hear the end of the sentence. This is an example of working memory. When a sensory perception or thought is not simply registered but is briefly held in mind, this is referred to as *working memory*. Working memory is extremely short-term and of limited capacity, but it is essential to normal mental functioning.

Sometimes working memory is conscious; for instance, you perform long division and mentally visualize your work; you remember a phone number while you walk across the room to the telephone, but only until you have dialed the number. This sort of conscious working memory requires mental visualization or repeating of the information to one's self.

Encoding, Storage, and Retrieval   Another way to think about memory is by focusing on how an experience is transformed into a memory. First, an individual registers a sensory perception or thought; this requires attention. Second, that experience may be stored as a memory. Third, the memory could be retrieved or recalled (*recall* being the conscious process of memory retrieval). These processes are referred to as encoding, storage, and retrieval. They take place over time and involve actual structural and physiological alterations in brain cell interactions.

EVALUATING PATIENTS

When evaluating patients, it is important to keep in mind that other cognitive functions, such as arousal, attention, and motivation, will affect memory functioning. Thus, *patients who complain about memory* may not be having trouble with memory per se; they may be distractible or have a clouding of consciousness. And *patients who do not complain about memory* may nonetheless have serious trouble with memory—and also with insight. Thus, as a clinician your first task is to determine whether your patient has a problem with memory storage, memory retrieval, memory registration, working memory, or with some other cognitive function altogether.

In clinical practice you will encounter patients who deny that they have any problems with memory at all, while their family members are reporting that they have significant memory impairments. This is not uncommon, especially in the presentation of many of the dementias, and argues for the importance of doing a screening mental status exam on all patients. It also underscores how crucial it can be to get permission to talk with family members or friends of the patient when you have any concern that your patient might have problems with memory.

On the other hand, when patients do say they are "having trouble with memory," it is important to ascertain precisely what they mean. Often the word *memory* is used loosely; what patients believe to be a problem with memory may be more appropriately attributed to difficulties in other areas of cognition. For instance, when patients report that during conversation they lose track of what they're saying and don't remember the point, this is more likely to be a problem with distractibility.

> *Doctor Dodd had a busy primary care office in the outpatient department of a local hospital. He came to see me because he "hated his job." The workload was heavy, and he complained about needing to stay later and later in his office each evening in order to complete his work. Recently, he had been threatened with a pay cut if he didn't finish his charts in a timelier manner. He was thinking of leaving medicine. He was 42.*
>
> *Then Dr. Dodd said, "I must confess that I've been worried about forgetting things. I double-check everything to be sure I'm not making mistakes. Maybe I have early Alzheimer's disease. My mother had Alzheimer's."*
>
> *In my office, Dr. Dodd was able to recall three out of three items after 30 minutes. I didn't think he had a problem with memory storage, but I wasn't ready to dismiss his difficulties as simply being a consequence of stress and an increased workload. In the process of doing a complete evaluation, Dr. Dodd told me about his long history of migraine headaches. He had tried many treatment approaches over the years. The latest had been topiramate, an antiseizure medication also used for migraine prevention that he had been taking for about a year.*
>
> *Although topiramate had relieved Dr. Dodd's migraines, he was willing to discontinue the drug when I reminded him that it is capable of having negative effects on cognition. We both wanted to know if this might be the underlying source of Dr. Dodd's difficulties, and indeed it was.*
>
> *Upon looking back, Dr. Dodd said that now he was aware of the "mental fog" he had been in for more than a year. Off the topiramate Dr. Dodd was much more efficient at work. He was able to leave the office at a reasonable hour and complete his charts on time. He also loved his work again.*

Dr. Dodd hadn't had a problem with memory itself. When he said that he was "worried about forgetting things," he was trying to convey his subjective experience, namely that his mental functioning had changed, that he wasn't as efficient or as sharp as he had been, that his processing speed had slowed, and that he worried about making errors. Topiramate is only one of numerous medications that can interfere with cognition and lead people to believe that their memory function is impaired and that they might even have a dementia. The side effects of medications always need to be top on your list of possible causes for memory complaints.

In addition, physical factors and medical disorders of all kinds may have effects on cognition that patients will find difficult to define and may call "trouble with memory." Sleep disorders will cause cognitive dysfunction on the basis of daytime fatigue. In addition, disorders of any endocrine organ, electrolyte imbalances, metabolic dysfunction of the kidneys or liver, infections, and a myriad of other medical conditions can lead to cognitive problems that may be dramatic or subtle and fluctuating—part of the presenting picture of a delirium.

Often patients with underlying medical conditions have problems with motivation, attention, concentration, processing speed, or clouding of consciousness. They may also have difficulties with what are called *executive functions*, including processes such as organizing information, planning, ordering or sequencing, prioritizing, generating strategies, working toward long-term goals, self-monitoring, and inhibiting responses to stimuli that are not relevant to the current task. Any of these cognitive difficulties may have a secondary, downstream effect on memory.

Psychosocial conditions also may lead to difficulties with memory functioning on the basis of a disruption in the individual's attention, concentration, and motivation; this in turn interferes with the initial encoding of experiences. This is commonly seen when an individual's capacity for engaging with the outside world is disrupted by a preoccupation with psychological trauma or stress, anxiety, depression or psychosis. It is well known that individuals with severe depression may present with memory difficulties that look like a dementia until the depression is treated and memory functioning returns.

Office Memory Testing   Neuropsychological testing may be necessary to ascertain whether a patient has a problem with memory storage, retrieval, or some other cognitive function that is having a secondary impact on memory. It is possible to do screening tests in your office. The most common test for registration is simply to ask a patient to repeat a string of numbers. Working memory is often tested by asking the individual to spell the word *world* first forward and then backward or to recite the months of the year backward. If an individual is able to do basic calculation, then asking the patient to serially subtract 7s from 100 also tests working memory.

To test memory storage and retrieval, one asks the patient to remember three words. Be sure to tell the person that some time later you will be asking what those words were. Have the patient repeat the words in order to know that he or she has registered them. Then go on to other parts of your interview to distract from the memory task. Finally, after a measured period of time, usually 15 minutes, ask whether the patient recalls those three words.

If a patient does not remember one or more of the words, the question is whether the individual has difficulties with memory storage or simply with memory retrieval. The approach that is used to differentiate problems with storage from difficulties with recall is to test whether the individual is able to recognize the word or words that they had seemed to forget from a list that includes those words as well as decoy words. Recognition of the original word or words implies that memory storage is intact.

TYPES OF MEMORY PROBLEMS

The following discussions will hone in on the different sorts of memory disturbances that you might find in your patients. Does the patient have ongoing problems with memory that may or may not have worsened over time? Or does the individual feel that his or her ongoing memory functioning is fine but that there are gaps in his or her memory? The following discussions will first address memory gaps and then ongoing memory difficulties.

Memory Gaps   When there is a temporary disruption in the physiologic process of memory creation as a consequence of significant head trauma, for example, clinically one sees certain characteristic patterns. These individuals will have a memory gap, a period of time for which they have no memory, even though they now have no problems with forming new memories. And this gap in memory will have certain features.

Here is an example.

I asked Eric about his medical history during our first psychotherapy session. He had been in a car accident several years before and had sustained a head injury. Eric said that he had been in the hospital for 5 days and in a coma for about 12 hours. "Apparently, I was thrown from the car. I actually don't recall the accident at all," he said. Eric told me that the last thing he now remembered from before the accident was drinking and laughing with his friends at a comedy club. The next thing he remembered was waking up in the hospital.

Eric had a gap in his memory, and this gap was for a period of time that extended back to before his auto accident as well as for some uncertain period of time after the accident. Eric's loss of memory for the time before the accident is called *retrograde amnesia*. His loss of memory for the time after the accident is called *anterograde amnesia*. The length of time that is lost to memory is considered to be one measure of the severity of the head trauma.

Retrograde Amnesia   Retrograde amnesia has certain characteristics. The most recent events are more vulnerable to being lost to memory. And as someone recovers, the more distant memories come back first.

> If we had seen Eric in the hospital soon after he emerged from coma, he probably would not have remembered having been at the comedy club, laughing and drinking with his friends. His last memory might have been from earlier in the day, perhaps having had breakfast with his mother, with whom he was living at the time.
>
> As Eric recovered during his hospital stay, he might have come to recall what had transpired after breakfast—a trip to the library to study. Only after more time had passed following Eric's emergence from coma would he have remembered lunch and then what happened on the afternoon of his accident, and finally the comedy club.

Disturbances of memory may take many forms. Eric is an example of someone who has a gap in his memory but whose memory functioning is otherwise entirely normal. This kind of memory disturbance is extremely common and is seen when some event leads to an interruption in the formation of new memories as, for instance, an incident involving head trauma, ECT, a complex or generalized seizure, stroke, brain hemorrhage, general anesthesia, and other disorders that cause loss of or a clouding of consciousness.

Blackouts   The term *blackout* refers to the loss of memory for a period of time during which an individual was intoxicated but not unconscious. Blackouts occur in people who drink heavily on a regular basis. Witnesses to the lost time period may know that the individual is intoxicated but often do not think that the person is *very* intoxicated. Here is a dramatic report of this syndrome.

> A 39-year-old salesman awoke in a strange hotel room. He had a mild hangover but otherwise felt normal. His clothes were hanging in the closet; he was clean-shaven. He dressed and went down to the lobby. He learned from the clerk that he was in Las Vegas and that he had checked in 2 days

previously. It had been obvious that he had been drinking, the clerk said, but he had not seemed very drunk. The date was Saturday the 14th. His last recollection was of sitting in a St. Louis bar on Monday the 9th. He had been drinking all day and was drunk, but could remember everything perfectly until about 3 p.m., when "like a curtain dropping", his memory went blank. It remained blank for approximately 5 days. Three years later, it was still blank. He was so frightened by the experience that he abstained from alcohol for 2 years. (Goodwin, 1995, p. 315)

Memory Gaps From Medications Medications of various kinds are known to cause periods of amnesia. For example, the sleep aid zolpidem and related drugs have been associated with automatic behaviors, including driving while asleep and sleep-related eating, for which the individual may have only vague memories or no memories at all (Hoque & Chesson, 2009).

Jared decided to stop taking zolpidem for sleep after he had the following experience. He had been planning a treasure hunt for his daughter's birthday party and was telling his good friend Steven about the details. After a few sentences into the conversation, Steven stopped him. Steven said that he had heard all of this—and more—from Jared, on the phone the previous night. Jared had no memory of that conversation. In reconstructing what had happened, Jared realized that on the prior evening he had taken his sleeping pill at 10 p.m. and then must have spoken with Steven on the telephone at about 10:30. It was "eerie to have no recollection whatsoever of a chunk of my life."

Sleep Behaviors Sleepwalking and sleep talking are well-known behaviors for which individuals may have no memory after awakening. In addition, patients may have either no memory or only a hazy memory for other types of behaviors that may occur during confusional arousals, including masturbating, sexual behavior with a bed partner, or sleep-related eating. These nighttime behaviors are frequently assumed to be psychological and may bring patients and/or their family members into a therapist's office.

Joe and Jane were referred to me for couples therapy. Joe was short and markedly overweight; Jane was tall and thin. Joe was a banker; Jane was a landscape architect. They were quite anxious during our first meeting, and it took until the third session for them to talk about the true reason for the consultation. Jane had a history of childhood sexual abuse, and it had taken years for her to feel comfortable having sex with her husband. Jane reported that during those years Joe had been patient, gentle, and kind.

Only now something disturbing had begun to happen. On several occasions, during the night, Jane had awakened to find Joe sexually aroused and on top of her. He was physically "insistent." Jane was unspeakably horrified. "This was rape. This was a replay of scenes from my childhood bedroom," she stated.

But Jane did not know what to make of the fact that Joe had only a foggy memory of just one of these episodes; Joe dimly recalled finding himself on top of his wife, in the middle of intercourse, and confused about "what was going on." He felt distressed about what he "was apparently doing" to his wife.

Joe wanted to understand what was going on, while Jane wanted to understand Joe's intentions. Was he angry with her for not having sex often enough? Was Joe lying? Was there a "darker side" to Joe, a malevolent part of him that she hadn't seen before and that she shouldn't trust? They both knew that the future of their marriage hinged on the answers to these questions.

After much exploration, it became clear that these nighttime episodes occurred under circumstances that set the stage for automatic behaviors during sleep. Joe had long before been diagnosed with sleep apnea; during the night, this would cause him to repeatedly move from deeper into lighter stages of sleep, closer to awakening. In addition, these nighttime episodes occurred when Joe would come home particularly exhausted and have a stiff drink close to bedtime; these factors exerted a force to keep him from awakening fully. And finally, the chances of these episodes occurring increased if the couple had tried to have sex before sleep but had failed to gain full satisfaction because of exhaustion or distraction by their children. This latter information about potential sexual frustration provided strong motivation that was both psychological and physiological.

I was struck by Joe's sincerity and honesty and believed that the evidence supported a diagnosis of sleep-related sex, similar to sleepwalking. Jane wanted to believe this, but she still had some doubts. She found it very comforting when she found a few articles from the scientific literature that reported cases of sleep-related sex.

Once the diagnosis was reasonably clear, it was possible for Jane and Joe to fully explore the meanings that these episodes had for them. We then proceeded to strategize about how to avoid the circumstances that led to these episodes. After six sessions, both Joe and Jane felt that their relationship was "back on track."

Transient Global Amnesia   Transient global amnesia is a relatively rare and short-lived syndrome, but it may be precipitated by significant, at times dramatic, emotional trauma such as receiving news of a child's death. Therefore, it is important for therapists to understand that this is not a conversion phenomenon.

Transient global amnesia is characterized by a transient but complete loss of ability to form new memories but without loss of insight. These patients are fully aware that something is the matter, and they are extremely anxious or even agitated. They will frantically ask the same questions over and over. "Where are we going?" "To the hospital." "Where are we going?" The individual is incapable of remembering any new information, even for a brief moment. Although there may be some retrograde amnesia, old information is not affected. In addition, no other area of cognition is affected.

This fascinating syndrome usually begins suddenly and lasts from about 2 to 12 hours. If it is not resolved by 24 hours, other diagnoses must be considered (Shekhar, 2008). In most cases it does not recur, but there remains a memory gap for the time during which the individual was affected.

Fugue States, Dissociation, and Total Amnesia   You are undoubtedly familiar with the occasional newspaper report of someone who turns up in an unfamiliar town with total amnesia. These individuals say they have no idea who they are or where they came from. It appears that they have lost all autobiographical memory. However, this presentation is not consistent with our understanding of how memory works. Total amnesia is a psychological phenomenon.

Fugue states and dissociation also may be psychological, but it is important to actively rule out organic disorders before feeling certain that you are dealing with a purely psychologically motivated phenomenon. In the case of fugue states, consider possibilities such as alcohol-related blackouts, medication reactions, or epilepsy. In the case of dissociation, when thinking about possible underlying causes one needs to be clear about exactly what the patient's experience is. Difficulties with attention or symptoms of narcolepsy may be mistaken for dissociation. Brief dissociative experiences also may represent seizure events, with or without an alteration in consciousness. The diagnosis of a delirium also must be considered in individuals who present with fugue states or who have dissociation.

ONGOING MEMORY DIFFICULTIES

Individuals who have trouble with memory storage will have difficulty learning new things; they will not recall experiences, even when reminded of them. If you think that one of your patients might have compromised memory storage, it is crucial to initiate an evaluation to identify the underlying physical cause.

When memory storage problems are minor and do not interfere with everyday functioning, patients are considered to have mild cognitive impairment. This category includes a heterogeneous population; over time some of these individuals will improve, some will stay the same, and others will worsen and develop overt dementias.

The dementias are extremely common causes for persistent and progressive disturbances of memory. In addition to the dementias, there are other physical conditions to consider in patients who have trouble with memory storage. Severe sleep apnea can lead to ongoing trouble with memory.

Persistent memory dysfunction might result from episodes when there was a loss of oxygen to the brain, such as might occur with a cardiac arrest. Carbon monoxide poisoning, either from a failed suicide attempt or from accidental exposure when an internal combustion engine is malfunctioning or poorly vented, can lead to delayed onset of neuropsychological deficits, including memory dysfunction.

Loss of Ability to Form New Memories: Korsakoff's Syndrome   This is another extremely significant and often permanent form of amnesia that is caused by thiamine deficiency. Most commonly, Korsakoff's syndrome is a result of alcohol use, but it may also be a consequence of dietary insufficiency of thiamine from gastrointestinal disease, anorexia nervosa, severe vomiting with pregnancy, a complication of bariatric surgery, or starvation.

In contrast to transient global amnesia, even when a patient is promptly treated with thiamine replacement, Korsakoff's syndrome is often not reversible. In addition, these patients have a striking lack of insight and often utilize confabulation.

> *Although it was many years ago, I still vividly recall a patient with Korsakoff's syndrome who was on a medical ward. I was a medical student on rounds with an attending physician. As we approached the patient's bedside, the attending physician reached out and shook hands with the patient.*
>
> *"Hi, Jack. Wait, did I see you last night?"*
> *"Yeah, doc. I saw you in that O'Neil's Bar."*
> *"Is that right?"*
> *"Yeah, had a few too many. And told some good stories . . . "*
>
> *The two of them went on like this. The physician then performed a mental status exam, revealing that this patient had a severe problem with memory storage. Only at that point did it dawn on me that the conversation I had just witnessed had been a demonstration of confabulation. The attending had led the patient with open-ended comments, and the patient had filled in with stories that were entirely fabricated.*

Language

INTRODUCTION

Language is an extremely complex human capacity that is central to interpersonal relating. Therapists are especially attuned to the nuances of any patient's word choice, to associative links, subtle inferences and assumptions, and to the emotional tone of the communication. We listen for affect and meaning. Rarely in our work, however, do we focus on the remarkable capacity for language itself.

Apart from rare exceptions, humans master language early in life. Family, culture, and education are factors that exert powerful influences on language. In addition, the biological basis of language is undisputed. Consider what British researchers found when they studied the KE family. Many members of this extended family were unable to learn some of the most fundamental aspects of grammatical structure. The problem was traced to a simple defect in the FOX P2 gene (Lai, 2001). This rare condition highlights the biological underpinning of language.

THE PHYSICAL BASIS OF LANGUAGE

Language involves the production and comprehension of meaningful communication. It includes both verbal and gestural elements. In normal individuals, all of the elements of language work together seamlessly, but it is not uncommon for someone's capacity for language to break down during adulthood as a consequence of underlying organic disorders. Most often individuals will lose only certain components of language. For instance, someone might retain the ability to comprehend but be unable to speak coherently. Or individuals may lose nouns from their speech (anomia).

By observing the types of flaws that can develop, scientists have been able to discern the underlying structure of language and its complex neurobiological substrate. Language was the very first high-level faculty that was shown to be associated with particular regions of the brain; therefore, the story of this discovery has a special place in the history of neurology.

In the mid-1800s, Pierre Paul Broca performed an autopsy on the brain of a man whose nickname was Tan. What was special about Tan was that during adulthood he had lost the ability to speak coherently; he was only able to say one word clearly, and apparently that word was "Tan." Remarkably, however, Tan retained the ability to fully comprehend what others were saying. When Broca examined Tan's brain at autopsy, he found damage to a region in the left temporal lobe that has been called Broca's area ever since. Broca hypothesized that this was the site of expressive language. Some years later, Carl Wernicke followed a similar approach and identified a different region of the brain that was associated with the comprehension of language. The work of Broca and Wernicke revealed that it is possible to separate the fundamental elements of language and to identify their neurological underpinnings.

Beyond these cortical regions of the brain that form the basis of language functions per se, many other brain regions are involved in the ability to utilize language for communication. Regions that process emotion are recruited. Memory systems are engaged. Frontal brain regions are involved in planning, organizing, initiating, and monitoring what we say. Language production also involves the coordination of multiple somatic systems, some of which are specialized for language, while others are utilized only secondarily for language. Speaking involves precisely timed breathing and airflow, but this is hardly the primary function of the respiratory system. An intact larynx and vocal cords, plus strength and coordination of the muscles of the mouth and tongue, are also crucial to verbal communication. Gestural communication requires the use of still other muscles.

Hearing and sight are utilized for receiving communication signals. Brain regions that would have been utilized for sight or hearing may become adapted for other systems of language in blind or deaf individuals. Sign language is a fully operational language that does not rely on hearing. Braille does not rely on sight. Not all of the world's languages have a written form, but when a written form does exist, writing and reading also utilize the brain's language systems.

THE ELEMENTS OF LANGUAGE

We now know that language consists of nonvocal and vocal elements that work together like instruments in a symphony, enhancing one another. Organic disease can disrupt the production and/or comprehension of any of these elements, so it is useful to have a working knowledge of the various components of language.

The nonvocal elements are gestural. Most often, gestures are movements that accompany verbal communication and add nuance and emphasis. But gestures also may be symbolic in the way words are (such as the hand positions for "OK" or "victory").

The vocal elements of language include the linguistic components, namely words and grammatical structure, as well as the nonlinguistic music of language: intonation, rhythm, pacing, pitch, and so on. In our work as therapists, we tend to focus conscious attention on a patient's words, on the narrative. But even more crucial to psychotherapy and to any effective communication are these nonlinguistic elements of language through which emotion and subtleties of meaning are conveyed.

The nonlinguistic vocal elements are called *prosody*. Prosodic elements of language tend to be less consciously processed, but they provide both nuance and emotional power to communication. They are also viewed as more authentic than the words, because words can be more easily manipulated.

Affective prosody communicates emotional nuance. Here is an example:

> *Husband: I offered to do the dishes. I don't understand why you're mad at me. Wife: Sure, you offered to do the dishes, but there were implied undercurrents. "I'll do the dishes, but I'll resent it." "I'll do the dishes, but you'll owe me." "I'll do the dishes, but I've worked hard all day, and really what have you done all day?" "I'll do the dishes, but why should I do the dishes?" "I'll do the dishes, but it's only to get you off my back." Now do you understand why I'm mad at you?*

In contrast to affective prosody, *linguistic prosody* clarifies intended meaning as when the speaker's pitch rises at the end of a sentence to indicate a question or when the tone signifies irony. Read the following two paragraphs aloud to see how the very same words can convey entirely different meanings depending on differences in pacing, stress, pitch, and so on. In written language, punctuation marks communicate how something is to be said. These notes to Jack were taken from Lynne Truss's book entitled *Eats, Shoots & Leaves: The Zero Tolerance Approach to Punctuation.*

Dear Jack,

I want a man who knows what love is all about. You are generous, kind, thoughtful. People who are not like you admit to being useless and inferior. You have ruined me for other men. I yearn for you. I have no feelings whatsoever when we're apart. I can be forever happy—will you let me be yours?

Jill

Dear Jack,

I want a man who knows what love is. All about you are generous, kind, thoughtful people who are not like you. Admit to being useless and inferior. You have ruined me. For other men I yearn! For you I have no feelings whatsoever. When we're apart I can be forever happy. Will you let me be?

Yours,
Jill (Truss, 2004, pp. 9–10)

Disturbances in the Production of or Comprehension of Language

Impairments in the production or comprehension of language are hall-marks of organic disease involving the brain. This is true for written or spoken language and for the linguistic or nonlinguistic components, the "words" and the "music."

Adult-onset organic-based disturbances in language may take many different forms. These include impairments in naming, comprehension, repeating, writing, generating language with a grammatical structure, speaking with a normal flow of discourse (fluency), the communication of emotion and meaning through variations in rhythm, pitch, and emphasis and/or the comprehension of these nonlinguistic prosodic elements of speech. These problems with language are extremely common and important.

Problems With Language: Aphasia

There are many types of disturbances in language (aphasias) that are possible, based on which areas of the brain are affected by injury. The symptoms that result depend more on the site and size of the injury than on the source of the injury, although treatment approaches would vary considerably depending on whether the problem originated from a hemorrhage, a clot, trauma (including injury from brain surgery), a tumor, or an infection.

When an individual's ability to utilize language is suddenly altered and remains impaired, it is generally obvious that a physical disorder is involved. But when language is disrupted for only a brief moment, unfortunately the temptation for denial is strong.

> *Mr. Broom, a 68-year-old grandfather, was visiting his family on the West Coast. All was well until he picked up the telephone to arrange for a taxi to the airport. As he later related, "Words just wouldn't come out right." He simply was incapable of producing meaningful language, though he was fully able to understand what other people were saying. He had no other symptoms; moreover, within minutes he was back to normal again. It was only at his wife's insistence that Mr. Broom was willing to call his doctor.*

Mr. Broom had not had thought blocking, a brief interruption in the flow of language that one may find in individuals with a serious depression. He was not exhibiting a conversion reaction from repressed feelings about returning home. This was a dramatic example of an acute disturbance of language production. Mr. Broom had had a transient ischemic attack (TIA), in which a brain region that is crucial to language *production* was temporarily deprived of sufficient blood oxygen and glucose. A TIA may be the harbinger of a stroke and needs immediate medical attention.

The specific type of aphasia syndrome that any particular individual will display will depend upon which brain region or regions have been affected. Some of the possibilities are brain areas involved in: the production of language, the comprehension of language, the connection of brain regions that are involved with understanding speech to those involved with output, and/or accessing the names of people and things. In all cases, these problems may be subtle or profound and disabling.

Clinically, one will see patients who have combinations of deficits. They may or may not be capable of: producing fluent (fluid) speech, comprehending the speech of others, repeating what an examiner says, and/or naming. When individuals have difficulty with the production of language, they may substitute incorrect words (semantic paraphasias), words with incorrect syllables (phonemic paraphasia), or non-words (neologisms). When patients lose nouns (anomia), they may produce "empty" speech. Patients with disturbances of comprehension will not recognize that their own speech makes no sense, yet they will produce speech that has normal fluidity (called fluency).

When patients have adult-onset disturbances in the arena of language, it is extremely important to not confuse these with the disturbances of thought that are associated with schizophrenia. At times a neurology or neuropsychiatry consultation may be necessary to make the distinction between aphasia and a thought disorder.

When a disturbance in the arena of language function begins gradually, it may not be clear at first whether the problem is organic. Keep in mind that some types of dementia can first present in just this way, with the insidious onset of disturbances of language. These dementia subtypes are referred to as semantic dementia or primary progressive aphasia.

DISTURBANCES IN UNDERSTANDING OR COMMUNICATING PROSODY

Disturbances in communicating or comprehending prosody are frequently subtle and can present as relationship difficulties. At a conference some years ago, the neurologist Dr. Kenneth Heilman told the story of a patient he had seen for a follow-up appointment. Here is how I remember the story:

> *Dr. Heilman was very pleased that his patient had had a full recovery after her right hemisphere stroke, but the patient's husband seemed less pleased and gestured that he wanted to talk with Dr. Heilman alone. The husband told Dr. Heilman that he was thinking of divorcing his wife and wanted to know if Dr. Heilman thought she could make it on her own. Dr. Heilman inquired further. The husband could not describe exactly how his wife had changed, but he was clear about one thing— since the stroke she was so different that it was no longer possible to have a meaningful relationship with her.*

Being the expert clinician that he is, Dr. Heilman proceeded to try to figure out what had changed. He discovered that the wife could not perceive the affective tone of verbal communications. In other words, when Dr. Heilman said something with neutral content (like "the boy is riding his bicycle") in a sad voice and then repeated the same words in a happy voice, the wife could not decipher the emotional difference that was conveyed by his tone, cadence, volume, and so on. The wife had a problem with comprehending this crucial nonlinguistic aspect of language, though she had no trouble with understanding the words.

Before the wife's stroke, apparently the husband would come home from work and tell his wife about the day. In that near-magical way that communication works, the wife would understand the emotions her husband was conveying. Since the stroke, that essential aspect of relating was no longer possible because the wife was unable to *comprehend* affective prosody.

In 1979, the neurologists Ross and Mesulam described a patient who had developed impairments in *producing* affective expression. The patient was a right-handed teacher who, like Dr. Heilman's patient, seemed to have had an excellent recovery from a right hemisphere stroke (but in a different region of the right hemisphere). When this patient returned to her job, however, she discovered that she could no longer control her classroom because she was unable to convey emotional weight or nuance when she spoke. This patient was able to perceive and interpret affective expression from others, and she reported feeling emotions inwardly, but she was not able to communicate these feelings through the music of her language (Ross & Mesulam, 1979).

OTHER DISTURBANCES IN THE REALM OF LANGUAGE

This section about disturbances of language would not be complete without a brief word about developmental disturbances that affect language. Although many of the inborn difficulties with language are diagnosed during childhood, it is not uncommon for adults to enter therapy with language impairments, including dyslexia, that have not been previously identified.

> *My teaching task was to introduce a small group of second-year medical and dental students to the mental status exam. Six times during the semester, we would gather on the psychiatry inpatient unit to interview patients. Afterward we would talk about the experience, and then the students were expected to produce a patient write-up.*
>
> *Pavel didn't speak up much during the meetings, but he seemed fully engaged. On the other hand, his write-ups were invariably turned in late, and while he did seem to grasp the material, his writing was atrocious. He used incomplete sentences, run-on sentences, subjects that did not agree with verbs, and incorrect punctuation. I found myself wondering how he had managed to get into medical school.*
>
> *Here is what I learned when I had a private discussion with Pavel. He had had a terrible summer. While traveling for two weeks in South America, he had been robbed at knifepoint. He was so deeply shaken by the experience that he had been unable to complete the research upon which his scholarship for medical school tuition depended. Now, months later, he was still trying to recover emotionally, and he was "desperate to finish the research project" before he could focus his energies on the semester's schoolwork.*
>
> *Moreover, he hadn't talked to anyone about the pressures he felt or the emotional trauma he had experienced. In fact, until we had our conversation, he hadn't quite realized how traumatized he had been by the robbery. I felt sympathetic. I encouraged Pavel to get some therapy, and I cut him a lot of slack when it came to deadlines. But I realized that none of this explained why Pavel's writing was so bad. He had graduated from an excellent college. English was not his first language, but he had lived in the United States from the age of seven, surely long enough for him to have become entirely competent in speaking, reading, and writing English. Yet no one had ever raised the possibility that Pavel might have a learning disability except for his first-year preceptor, a surgeon at the medical school. That was only 1 year before; Pavel just hadn't believed it.*
>
> *But this time was different. Mine was a second opinion, and I was a psychiatrist. When we dug deeper into Pavel's educational experience, he told me that he thought he had "gotten by" despite his language difficulties in part because his teachers knew that he was smart and attributed his areas of weakness to English being his second language. He also told me that no matter how much feedback he had received in school over the years, none of it made any difference. He was never able to read any faster or write any better. His strategy for getting through college had been to take only courses that required minimal reading and no papers. Eventually Pavel had neuropsychological testing that confirmed that he had a language-based learning disability.*

Another type of developmental learning difficulty that is commonly misinterpreted involves impairments in the ability to interpret nonverbal communications including facial expressions. This is a significant impediment to social relations that may be confused with social phobia and other anxiety disorders or with an autism spectrum disorder.

Individuals with autism spectrum disorders may have other disturbances involving language. They may speak in a singsong tone, have a flattening of prosody, or hum to themselves. In addition, they may be loquacious and pedantic; their speech is often professor-like, encyclopedic, and devoid of emotional content. The usual turn-taking that characterizes normal conversation may be absent, and the individual may not be able to take the listener's level of interest into account.

Tourette's syndrome is characterized by tics, which may be verbal. Verbal tics may take the form of impulsively articulated simple sounds such as grunts, groans, growls, whistling, snorts, or complex words or phrases. Rarely, patients may have *copprolalia*, in which they utter curses or socially taboo words or phrases.

Other disturbances in the realm of language that are significant signs of organic disease include abnormal repetitions, either *palilalia*, which is simple echoing of one's own words, or *echolalia*, involving echoing what someone else has said; the new development of stuttering; loss of ability to comprehend music or to sing; loss of ability to decipher written language; and loss of ability to write comprehensible language.

DISTURBANCES IN SPEECH QUALITY

It is important to distinguish disturbances of language itself from disturbance in the quality of speech sounds. You might notice changes in voice tone or pitch, trouble with articulation, slurred speech, developing a new foreign-sounding accent, or speech that is soft in volume. These may be are signs of underlying organic problems. Many disturbances in speech quality are caused by physical abnormalities in the parts of the body where sounds are produced: the throat, larynx, and vocal cords. The potential underlying causes range from benign nodules on the vocal cords to malignancies in the region of the lung; all require medical attention.

There also are disorders that originate in the brain or the endocrine system and that will have an impact on speech quality. These disorders are significant for often being covert, easily misinterpreted, and capable of affecting other aspects of the individual's mental status. At times one might suspect that a patient could be producing some of these changes in speech consciously or for unconsciously motivated reasons, but it is wise to first rule out the possibility of an underlying physical problem.

Here are a few of the disorders that may lead to changes in speech quality as well as alterations in other aspects of mental status.

When a patient speaks in a low volume and the psychotherapist has to strain in order to hear, a variety of interpretations are possible. Perhaps the patient is unconsciously testing to see how motivated the therapist is to hear the patient's story. Maybe the patient is being covertly hostile; he doesn't want to do *all* the work. Before settling on a psychodynamic interpretation, however, one needs to be sure that this patient does not have Parkinson's disease or a related disorder that is known to produce low speech volume.

A newly developed unusual style of speaking or a foreign-sounding accent may seem entirely affected. Again, think twice before settling on this conclusion; foreign accent syndrome has been described in patients who suffered strokes or head injuries (Blumstein, Alexander, Ryalls, Katz, & Dworetzky, 1987). In these cases, brain damage causes individuals to pronounce words in a slightly different way than they did before their brain injury; the result is that individuals sound as though they are speaking their native language with a foreign accent, albeit one that is not identifiable.

Slurred speech is commonly associated with excessive alcohol or drug levels but also may be a symptom of diseases that affect the cerebellum. Slurred speech may be seen in strokes, in serotonin syndrome, in severe or repeated lithium toxicity, and in amyotrophic lateral sclerosis. Insufficient thyroid hormone is known to lower the pitch of one's voice and to produce depression or in, rare instances, psychosis.

THOUGHT DISORDERS IN CONTRAST TO LANGUAGE DISORDERS

Therapists are generally more familiar with disorders of thought content or organization than with disturbances of language production and/or comprehension. In contrast with disturbances of language, thought disorders are problems in the organization of the content of the communication, the associations, goal-directedness, and underlying logic. Thought disorders, especially loose associations, word salad, clang associations, and neologisms, are most strongly associated with schizophrenia. But being circumstantial and/or tangential may also occur with neurological disorders, including untreated, long-standing seizure disorders or multiple sclerosis.

When an individual is circumstantial, he or she produces perfectly grammatical sentences that are fluid (fluent), that communicate emotion and meaning through nuances of tone, cadence, and so on. In other words, the problem is not with language per se. The problem with circumstantial speech is that, although the patient is headed toward some goal such as explaining how she came to be admitted to the hospital, his or her account is long-winded, giving minute details and unnecessary background information.

One extremely bright individual was unusually insightful and succinct in describing her own circumstantial speech to me. She used this sound bite: "Ask me what time it is, and I'll tell you how to make a clock." The circumstantial patient does eventually make the point or answer the question, but it takes a long time to do so. In contrast, a patient with tangential thinking never does reach the goal of the discourse but rather spins out a logical train of associations that get further and further from the point. In either situation, the experience for a listener is one of feeling impatient and frustrated and wanting the individual to get to the point.

When a patient has loose associations, the logic of the flow of words is even more disrupted; the sequence of thoughts may be based simply on the sounds of words (clang associations), very personal associations, or even seemingly random mental leaps. With even further disruption in the underlying logical organization of thought, one may see flight of ideas or word salad, patterns of thought that may be virtually incomprehensible.

Patients whose thoughts are circumstantial or tangential, who have loose associations or who exhibit word salad, do not have a problem with language itself but with the organization of what is expressed through language. The more disorganized the individual's thinking, the more difficult it becomes to distinguish a thought disorder from a disorder of language production. This is very important to keep in mind, especially if you see an individual who develops what looks like a thought disorder late in life. You will want to be sure the problem is not aphasia.

Perseveration in Thought or Action

Perseveration is behavior that is involuntarily repetitive; the first instance of the behavior is appropriate, but it is then repeated even when the context has changed and the behavior is no longer sensible. Whether in speech or action, perseveration may be conceptualized as a failure to update the goals for which the original behavior was produced and a failure to shift set with changing circumstances.

> *One dramatic example of perseveration is the story of a man who set out to shovel snow from his driveway. He appropriately began by shoveling all the way down one side of the driveway, but then he continued into the street, across the street, and then down the block.*

Here is another example from a mental status examination:

> *An elderly woman was asked to draw a house. She began by sketching a good-looking first floor, including several windows. She then added on a second floor with windows, and then a third floor, a fourth, a fifth, and on and on.*

On the screening questionnaires that patients may be required to fill out in some clinics, you might see perseveration in the form of 3's with too many loops, m's with too many humps, or the erroneous repetition of letters or numbers in a zip code or phone number.

In the context of an interview, any perseveration is highly significant, even if there are only one or two instances. One commonly sees perseveration manifested in the following way. The individual is asked a question to which he or she responds appropriately. But then, that answer to the first question bleeds into the response to the next.

Examiner: How old are you?

Patient: 52 years old.

Examiner: And how old is your daughter?

Patient: 52.

Often individuals who exhibit perseveration on some tasks will have poor follow-through (impersistence) on others. That is, if asked to subtract 7 from 100 in serial fashion, they may easily lose track of the task after the first or second computation. Or on trails B, a test that involves connecting alternating numbers and letters in sequence (1-A-2-B-3-C), an individual might simply revert to connecting sequential numbers, omitting the letters entirely.

Perseveration is a highly significant finding, indicating the presence of an organic disorder. It may be seen in a vast variety of brain diseases including autism and may be a feature of delirium.

Automatic Behavior

Automatic behaviors are rote, robot-like behaviors in which the person is not responsive to other individuals. Automatic behaviors are reflective of an altered state of consciousness. Most often these behaviors are simple, repetitive, purposeless acts that are performed in a clumsy fashion. Examples include typing the same letter over and over on a computer, groping, chewing, picking at one's clothing, or smacking one's lips. Automatisms also may be verbal, such as repeating a phrase over and over or shouting. More complex activities sometimes may be seen, but these never require conscious thought, complex decision making, or problem solving. Examples include walking downstairs and out of the house, running, or disrobing. Automatic behavior is associated with organic disease, especially seizure disorders and narcolepsy.

For a good example of automatic behavior, let's return to my patient Joseph, the computer firm manager who had partial seizures. It was Joseph's powerful emotional experience of being back on the playground of his youth that eventually convinced him to get a seizure workup, but he had been having another disruptive symptom that contributed to his decision.

> Joseph was embarrassed to tell me that he had been having some peculiar experiences, and he didn't know what to make of them. He would find himself saying things, involuntarily, and often inappropriately. "No way." "Hell!" He said things that "didn't make sense" and at random moments. What's more, sometimes those random moments were in the middle of business meetings. Joseph would try to "bluff his way out" of these situations. After an involuntary utterance, he would cough loudly or drop something on the floor in an attempt to create a diversion. Joseph was confused about what was going on—and he was worried.

These verbal automatisms provided still more evidence that Joseph had a seizure disorder.

Environmentally Dependent Behavior

These unusual behaviors are called environmentally dependent or stimulus bound in that they refer to unmediated, automatic responses to objects and people in the immediate environment. The key to understanding these behaviors is to grasp the notion that these patients have an absence of internal, inhibitory control. On the basis of neurologic dysfunction, the individual is lacking the capacity for personal autonomy. The behavioral responses are called forth in an automatic or reflexive way by the specific, external stimuli.

When the external stimulus is a person, the behavior is called *imitative*. Examples of imitative behavior include a patient mimicking the natural gestures of an examining physician. The doctor might scratch his forehead or bend forward; the patient follows suit. The doctor holds up one finger and asks the patient to fix his eyes upon that finger. In response, the patient holds up one finger. Even if the patient is told that there is no need to do what the doctor is doing, and even when the patient seems to fully comprehend, he or she persists nonetheless.

When the external stimulus is an object or objects in the environment, the behavioral response is called *utilization behavior*, referring to the fact that the patient often uses the object in the way that is naturally called for by the nature of the object. For instance, the therapist's reading glasses might be sitting on the desk near the patient; the patient picks them up and puts them on.

Another example of stimulus-bound behavior may be observed during neuropsychological testing when the tester draws a shape on a piece of paper and asks the patient to copy it. The intention is for the patient to duplicate the figure on the same page, but next to the original one. Instead, the patient takes the pencil and draws right on top of the psychologist's figure. Or, in another example, the patient is given a piece of hospital stationery and is asked to write a sentence of his or her own choosing; the patient copies the letterhead. These behaviors occur even when these individuals seem to fully understand what is being asked of them.

Imitative behavior and utilization behavior are fairly unusual and easy to misinterpret as psychologically driven. One might be apt to hypothesize that the individual exhibiting these behaviors has inappropriate boundaries or is being provocative. But this kind of reactivity to external stimuli is based on disease of the frontal lobes or lesions that disconnect the frontal lobes and limit their modulating influence on behavior.

In William Alwyn Lishman's classic book *Organic Psychiatry*, he gives these unforgettable examples of utilization behavior.

> Thus when taken into a room containing a buffet, his patient laid out the glasses and offered him food, spontaneously behaving like a hostess. Confronted with makeup she used it immediately, and seeing wool and knitting needles began to knit. Another patient, when taken into a bedroom with the sheet turned back, got undressed, went to bed and prepared to go to sleep. On hearing the word 'museum' while in an apartment he began methodically to examine the paintings on the wall, and walked from room to room inspecting various objects. (Lishman, 1987, p. 79)

Apraxia

Apraxia is a disturbance in the ability to perform learned motor movements or routines (e.g., brushing teeth, dressing, using tools, putting a letter into an envelope) when it is not because of any weakness or paralysis. Apraxia results from a disturbance in the brain's organizing and sequencing of motor behavior. Apraxia is a clear sign of underlying organic pathology. Apraxia will show up in individuals as an inability to perform simple tasks or to dress or feed themselves. These patients may put socks on top of shoes or find themselves entirely flummoxed as to how to get into a sweater.

When testing for apraxis, an examiner might ask Mr. Jones "to show how he hammers a nail" or "to pretend to use a scissor." Or one might ask Mr. Jones to "take a bow" or "show how to bat a baseball." Keep in mind that apraxia may involve one side or both sides of the body. Also, it may be difficult to distinguish patients who have apraxia from those who have trouble with the visuospatial organization that is required to accomplish certain motor tasks.

Agnosia

The term *agnosia* ("without knowledge") is also a clear sign of an organic disorder. There are many types of agnosia; each involves the loss of ability to know what something is despite intact memory and sensory perception.

Someone with a visual agnosia, for instance, would be able to see a drawing of a cactus but would have no idea what the object was. In contrast, individuals who have a problem with naming (*anomia*) would be able to describe what the picture represented, even though they couldn't produce the actual name of that particular object. They might say something like, "It's green, prickly, and grows in the desert." The individual with a visual agnosia would simply have no idea what he or she was looking at.

Prosopagnosia is a kind of agnosia; it is the inability to recognize faces. Depending on how severe the prosopagnosia is, individuals may have only slight difficulty recognizing people out of context or they might be entirely unable to distinguish faces one from another. Individuals who have prosopagnosia will often learn to recognize people by cues such as the sounds of their voices, how they walk, or the style of haircut or beard they sport.

> *Many years ago I treated a middle-aged couple, Sam and Samantha. Sam had been successful financially as a consequence of having been an early non-technical employee in a successful tech start-up company. Samantha took care of the home, their four children, and "my fifth child" as she referred to her husband. Samantha had an intuitive sense of Sam's needs and was resentful of the amount of care that she felt Sam required. When this couple first came to see me, they had no conscious awareness of Sam's numerous neuropsychological impairments.*
>
> *In addition to substantial clumsiness and difficulties with sustained attention, Sam had an auditory processing disorder that made it difficult for him to time his entry into group conversations. "By the time I figure out what I'm going to say, they're already onto another topic."*

Sam also had prosopagnosia. These neuropsychological problems were not identified until I referred Sam for neuropsychological testing. Once the couple received feedback from the tester, they became aware of the many compensatory mechanisms they had developed, quite automatically.

With regard to the prosopagnosia, Samantha said, "Sam rarely goes anywhere alone . . . except to work, where he knows all the players in his department; he knows just exactly how each of them walks, talks, and dresses. And on the weekends, if we're in the market together and run into someone we know, a neighbor for instance . . . I'll say to the neighbor, 'Oh, hi, Jim or Peter or Suzie' or whoever it is. 'Your weeping cherry tree has been just beautiful this season.' I now realize that I'm careful to say the person's name and also something that will let Sam know who this is. Otherwise he'd be lost."

Despite their similar names, the contrast between Sam's deficits and Samantha's social sensitivity and verbal agility could hardly have been greater. They were both loving and smart, and they made an excellent team. This sense of mutual respect and teamwork was only improved after we identified and worked on the feelings they both had about these neuropsychological deficits. For Samantha, the resentment had been conscious, though she now understood the true nature of her husband's needs. For Sam, the sense of being defective and the guilt about being a burden ran deep and as far back into his past as he could remember.

Prosopagnosia, whether mild or severe, is readily interpreted as anxiety driven. Individuals with prosopagnosia may present with a reluctance to engage socially. They may not be aware that their underlying motivation is to avoid situations in which they will not recognize people who expect to be recognized. A variety of possible misdiagnoses may ensue, especially social phobia.

One particular patient with prosopagnosia and visual agnosia was the inspiration for Oliver Sack's fascinating and widely read book *The Man Who Mistook His Wife for a Hat and Other Clinical Tales*. More recently, Dr. Sacks has written about his own experience of having prosopagnosia.

At the age of seventy-seven, despite a lifetime of trying to compensate, I have no less trouble with faces and places. I am particularly thrown if I see people out of context, even if I have been with them five minutes before. This happened one morning just after an appointment with my psychiatrist. (I had been seeing him twice weekly for several years at this point.) A few minutes after I left his office, I encountered a soberly dressed man who greeted me in the lobby of the building. I was puzzled as to why this stranger seemed to know me, until the doorman greeted him by name—it was, of course, my analyst. (This failure to recognize him came up as a topic in our next session; I think that he did not entirely believe me when I maintained that it had a neurological basis rather than a psychiatric one.) (Sacks, 2010, p. 37)

Two other agnosias are deserving of special mention: simultagnosia and finger agnosia. Finger agnosia is the loss of ability to distinguish the different fingers. This particular agnosia is part of an important neurological syndrome called Gertman's syndrome, which helps neurologists to localize a brain injury.

Simultagnosia is the inability to see more than one visual stimulus at a time. In order to understand how individuals with this agnosia might behave, consider looking at a picture of a beach scene. A normal individual would find it easy to take in the big picture as well as all of the details: the sand, the horizon, the surf, children in the foreground who are building a sand castle, teenagers playing beach volleyball in the corner, and so on. But someone with simultagnosia would only be able to take in one detail at a time. "Oh, this is a picture of a foot, a barefoot. Oh, it's a boy."

Adult-Onset Difficulty With Reading, Writing, Drawing, or Calculating

Highly indicative of an underlying organic disorder is the loss of a cognitive capability that an individual once had, and this is certainly true in the arenas of reading, writing, drawing (constructional ability), and/or calculating. When evaluating a patient, what matters is not how well the patient performs relative to other individuals. What is important is whether that particular individual's performance has declined compared with his or her previous level of functioning in these various areas of cognition.

In order to make that assessment, first the clinician must try to ascertain the person's highest prior level of functioning. This may be very difficult, if not impossible, to know for sure, especially because there is enormous variation in performance in these various domains within the general population. Many factors contribute to that variation, including educational experience, socioeconomic background, and innate abilities.

Sometimes a decline in functioning will be obvious, as when an accountant has trouble balancing her checkbook or an artist cannot draw a three-dimensional cube during your office exam. On the other hand, one should not assume that, in the past, the accountant was able to balance a checkbook or that the artist was able to draw. Keep in mind that areas of cognitive weakness and frank learning disabilities, are extremely common, even in people who are highly successful, because so many individuals are able to make effective adaptations to areas of relative cognitive weakness.

In order to try to ascertain whether an individual has declined in functioning from a previous level in a particular cognitive domain, you might try some of the following suggestions. Most important, obtain the records of any prior neuropsychological testing, even if it was administered during grade school. Seek out knowledgeable and reliable observers who have known the patient well and for a long time, perhaps a primary care physician, a prior therapist, a neighbor, or relative. Look into the patient's academic and employment history as these may offer a rough indication of past levels of ability: highest grade in school, old report cards, occupation, highest level of employment, any standardized testing scores on SATs, ACTs, GREs.

If you are concerned that a patient might be declining in mental capacity, it is useful to arrange for the individual to have a battery of neuropsychological testing. This will not only give you a snapshot of the patient's cognitive capacities in the present but also will establish a baseline with which to compare that person's functional state in the future. A pattern of deterioration may only become unequivocal as you track the patient over time.

The Executive Functions

The "executive" functions of the brain are so named because they function in a way that is analogous to the CEO of a corporation or the conductor of an orchestra. The executive functions harness, direct, and coordinate other specific cognitive abilities for goal-directed behavior. Some of the capabilities that are included in the category of executive functions are planning, organization, prioritizing, goal setting, sequencing, initiating, self-monitoring, inhibiting impulsive responses, and anticipating future consequences. Patients may have disturbances in some areas of executive functioning and not in others.

It is important for mental health practitioners to be familiar with the concept of executive functioning. Many individuals who enter therapy have difficulties in day-to-day life as a result of problems in executive functioning that interfere with their ability to effectively utilize their other cognitive capacities. Patients who have trouble with executive functioning may be very smart, and they may have what seem to be reasonable goals; nonetheless, these individuals may be frustrated in reaching those goals because of trouble with developing a step-by-step strategic plan, prioritizing, initiating action, anticipating difficulties, monitoring their progress, course-correcting, and/or following the plan through to completion.

Problems with executive functioning may be inborn. Individuals with attention deficit hyperactivity disorder frequently have difficulties in this arena. In addition, any diseases that have a direct or indirect effect on the frontal lobes of the brain may present with problems of executive functioning, including tumors, dementia syndromes, trauma, infections, multiple sclerosis, and so on. Delirium will produce reversible, global problems with executive functioning.

Chapter 10

Important Aspects of the Patient Assessment— A Second Look

unknown unknown

Introduction

This chapter focuses on aspects of a patient's history that may be over-looked or only superficially investigated in daily practice. Yet these very areas of the history may be the source of important clues to a covert medical condition. An especially thorough inquiry is called for when you are faced with a stalled treatment or a mystery diagnosis; when you encounter a problematic clinical situation that eludes understanding; when a new patient has an unusual presentation; when an ongoing patient is not getting better or actually getting worse despite good treat-ment. These are times when it is important to cover all the bases in your investigation and when it may be fruitful to circle back and carefully search again for evidence of possible hidden physical disorders. And, you may need to look for clues in unlikely places.

You will want to be sure that you have conducted a thorough mental status exam and that you have discussed the onset and history of the present illness with your patient. In order to be sure you have garnered all of the important details, it might be necessary to go over this territory on more than one occasion with the patient and possibly also with the family. Then move on to look into the following areas: current physical symptoms, family medical history, and personal medical history.

Impediments to Exploring Physical Symptoms

When searching for possible covert physical disorders, it may seem that there is no more obvious approach than to ask patients about the details of their physical symptoms and about their personal and family medical histories. Yet, clinicians often do not explore these areas directly, and patients don't necessarily volunteer the information they may have. Even when patients have a specific medical diagnosis, they may not provide this information to their mental health practitioners. The message here is that you have to ask. Ask about a patient's medical and family history and about physical symptoms.

Understandably, many therapists have some degree of reluctance to ask about these topics. The somatic arena may be entirely unfamiliar territory. This book is an encouragement for you to begin exploring the physical terrain in order to get the full picture of a patient's situation and also to prepare for making necessary referrals. Your comfort in exploring this arena with your patients is also likely to make it easier for them to discuss their symptoms and their personal and family medical histories with you.

When a patient does reveal information in the somatic arena, you may not know exactly how to respond. All clinicians have times when they encounter areas about which they have limited understanding. It is at these times that one becomes aware of how the clinical interview is driven by theories generated in the mind of a practitioner, who is trying to figure out the source of the patient's difficulties. Questions that a clinician poses to a patient are shaped by that clinician's fund of knowledge. For example, it is only once you've learned that depression may be accompanied by vegetative symptoms that you begin to regularly ask patients with a depressive mood about their appetite, weight, energy level, sleep, and libido. Similarly, it is only when you know how to distinguish the possible underlying causes of recurrent headaches that you will know the most pertinent questions to ask. For instance, if there is a family history of tuberous sclerosis or neurofibromatosis, headaches could indicate the presence of a brain tumor.

When faced with a patient who might have an underlying somatic disorder, it is possible for any clinician to begin to collect information from the patient and possibly from his or her family. You can ask and ought to ask about when it started and what it felt like. As you learn more, your questions will become more targeted, more illuminating, and more useful in discriminating one underlying diagnosis from another. However, keep in mind that although you may be able to learn a great deal from your patient about his or her medical history and symptoms, it would *not* be appropriate for you to take responsibility for investigating their full significance without suitable medical training.

Let's suppose that the patient tells you she has leg cramps, or night sweats, or that she has noticed a change in her bowel habits, or any of an uncountable number of other possible symptoms. What do these symptoms signify? How serious are they? What could be causing them?

LEARNING FROM CONSULTANTS

As a practitioner's fund of information grows, his or her theories will broaden, and the nature of the inquiry will expand. This is true in every field of clinical care. No matter what the specialty or level of expertise, each practitioner regularly comes face to face with the limits of his or her knowledge, for we are now living in a time when the scientific understanding of health and disease is expanding at an astronomical rate. The use of expert consultants is a fruitful way to learn while also providing your patient with a sound medical opinion.

It is always crucial to keep in mind that there are things that *you do not know are known.* You will want to refer your patient for consultations to clinicians who have a broader knowledge base in the area of your patient's difficulties. This process of referring patients to practitioners with more expertise occurs in every area of health care. A chain of increasingly specialized consultations not only benefits patients, but it also provides referring clinicians with an opportunity to learn.

Let's look at an example of this learning chain.

> *The patient's chief complaint goes like this: "I sleep at least 10 hours every night, and I'm still tired during the day." This patient also feels "depressed and anxious" and has "mind fog." She is hesitant to bring up her somatic symptoms. She has muscle aches, headaches, and abdominal pains. Sometimes she limps, and she fears that her "hearing is going." This has been going on for years, but she's getting worse. "My family thinks I'm a hypochondriac."*

Perhaps this patient has a depression, an anxiety disorder, or somatization disorder. These are common possibilities. But what if I told you that this patient has a rare disease? Let's suppose that she has a mitochondrial disorder. Mitochondria are tiny but complex organelles that are present in virtually every cell of the body, hundreds per cell in many cases. Mitochondria produce all of the power for cell functioning. Curiously, mitochondria have DNA of their own, because eons ago mitochondria are believed to have been freestanding microorganisms that became incorporated into cells as we now know them. When there is a mutation in the mitochondrial DNA or in the part of a cell's nuclear DNA that is involved in mitochondrial function, the consequence is inefficient energy production. The form that a mitochondrial disorder takes in any one individual will depend on the specific mutation that is involved, the number of mitochondria that are affected, the organs that have a heavy burden of cells with malfunctioning mitochondria, and the energy demands of that organ.

Because the mitochondrial disorders have been described only relatively recently, they might be entirely unfamiliar to a psychotherapist or to a primary care physician who has not read the latest clinical journal reports. Nonetheless, one of these clinicians might decide to refer the patient for a consultation—perhaps the patient is getting worse; perhaps there has been a documented hearing loss. Perhaps a review of the family history has revealed that the patient's mother and grandmother died from mysterious disorders that affected multiple organ systems; this might raise the question of whether there is a genetic disease in the family.

The patient might be referred to a sleep specialist because of her fatigue or to a neurologist because of her limping. These specialists are more likely to know something about mitochondrial diseases, because they tend to be consulted about patients with problems that are difficult to diagnose. Their job involves focused thinking about rare disorders. Perhaps the consultants have seen patients in the past whom they thought had mitochondrial disorders. Perhaps they went on to refer their patients to a mitochondrial disease expert.

The expert in mitochondrial diseases undoubtedly has seen many patients with different varieties of mitochondrial disease. That expert has also seen individuals who looked like they had a mitochondrial disease but didn't. And that expert has followed patients who had a mitochondrial disease over time; he or she knows how they fare and what kinds of things help or make the symptoms worse. The expert also is familiar with the published scientific literature as well as the cutting-edge ideas that are currently under investigation about this class of diseases. To the expert, the mitochondrial diseases are old hat.

Each clinician along the chain has an opportunity to learn from the practitioners who know more about this disorder. Also, each clinician along the chain has an opportunity to learn from the patient. What is it really like to feel exhausted, to cope with recurrent headaches, or to have symptoms that no one has been able to explain? This is also an opportunity to read about your patient's disorder as a way to increase your fund of knowledge.

Present Illness

Learning about the present illness in detail is the starting point of every investigation. This is true whether you are seeing a patient for the first time or reconsidering your case formulation after years of treatment. Even if the present illness began years earlier, it is important to keep in mind how much information can be gained from gathering a full picture of the onset of the patient's difficulties. The pattern of emergence of any disorder is often characteristic and extremely useful to clarify in honing in on a diagnosis. In addition, the picture of any disorder is often clearest at the outset before the proverbial waters have been muddied by numerous treatment attempts or by complications that may have developed. Early on the picture is not yet clouded by diagnostic theories that have been formulated and believed in by the patient, the patient's family and friends, and most importantly the health-care practitioners.

Listen vigilantly for any behavioral evidence that might indicate the presence of a covert medical illness. Be mindful that the patient is presenting a very personal narrative. Listen carefully to this experiential perspective, but simultaneously, look beyond the explanations that the patient presents. Just as you would consider alternate psychodynamic interpretations in trying to understand an individual's experiences, consider also whether an underlying medical disease that is out of the patient's awareness might have generated any of the individual's behavior.

Here are some examples of this kind of thinking: The patient reports that the present illness began when he lost his job; you wonder, "Did he have an early dementia?" The patient says he became an alcoholic in his late thirties; you think, "Huntington's disease? Frontal lobe brain tumor?" The patient comes in with 10 pages of notes and talks about a dramatic religious conversion; you think, "Temporal lobe seizure disorder?" The patient is in academic difficulty; you think, "Attention deficit hyperactivity disorder, learning disorder, narcolepsy or other sleep disorder?" The family reports violent outbursts in a young man; you wonder whether the patient is using drugs or if he might have a history of brain injury. These examples do not convey the complete differential diagnoses of these behavioral changes, but they demonstrate how it is possible for a clinician to begin to include medical diagnoses on the list of possibilities.

Physical Symptoms

When inquiring about physical symptoms, it is useful to begin with open-ended questions such as: Do you have any physical symptoms? Any discomforts? Any changes in body functions? Do you notice any changes in how your body looks or works? If the patient responds with specific physical complaints or observations, follow up by asking for more details. In the same way that you would explore more familiar psychological symptoms such as irritability or feeling suicidal, you will want to inquire about onset, timeline, intensity, waxing and waning, what brings it on, or makes it worse or better. Although the content here may be less familiar to you, it is important to explore patients' experiences of their symptoms.

After you have followed up on a patient's response to your open-ended questions, consider using a verbal or written checklist of symptoms to cover the variety of symptoms that might emerge as a consequence of diseases in the different organ systems. Many clinics and private practices utilize a paper or computerized checklist format for this review of systems; outlines are available on the Internet. Taking a quick inventory of this sort facilitates recall for patients. It also cues patients to recognize that certain of their experiences are noteworthy. In addition, it may make it easier for individuals to bring up symptoms they find embarrassing.

Information Flow Between Mental Health Practitioners and Medical Personnel

If you discover that your patient does have some physical symptoms, it is important to inquire as to whether he or she has told a physician about them. Ask about whether the symptoms have been investigated and what has been determined. With permission, be sure to obtain the medical records and speak with clinicians the patient has seen. The patient's physicians may have important information that the patient has not conveyed to you. I will never forget the lesson learned from a patient I referred to a neurologist for a consultation. The patient and her husband returned to see me after they had had a final meeting with the consultant. All the testing had been completed.

> *"How did it go?" I asked.*
> *"Oh, everything is fine. A clean bill of health!" They concurred.*
> *But when I called the neurologist, he told me that my patient had multiple sclerosis. He also was clear that he had told this to both the patient and her husband.*

Medical caregivers have information that may not get to you via the patient. In the same way, information you have as a therapist may not get to other caregivers via the patient, even if you have fully discussed something with the patient and asked that individual to tell his or her PCP or medical specialist. Accurate information flow is central to good care, and often therapists have crucial data to contribute to the diagnostic process.

Patients may reveal to their therapists information that they have not yet provided to other health-care practitioners, including their PCPs.

This is understandable. For one thing, therapists often see patients on a regular basis over time, and they tend to spend more time with patients at each meeting than most other clinicians do. Having an ongoing relationship allows mental health clinicians to hear about and observe the ups and downs of symptoms in close to real time. With this kind of continuity, it is easier to develop a sense of the waxing and waning of a patient's symptoms and the degree to which those symptoms are affecting the patient's daily life.

Although trust is central to all practitioner-patient relationships, therapists often work directly on the therapeutic relationship. This allows therapists to help patients with emotions that may be obstacles to talking about symptoms, such as feelings of fear, shame, self-doubt, embarrassment, or anxiety.

One primary care doctor told me about a patient who had been in his practice for 8 years before she told him that she had nocturnal enuresis. Nocturnal enuresis is medical-ese for nighttime bed-wetting. This 35-year-old patient had been horribly embarrassed about her frequent episodes of middle-of-the-night urinary incontinence. It had gotten in the way of her embarking on an intimate relationship. Her therapist had helped her to find "the words and the courage" to tell the PCP about her bed-wetting. After that, a workup revealed that the patient had been having nighttime seizures. Anticonvulsant medications fully resolved this symptom.

Patients will tell their therapists about many important symptoms before they tell anyone else, such as incontinence of urine or feces, impotence, drug use, drinking too much alcohol, unusual sexual interests, academic difficulty, intrusive thoughts that the patient finds abhorrent in some way, private rituals, visions, violent episodes, thinking one is "going crazy," "losing one's mind," or "getting demented." Often therapists will help individuals to figure out and articulate what they are experiencing, thus enabling them to present the situation more clearly to a primary care physician or specialist. Here is an example.

A couple comes to therapy for the first time in their 45 years of marriage. The wife says that the husband has been abusive to her. He has hit her several times, giving her a black eye on one occasion. When you inquire as to what these fights are about, you discover that there are no real fights at all. These incidents only occur in the middle of the night. The husband feels terrible. "They happen in my sleep. I don't even know I'm doing it." The husband likely has REM sleep behavior disorder. You refer them to a sleep specialist.

Family Medical and Psychiatric History

The patient's family history of medical and psychiatric problems becomes all the more important if you suspect the presence of a physical disorder. Not only are we interested to learn about the psychological climate that surrounded the patient during his or her formative years, but we are also interested in discovering any biological factors that might be operating. Given that family members have shared a living environment with the patient, in addition they may have shared infectious or toxic exposures. And we are interested in knowing if the patient may have inherited any disorders.

Ask the patient to methodically go over the family members in each generation and how they are biologically related. For family members who are deceased, what did they die from and at what ages? What medical or psychiatric diseases did they have? Were there any unexplained accidents, diseases, hospitalizations, or deaths in family members? Inquire about the details. If there is a history of a family member receiving ECT (shock therapy) or being institutionalized, especially if the treatment was in the distant past, it is often impossible to know whether the individual was being treated for a depression, mania, psychosis, dementia, or medical condition with mental manifestations. Keep in mind that suicides, violent behavior, and alcohol abuse may be associated with a variety of underlying medical diseases.

When taking a family and psychiatric history, keep your perspective. Diagnoses made by others, sometimes decades earlier, may not have been accurate. In addition, distortions of memory and the psychological effects of shame and embarrassment about certain disorders will influence the reliability of any information you might obtain about the family.

GENETICALLY TRANSMITTED DISORDERS

Here are some things to keep in mind when thinking about the possibility of a genetic disorder. Naturally, the focus needs to be on the individuals to whom the patient is biologically related: grandparents, parents, siblings, children, grandchildren, parents' siblings, and siblings' children. If an ancestor died at a young age in an accident or from an infectious illness, it is impossible to know whether he or she would have developed a genetically influenced disease if he or she had lived to a riper age.

When evaluating the information you gather, remember the clinical maxim: You cannot be sure who the patient's father is. In this current era, when reproductive technologies include not only the use of donor sperm but also donor eggs, one may not know for sure who the mother is either.

This text does not address itself to the myriad of genetic disorders that are symptomatic early in life and diagnosed during childhood, but this book does apply to those developmental disorders that are sometimes overlooked during childhood and first diagnosed during adulthood, such as attention deficit hyperactivity disorder, learning disabilities, dyslexia, neurofibromatosis, and high-level autism. In addition, this book includes genetic disorders that may not be symptomatic until adulthood, some of which are Huntington's disease, Wilson's disease, acute intermittent porphyria, and the mitochondrial diseases.

Diseases with a genetic component vary considerably in their mode of inheritance and their clinical expression. For some genetic diseases, it is clear that, if you have the gene, you get the disease. These are conditions such as Huntington's disease in which, on a statistical basis, half of an individual's children will have the disorder. With other genetic disorders, the mode of inheritance is more uncertain and variable. For instance, the mitochondrial diseases are virtually always transmitted from mother to daughter, but the severity of the disease and the organ systems affected will vary. In neurofibromatosis the same genetically inherited disease may express itself with varying degrees of severity in different family members. Neurofibromatosis is a neurocutaneous syndrome, one of a number of lifelong disorders that display specific skin manifestations in addition to symptoms related to nervous system involvement. Neurofibromatosis 1 is frequently associated with learning disabilities; individuals with this disease also may develop tumors in the brain.

Most of the genetically influenced disorders that mental health clinicians encounter are a consequence of multiple genetic factors that contribute to the development of the disease, along with environmental factors. This is believed to be the case with bipolar disorder, schizophrenia, and obsessive-compulsive disorder, for example. Most dementias also are determined by multiple genetic factors.

Personal Past Medical History

Inquire about the patient's complete, past medical and psychiatric history. Obtain any medical records that may be available, but do not assume that past diagnoses have been accurate. Remember that some illnesses are only accurately diagnosed in retrospect. For instance, past episodes of transient somatic symptoms with depression may turn out to have been early incidents of multiple sclerosis. Fleeting psychotic events, first thought to be regressive psychological experiences, may later be more completely understood to be seizure related, medication or drug related, or attacks of acute intermittent porphyria.

In addition to any clearly defined illnesses, has the patient had any mysterious, undiagnosed problems or persistent or recurrent symptoms? Are there any physical or mental experiences that the person hasn't mentioned to anyone, thinking they were too trivial? Has the patient had experiences that led to worry about going crazy or becoming demented?

RISK FACTORS

Specifically ask about evidence of developmental disorders during childhood and about factors that may be associated with enduring effects on the brain. Knowing specific details will help in assessing how serious these problems were and whether they might still be affecting the patient's clinical presentation.

- Did the patient have an early or a difficult or traumatic birth?
- How was the patient's mother's health during pregnancy with the patient? Did she use drugs?
- Were the individual's developmental milestones delayed?
- Has the patient changed his or her handedness?
- How did the patient do in elementary school? Middle school? High school?
- Is there any history of head trauma during childhood or adulthood? Inquire specifically about any auto accidents, falls, slips on ice, sports-related injuries, physical or sexual abuse, torture, military trauma, or falling as a result of intoxication, seizures, or other medical disorders that can lead to a sudden loss of consciousness.
- Has he or she ever been unconscious and for how long? Was there amnesia? What period of time was lost to memory? Was there a hospitalization and for how long?
- Has the individual ever had encephalitis or meningitis?
- Has the patient had exposure to Lyme disease?
- Has the patient ever had a sexually transmitted disease?
- Does the individual have any risk factors for HIV (e.g., unprotected sex, blood transfusion, or IV drug use)?
- Does the patient have high blood pressure, atherosclerosis, or diabetes? Over time, these conditions may have a significant impact on the brain.
- Has the patient ever been hospitalized and why?

- Has the patient had chemotherapy or radiation therapy? What was the diagnosis?
- Has the patient had surgery? What kind of surgery? Was the patient on a heart/lung machine?

MEDICATIONS AND OTHER SUBSTANCES

Inquire about any and all medications and other substances that the patient has consumed, including over-the-counter medications, herbal preparations, natural remedies, ritual or religious healing formulas, vitamins, hormones, nutritional supplements, and illicit drugs (including their route of administration) and alcohol, either home-brewed or store-bought. Has the individual smoked cigarettes? Does he or she take any prescribed medication in correctly? Has the patient ever accidentally or purposely overdosed? Try to ascertain the time course of the individual's medication, alcohol, or other substance use to determine if there is any correlation with the onset of the patient's presenting symptoms. It cannot be emphasized enough how important this information is.

Drugs and substances of all kinds, either alone or in combination, can have potent effects on a person's mental state. Look up the reported side effects and drug-drug interactions of any substances your patient is taking. Utilize the Physician's Desk Reference, reliable Internet databases, or other authoritative, comprehensive sources. Phoning a pharmacist also may be extremely helpful. Remember that medical conditions that "come out of a bottle" are very common, relatively simple to diagnose, and, with the exception of the addictions, also easy to cure.

Although a patient's substance use or abuse may be prominent in the presenting clinical picture, it is important to keep in mind that medical and/or psychiatric conditions may be driving that substance use. Here are some examples involving somatic disorders. Untreated attention deficit hyperactivity disorder is commonly associated with the use of caffeine, nicotine, alcohol, cocaine, and other people's stimulant prescriptions. Individuals with narcolepsy may depend on NoDoz and stimulants. Alcohol, sedating antihistamines, and sleeping pills of all kinds are used when patients have trouble with falling asleep; they may not realize that their problem with sleep onset stems from restless legs syndrome, attention deficit hyperactivity disorder, a circadian rhythm disorder, or excess caffeine intake.

TOXIC EXPOSURE

Toxic exposure is a more frequent cause of mental symptoms than the reader might suppose. Uncontrolled supplements and herbals may be contaminated with toxic ingredients. The workplace is another important potential source of exposure. Be especially cued to listening for exposure to lead, mercury, arsenic, manganese, or thallium. These substances are capable of producing a clinical picture with prominent mental symptoms. Particularly vulnerable are miners, smelters, firefighters, recycling or demolition crew members, chemists, agricultural workers, dentists, painters, lab technicians, emergency first responders, and possibly military personnel.

A suicide attempt or being the victim of a fire also may be a source of toxic exposure. In some communities and in many third-world countries, environmental toxins are common, and contaminated water or air pollutants may affect whole communities. Though extremely rare, attempted murder should not be dismissed as a possibility.

Examples of unsuspected toxic exposure are myriad and include carbon monoxide diffusing into a home from a malfunctioning furnace; lead released when acidic drinks were served from inadequately fired ceramic urns with lead-based glaze (Matte, Proops, Palazuelos, Graef, & Hernandez Avila, 1994); accidental ingestion of lead shot (Gustavsson & Gerhardsson, 2005); lead released into the air when lead-based paints were sanded from old buildings or bridges (Lead poisoning among sandblasting workers—Galveston, Texas, March 1994, 1995); herbal remedies contaminated with arsenic, lead, and other heavy metals (Lynch & Braithwaite, 2005); thallium-contaminated cocaine has been reported; arsenic may be released into the air from burning of coal that contains high levels of arsenic—a serious problem worldwide (Liu et al., 2002).

When toxins are a factor in causing illness, other individuals who have been exposed will also be affected. Inquire about whether co-workers, family members, housemates, neighbors, or others have had symptoms similar to the patient's. Have any pets been ill?

TRAVEL

Inquire about the patient's travel and any changes in residence, both recent and in the past, both within and outside the United States. Ask about military service experiences. Keep in mind that the prevalence of different infectious diseases varies greatly in different regions of the United States, as well as in areas around the globe.

Inquire about experiences that increase the likelihood of infection while traveling: having been bitten by insects, spiders, dogs, monkeys, bats, or other animals; swimming in fresh water; drinking or using ice made from potentially contaminated water; eating raw meat, fish, or shellfish; eating uncooked foods that were washed in the unsanitary water. Inquire about vaccination history and whether the individual took medications to prevent malaria. Be sure to ask whether the individual actually followed the directions in taking the antimalarial medications.

Mental symptoms from an infectious disease may emerge days, months, years, or even decades after first exposure. In some cases, this delay is because of the incubation period of the illness (i.e., the time between exposure and the first appearance of symptoms). Rabies, for instance, has an incubation period of up to a year. With other infectious diseases, after the systemic illness appears to have ended, the organism still may lie dormant in the brain; the mental manifestations of the disease may present only years later. This mechanism occurs with syphilis, HIV, Lyme disease, and some parasitic infections.

Many individuals have lived and worked where standards are low for workplace safety, food purity, air and water quality, and the control of toxic pollutants. These individuals may have an increased risk of having been exposed to toxic substances. In addition, consider the risk of having suffered from poor nutrition or physical trauma, including torture, which may have enduring effects on the brain and behavior.

WEIGHT AND NUTRITION

It may be only after a patient has lost or gained a considerable amount of weight that the possibility of an underlying physical problem is actively entertained. Inquire about any significant recent changes in the patient's weight, either up or down. Try to get this information in actual pounds. Some individuals will feel that a gain of one pound is catastrophic. Others will be glad to have lost 20 pounds "without trying," even though this may indicate a serious underlying medical problem.

If a change in weight is out of proportion to changes in the patient's eating and exercising, this raises the question of whether other forces are operating. The patient might have experienced a shift in metabolic functioning because of a disorder of the endocrine system or as a consequence of taking certain medications, including many psychotropic drugs. A loss of weight, sometimes of dramatic proportions, could signal the presence of other significant conditions: a malignancy that might be covert, a parasitic infection, HIV, or diseases that cause a lack of effective absorption from the gastrointestinal system.

In addition to the detrimental affects of serious starvation, deficiencies of specific nutrients are capable of producing mental symptoms, especially B12, thiamine, or niacin. Inquire about the patient's past and present nutritional status, looking for conditions that would predispose someone to malnutrition or vitamin deficiency diseases. Is the individual a vegetarian or a vegan? Does he or she take vitamin supplements? Has a patient's pregnancy been associated with severe vomiting? Nutritional concerns arise when an individual is too paranoid to eat or too disorganized to prepare or obtain balanced meals as a result of dementia or psychosis. Alcoholism also can have a significant impact on nutrition and may be associated with the severe mental effects of thiamine deficiency.

It is extremely important to guard against assuming that someone who is thin has anorexia nervosa. One must make the diagnosis of an eating disorder on the basis of the clinical criteria that are associated with anorexia nervosa, including the individual's eating patterns, such as bingeing, purging, patterns of restricting food, and distortions of body image. If a patient does have an eating disorder, keep in mind that distorted eating behaviors may lead to disruptions in normal physiology, upsetting the crucial electrolyte balance of the body, causing erosion of tooth enamel, scarring of the esophagus, and so on. Some of these conditions may be life threatening.

Two sleep disorders are associated with eating disturbances, and these will provide a transition to the next topic—sleep. Does the patient eat in the middle of the night? If so, does he or she have memories for these nocturnal binges or simply find candy wrappers and crumbs or a mess in the kitchen as "evidence" in the morning?

Individuals with *sleep-related eating disorder* have repeated nighttime arousals during which they engage in compulsive eating while in an altered state of consciousness. They may have a dim awareness or full amnesia for their nighttime binges.

Patients with *night-eating syndrome* display sleep-onset insomnia that is associated with compulsive, binge-like eating after dinner. These individuals consume most of their calories after the evening meal and often have a loss of appetite in the morning. They also may have nighttime arousals associated with eating, but these are generally in a full state of alertness (Winkelman, 2003).

SLEEP

Sleep is a complex phenomenon. A good night's sleep is necessary for optimal mental functioning. A healthy life, both physically and mentally, will maximize the likelihood of a good night's sleep. When evaluating a patient who has trouble with sleep and who also has daytime mental symptoms, it is often difficult to know which is causing which.

On the one hand, sleep is sensitive to disruption from numerous sources, including stress, mental disorders, and underlying medical disease. It is also affected by medications, alcohol, illegal drugs, caffeine, an environment that is noisy, too hot, or too cold, and so on. Therapists are ordinarily aware of how often a mental disturbance can lead, secondarily, to disruption of sleep (a secondary sleep disorder). In these situations, we expect the patient's sleep to return to normal after we have effectively dealt with the psychological problem, be it depression, anxiety, another mental disorder, or situational stress.

On the other hand, it is important to keep in mind that there are primary disturbances of sleep, including sleep apnea, restless legs syndrome, narcolepsy, and periodic leg movements of sleep, that may lead individuals to suffer secondarily with excessive daytime fatigue. These primary sleep disorders may lead to a multitude of prominent downstream effects: depression, anxiety, difficulty with concentration, slowed mental processing, declining work performance.

In order to provide optimal treatment, it is important to assess whether the patient has a primary sleep disorder, a secondary sleep disorder, or both. You might begin by simply asking, "How's your sleep?" But that is not enough. The behavioral neurologist Albert Galaburda tells the story of one of his patients who turned out to have severe sleep apnea. In answer to that open-ended question, his patient answered, "My sleep is fine. I can fall sleep anytime, anywhere." This is a classic symptom. The patient could fall asleep anywhere, anytime because he was always sleep deprived!

When inquiring about an individual's sleep, keep in mind the variety of problems individuals may have with sleep. Some patients have trouble falling asleep; others have trouble staying asleep; some individuals take a long time to fully wake up; some have disturbances in the rhythm of their sleep cycles, whereas others have abnormal sleep-related movements, abnormal breathing, or abnormal eating behaviors related to sleep, night terrors, nightmares that they may or may not act out during sleep, or sleep-associated seizures.

When taking a sleep history from the patient, keep in mind that the individual's bed partner may be the only one who knows about certain of the patient's nighttime behaviors. Here are some of the important questions to ask:

- What is your usual sleep routine? At what time do you generally get into bed? How long does it take you to fall asleep? How long do you stay asleep? When do you awaken? When would you wake up if you didn't use an alarm?
- What is your bedtime routine? Is there a calming-down period before sleep?
- Are the bed and the bedroom comfortable for sleeping?
- Are there things that wake you during the night, such as having to urinate, heartburn, children climbing into bed, bed partners snoring, etc.?

- Do you feel rested when you awaken from sleep?
- Are you tired during the daytime? How tired? Do you fall asleep at red lights? In meetings? During conversations? After meals?
- Do you nap? For how long? Are the naps restorative?
- Do you snore? Does your bed partner say that you snore?
- Do you make unusual, sleep-associated breathing noises or have periods of not breathing? Does your bed partner report any of these?
- Do you have any abnormal sleep-associated body movements? Does your bed partner report these? How do the bed linens look in the morning?
- Do you have any funny feelings in your legs? Does anything make these sensations go away?
- Do you have nightmares? Do you ever act on your nightmares during sleep? Have you ever hit your bed partner during sleep? Have you ever injured yourself during sleep?
- Do you ever have experiences that feel like nightmares but that are devoid of the imagery and content of dreaming (night terrors)?
- Do you ever have incontinence during sleep?
- Do you ever bite your tongue during sleep?
- Do you ever walk in your sleep?
- How much caffeine do you consume and at what times of day? In your inquiry be sure to include coffee, tea—including green tea, caffeinated sodas, chocolate, and decaffeinated beverages.
- Do you use medications that might have an impact your level of wakefulness, such as stimulants or sedatives?
- Do you use any pills to help with sleep?

PSYCHOMOTOR ACTIVITY

Psychomotor activity is another arena that is commonly affected by organic conditions as well as functional ones. There are two ends of the spectrum, diminished psychomotor activity and increased psychomotor activity. On the lower end, it is important to differentiate several symptoms that are readily confused. Fatigue, weakness, loss of stamina, and apathy are terms that are often used interchangeably by patients. These should be differentiated one from another, as they have distinct meanings as well as different diagnostic significance. They are all commonly mistaken for depression. On the high-energy end of the spectrum, it is important to distinguish restlessness, agitation, hyperactivity, irritability, and excessive exercising. These also have widely different diagnostic significance.

SEXUAL FUNCTIONING AND INTEREST

Inquire as to whether there have been any changes in the individual's level of sexual interest. Has the patient had difficulties in sexual functioning, such as maintaining an erection, reaching orgasm, vaginal lubrication, or pain during intercourse? Changes in libido and sexual functioning may be sensitive markers for psychological disturbances and/or physiologic changes.

Though less common, it is also important to ascertain whether there have been changes in sexual behavior. This category would include disinhibited or uncensored social behavior, such as telling erotic jokes in inappropriate settings, or making sexual advances to strangers. An early symptom of what might later become a more obvious change in personality might be an uncharacteristic sexual affair. In addition, a change in the type of preferred sexual activity could be significant if it is truly new and not simply the freeing of a long-held but previously secret desire. For instance, someone who switches from enjoying typical romantic sex to a preference for dominance and bondage or unusual erotic objects could have an underlying neurological problem.

OTHER CHANGES IN BEHAVIOR

Here are some other behavioral changes that are notable. It may be useful to inquire about the following, as you might uncover new information:

- Religious conversions may be associated with certain neurologic disorders.
- Changes in handwriting may be evidence of tremors or problems with coordination. Writing becomes smaller with Parkinson's disease.
- Changes in reading habits or TV-watching might signal cognitive changes.
- Trouble with the law and any history of arrests is important information, especially if this is new behavior.
- Changes in the area of language, such as diminished comprehension, being more or less talkative, a change in accent, stuttering, word-finding, and so on are strongly associated with organic disease.
- Automobile accidents, including minor accidents, may be significant in revealing any deficits that interfere with driving. Are there dings on both sides of the car or only on one side, implying a possible sensory or attentional deficit on that side? How comfortable are others with the patient as a driver?

- Addictive behaviors that are new are worthy of notice. Impulse disorders such as pathological gambling have been associated with certain treatments for Parkinson's disease.
- Falls with or without loss of consciousness are important symptoms that need medical follow-up.
- Is there a change in gait or trouble with walking?
- Are there changes in the patient's behavior in social situations?
- Has the patient's work situation changed and what are the reasons for this?
- Has the patient's educational situation changed and what are the reasons for this?
- Is the patient aware of having been exposed to any illnesses?

Activities of Daily Living

It is useful to go over the individual's activities of daily living and to ascertain whether there have been any changes in areas of functioning such as:

- Maintaining friendships
- Hobbies
- Handling personal finances
- Driving
- Caring for others, including pets
- Mobility
- Shopping for food and preparing meals
- Managing personal hygiene and grooming
- Dressing
- Toileting

Chapter 11

Extended Clinical Vignettes— Working With Patients

Introduction

Extended clinical vignettes are used in this chapter to illustrate how to work with patients when one suspects that an organic component is contributing to or causing the patients' problems. This chapter also presents fundamental attitudes and approaches that facilitate creative and effective clinical work; these are what the educational theorist Theodore Sizer called intellectual habits or habits of mind (Sizer, 1997).

Habits of mind are deeper and broader than the myriad of important strategies that have so far been presented: interviewing techniques, being thorough in your investigation, thinking about the timeline of an illness, distinguishing a sign from a symptom, and so on. Habits of mind are fundamental approaches to the acquisition of data, to problem solving, and to a deep engagement with the diagnostic task. The following habits are crucial in detecting covert physical illnesses in your patients, and they are important in working with patients in treatment:

- Taking it on
- Thinking diagnostically
- Monitoring all your perceptions as data
- Thinking scientifically
- Practicing persistence and patience
- Tolerating uncertainty and helplessness
- Dealing with inevitable blind spots
- Cultivating learning and a spirit of curiosity

Each extended clinical vignette in this chapter will be used to illustrate one of these habits of mind, but each narrative actually illustrates many of them. These clinical stories are true-to-life. They attempt to capture complex realities. They do not necessarily have happy endings. All of the loose ends may not be tied up at the end of the story. We might not know for sure what was the matter with the patient. These accounts are peopled with individuals who are difficult to work with, patients as well as clinicians. This chapter is not about working in an ideal world but about doing the very best one can in the face of difficult realities.

Taking It On

Take it on. This is the first order of business no matter what the clinical situation, whether you are seeing a patient in a private psychotherapy office, a school, or a nursing home, whether you are a consultant or a long-term therapist. At first glance, "take it on" may seem like very basic advice, and it is—basic, fundamental, yet difficult to accomplish. What I am suggesting is that you take full responsibility for actively thinking through what is the matter with your patient, that you commit yourself as though you were the first and only clinician the patient would see. This means operating with the idea that if *you* don't do it, it won't get done.

Accomplishing this may require a shift in mind-set. You are not just stepping in but rather stepping up. This may be particularly difficult to achieve when working as part of a team, especially if the team is informally configured. Under these circumstances, the natural tendency is for a diffusion of responsibility to develop.

On a treatment team in a busy clinical setting, efficiency is a priority and responsibility is generally distributed. It is common for team members to take at face value another clinician's understanding of a patient, including any working diagnoses. It is also common to get the history from the chart or from the prior therapist. This practice tends to perpetuate oversights and errors and to minimize the discovery of new, potentially important information. As a team member, it is easy to assume that someone else has a complete picture of the patient's situation in mind, that someone else has taken responsibility to review the chart, check on the full medical history, spoken with the family members and former therapist, and so on. One of my students told me the following story that is illustrative of this point.

> *The student was assigned to an inpatient psychiatry unit where she was one of a team of professionals who were taking care of a 50-year-old woman with a history of bipolar disorder. The woman was particularly memorable to my student, because this was the first time she had seen someone who*

was truly manic. She also got to observe the patient's behavior over many weeks, because during this hospitalization the patient's mania did not respond to any of the usual treatments. The staff became worn out and discouraged.

A breakthrough in the case came when a trainee in neurology began his 1-month training rotation on the psychiatry service. This young neurologist interviewed the patient. He reviewed all of her records and noted that something important had been overlooked. The patient had a history of lung cancer. Knowing that lung cancer has several ways of affecting the brain, this information started the whole team onto a new line of investigation.

This patient was found to have paraneoplastic syndrome, which is rare but known to cause dramatic mental status changes. The mechanism behind this syndrome is complex. A recurrence of this patient's lung cancer triggered the production of antibodies that kept the cancer under control and therefore hidden. But the antibodies also cross-reacted with parts of the patient's brain, leading to her prominent mental symptoms.

In this patient, the cancer was from the lung and the manifestation was mania. In other patients, the cancer might be ovarian or testicular and the manifestation might be a psychosis. What is important here is that any member of the team could have made note of this patient's history of lung cancer, a tumor that frequently recurs and often metastasizes to the brain. It turned out that this patient had a more obscure mechanism for her treatment-resistant mania, but any professional on the team could have drawn attention to the possibility that lung cancer was a covert factor. It took someone who was new to the situation to discover this crucial factor; it took someone who made a commitment to thinking through the case from start to finish like a new detective on the job.

Here is another example of how there can be a diffusion of responsibility when patients are cared for in an institution over long periods of time.

One day in supervision, Jason, a fourth-year resident in psychiatry, asked me if he could present a "psychopharm" patient rather than discuss one of the individuals we had been following from his psychotherapy clinic. Jason was perturbed and confused because his patient had been behaving in ways that were out of the ordinary, and he didn't know what to make of it.

Mr. Kraft was a middle-aged patient who had been referred to the clinic 10 years earlier for an anxiety disorder by the primary care physician who continued to follow him. Mr. Kraft was well known in the outpatient psychopharmacology clinic as a kind and reticent true gentleman. He was also well known because he had been going to the clinic for a long time, handed on from resident to resident every 2 years. Jason was his fifth psychiatrist.

In this context, everyone was astounded when Mr. Kraft left an irate message for Jason on the clinic's after-hours general voicemail. Jason tactfully brought up the matter of the phone message at Mr. Kraft's next appointment. Mr. Kraft was quite disturbed by this discussion, because he had no memory of making any such phone call!

Then the patient told Jason that recently another strange thing had happened; over that past weekend, neighbors in his apartment building had called the police and complained that Mr. Kraft had been "yelling and stomping around" in the hallways. Mr. Kraft had no memory of doing those things either. I could tell that Jason's intuitive sense was that Mr. Kraft had real amnesia for these incidents.

Jason and I talked about the possible diagnostic causes of episodic behavior of this sort. The list included problems with drugs or alcohol including blackouts, episodes of dissociation (perhaps in association with posttraumatic stress disorder), or a seizure disorder that might have a variety of possible underlying causes (e.g., a brain tumor, a history of head trauma, a genetic predisposition, or alcohol withdrawal).

In light of this discussion about the diagnostic possibilities, Jason and I reviewed Mr. Kraft's history. It was the first time that Jason had read carefully through the previous years of notes. When the primary care physician had first referred the patient to the clinic 10 years earlier, she had wanted the patient to be treated with medications for an anxiety disorder. That anxiety disorder had begun a few months after Mr. Kraft had been in a serious car accident. It was clear that Mr. Kraft had been very upset by the accident and that his primary care physician had believed that this was the precipitant for his anxiety. It was also clear that the auto accident had involved some head injury, but it was not clear how serious that head trauma had been.

In the clinic, Mr. Kraft was first treated with an antianxiety medication. Over the years, a variety of different antianxiety drugs as well as a number of antidepressants had been tried. A fairly high dose of clonazepam was settled on as the most helpful of the options; clonazepam is an antianxiety medication that, like many antianxiety drugs, also has anticonvulsant properties. Everyone accepted that Mr. Kraft was suffering from an anxiety disorder: the patient, the primary care physician, the numerous residents over the 10 years, and presumably their supervisors.

Yet over this time period as a succession of residents cared for Mr. Kraft, the patient went from being a productive, competent engineer to a more and more reclusive man who was on long-term disability by the age of 55. None of the clinicians caring for Mr. Kraft seemed to have made note of the steady decline in Mr. Kraft's life, and now Jason was reporting this odd, uncharacteristic behavior. Jason and I began to look more carefully at the working diagnosis of an anxiety disorder. We focused on what exactly constituted Mr. Kraft's anxiety symptoms. It turned out that they were mostly episodic. He complained of feeling "fear" and "dread."

Jason and I began to hone in on our list of possible diagnoses. Now we were looking for a diagnosis that would not only explain the patient's recent odd behavior but that would also explain his downhill course and his episodic symptoms of fear and dread. There were two main items on the list. The first was a covert drug or alcohol problem. The second was a partial seizure disorder (possibly secondary to his head trauma) that had worsened over time until he had a partial complex seizure manifest as verbally explosive behavior with a disturbance of consciousness and subsequent amnesia for the episode. Now we had diagnostic notions with strong explanatory power.

Next, we plotted a course of action to try to make a definitive diagnosis. The first step was for Jason to have a full discussion with the patient. In the next psychotherapy session, Jason explained that he had reviewed the history and had been thinking quite seriously about the big picture of Mr. Kraft's last 10 years, including the recent behaviors that had been so disturbing and puzzling for everyone, including the patient. Jason told the patient that he had begun to question whether an anxiety disorder was the full explanation. The patient was very glad to have his doctor's diagnostic thinking fully focused on his difficulties. He was happy to answer Jason's questions.

He only had "a glass of wine at dinner, sometimes two." No, he "never took drugs, other than the ones that were prescribed." Jason believed him. As for the seizure disorder idea, Mr. Kraft stated, "That seems utterly impossible!" Of course, he agreed that Jason could "have a full discussion" with his primary care doctor.

Jason presented the primary care physician with the historical and symptomatic evidence that Mr. Kraft might have developed a complex partial seizure disorder and that a neurological workup was appropriate. But Jason failed to persuade her to reconsider her original diagnostic impression. The primary care doctor did not think that a neurological consultation was needed. Jason also tried his best to persuade the patient to see a neurologist, but the patient said that he trusted his primary care doctor and adamantly asserted, "I can't possibly have a seizure disorder."

Jason and I talked a lot about Mr. Kraft's situation. We talked about why the patient might be so resolute about dismissing the possibility of having a seizure disorder; we hypothesized about what this potential diagnosis might mean to him. We pondered how upsetting it was to

witness a patient worsen "during your watch." We elucidated how diffi-
cult it is to distinguish a seizure disorder from episodes of panic or anx-
iety. We underlined how important it is for each new clinician to
rethink a patient's diagnosis and how difficult it is to find time for this
in a busy clinic. We remarked on how you can't unquestioningly rely on
the primary care doctor to rule out organic disease.

It was June; Jason was about to graduate and hand Mr. Kraft over to
yet another resident. Jason passed all this information along to Mr.
Kraft's next resident in the psychopharmacology clinic. We hoped that
Mr. Kraft would eventually agree to a neurology consultation. If he did
have a seizure disorder, there would be more effective treatment available
for him.

What are the lessons to be learned here? Especially when one has a
difficult patient, or a treatment that feels stuck, it is useful to start with
a fresh look and a determination to figure out how to understand what
has happened to the patient over time, what the initial causes of trouble
were, what has led to improvement or deterioration. This can be an
engaging and interesting challenge; let it be the focus of your attention.
Remember that it is possible for a string of well-meaning, well-trained
clinicians to miss important diagnoses.

The common practice of delegating the task of ruling out a medical
disorder to the primary care physician or the psychopharmacologist is
fraught with difficulty. These clinicians are also pressed for time, making
it unlikely that they will take on the task of rethinking the whole timeline
of the patient's narrative and revising their diagnostic impressions.
Research has been shown that it is difficult for clinicians to shift their
mindset once they have decided on how to understand a patient's symptoms. This is known as *anchoring* (Croskerry, 2003). Primary care physicians and psychopharmacologists often have settled on the patient's
diagnoses and limited their role in caring for the patient; visits may be
focused narrowly on current problems.

In addition, given that patients commonly switch primary care
doctors and psychopharmacologists as their insurance changes, the physicians may not actually know the patient or the complexity of the
patient's clinical situation as well as you do. When seeking consultation
from physicians, be sure to fully communicate your understanding of the
patient and your reasons for suspecting that he or she may have an
underlying medical disease. It is frequently helpful to do this in writing
in addition to having a phone conversation with the consultant, always
with the patient's permission. This will facilitate a medical workup that
is targeted to ruling out the pertinent diagnostic possibilities. Do not be
hesitant to encourage the patient to seek a second opinion if you are

concerned that the first clinician may have overlooked an underlying medical disease. Taking it on means taking on the ultimate responsibility for oversight and coordination.

Diagnostic Thinking

Figuring out the patient's diagnosis or diagnoses is an indispensable first step in providing effective treatment. It is easy to forget this crucial task as one is swept into the role of caring for an individual patient. Day-to-day management decisions readily take center stage. Is the patient suicidal? Do you have permission to talk to this patient's spouse? Where will the homeless woman sleep tonight? Do you need to report the possibility of child abuse in this case?

Management thinking focuses directly on what to do in the present, while diagnostic thinking focuses on what is fundamentally the matter. Clinical management decisions are essential, but they are quite different from making a diagnosis as a first step in generating an effective, long-term treatment plan. Think of how differently you would approach the treatment of a patient who has little motivation to get back to work if you knew that the patient had: (a) major depression, as opposed to (b) antisocial personality disorder, or (c) early Alzheimer's disease versus (d) a benign brain tumor with apathy, or (e) terminal pancreatic cancer presenting as a severe depression. A plan of action is best formulated when informed by knowledge of the patient's underlying diagnosis. In other words, having a diagnostic understanding of the problem will actually help in making management decisions.

Another distraction from thinking diagnostically occurs when clinicians focus exclusively on understanding the patient's psychodynamics. A psychodynamic approach involves coming to see the unique ways in which this individual thinks, feels, and experiences the world. The psychodynamic therapist comes to understand the special meanings that a particular patient gives to events and from what personal experiences those meanings have been derived.

Making a diagnosis, on the other hand, involves recognizing characteristics that your patient shares with other individuals who have the same disorder, whether it is a somatic or mental disorder. Seeing a pattern of commonality requires a view from a somewhat different perspective than that required in understanding the inner world of an individual. Being a good clinician requires both psychodynamic and diagnostic thinking.

A psychologist told me about a consultation he had done for a younger colleague. This story may serve as an example of how an empathic, psychodynamic approach can crowd out crucial, diagnostic thinking, to the detriment of the patient. Both are needed.

This story also illustrates an effective consultation for a stalled therapy.

> The patient was a 35-year-old, Catholic dentist who had attended church-affiliated schools as a youngster. He had worked on many issues during his 5 years in psychotherapy, but what had really motivated his weekly visits to the therapist was one very specific symptom. "I just can't stop thinking about nuns and priests having sex with one another. And what kind of person thinks like this?" The patient was plagued by this symptom and tortured by its implications. He noted that he had spent 5 years in therapy, delving into his personal history and exploring innumerable, possible motives for these thoughts; nonetheless, the thoughts had remained unchanged.
>
> The consultant was thinking diagnostically when he made two important observations. First, he noted that these thoughts about the nuns and priests felt alien to the patient. Second, the consultant found his attention drawn to odd, repeated movements of the patient's neck. He asked the patient about this. "Oh, that's just a gesture I make when I'm nervous."
>
> Like a good diagnostic and scientific thinker, the consultant now had a possible diagnosis in mind. Intrusive thoughts that did not respond to psychotherapy plus a possible motor tic might add up to Tourette's syndrome. He proceeded by asking further questions, looking for information that would either disprove or confirm his theory. The clincher was an additional piece of history: The patient's younger brother used to bark. This was supporting evidence for the diagnosis of Tourette's syndrome—a family history.
>
> The consulting psychologist referred the patient to a specialist in Tourette's syndrome. Here the patient learned that individuals with Tourette's syndrome frequently have intrusive thoughts and that these thoughts are entirely involuntary. The patient was very relieved to hear this but not entirely convinced that he had this disorder.
>
> The specialist then explained that individuals with Tourette's syndrome have movements (like the patient's odd neck twisting) or vocalizations (such as the patient's brother's barking) that are called tics. These tics are preceded by a buildup of unpleasant sensations or tensions that can only be released by ticking. In other words, patients are able to suppress the tics for awhile, but eventually the internal sensory experience makes it more and more difficult to refrain from the action. This description matched the patient's experience precisely.
>
> The specialist then offered some medication options, but the patient declined. He felt that he had just received from the specialist the treatment he

had needed all along. Really, what had disturbed him so profoundly had never been the symptom itself; it had been the meaning of the symptom. The diagnosis of Tourette's syndrome gave him clear assurance that his thoughts about nuns and priests having sex did not reflect on his morality or on the goodness of his soul.

This case illustrates a further point bearing on psychotherapy; when a patient gains a correct diagnostic understanding of a symptom, it often is both clarifying and relieving. For many individuals there is a sense of relief at simply knowing the true nature of the situation and having a name for what is wrong. There also may be renewed hopefulness.

To be sure, patients' reactions to the discovery that they have a medical disorder will be complex and can complicate the therapeutic relationship in numerous ways. One patient told me that it was "hard to learn" that she had attention deficit hyperactivity disorder. She clarified that even though this diagnosis offered her the hope of treatment and the possibility that she might be more effective in her life, it also required that she rethink her memories and her concept of herself. In addition, she was angry about not having known about this sooner and also angry that it was true.

Monitor Your Feelings as Data

Thus far, this book has focused mainly on data that resides in the patient. How does the patient look and behave? What does the patient say that he or she feels? But there is additional information available to us. As clinicians, as human beings, we respond to our patients on a millisecond-to-millisecond basis. These internal reactions are an important potential source of information about our patients, and these warrant some attention.

SENSORY EXPERIENCES AS INFORMATION

Let's first look at our sensory experiences. In evaluating patients, we are mainly aware of relying on sight and hearing to provide data for our clinical assessments. How does the patient look? What do the facial expressions and gestures convey? And what does the tone, the cadence, and the quality of his or her voice communicate?

Other ways of perceiving are always operating as well. Smell sometimes provides important clues about a patient. Consider, for instance, the body odor that tells you someone has not washed for weeks or the bad breath related to poor oral hygiene. These may be the consequence of a disorganizing disease process such as a dementia or a severe psychosis. The aroma of alcohol is another important clinical clue, as is peppermint breath, which may be evidence of an effort to cover up the smell of alcohol or tobacco. In addition, experienced clinicians are attuned to other odors that can result from disorders of metabolism, nutritional deficiencies, toxic states, and certain skin diseases. For instance, arsenic poisoning is associated with the smell of garlic, cyanide poisoning with the odor of bitter almonds, kidney failure with ammonia, liver failure with rotten eggs, and the metabolic derangements caused by starvation or diabetes are associated with a fruity smell (Senol & Fireman, 1999).

THE THERAPIST'S FEELING STATE AS INFORMATION

Your feeling state and mental associations upon interacting with a patient are also important sources of information. Some patients will give you the creeps or repulse you, make you mad, lead you to feel frightened, stuck, withholding, ineffectual, or helpless. There are a thousand variations. Have you noticed, for example, how you might feel comfortably competent with one patient and then remarkably incompetent during the very next hour with a different individual? This kind of data—information that comes from personal reflection—may provide important clues about a patient's psychological makeup and modes of relating. It is also possible that you might be reacting to patient behavior that is actually a sign of some underlying physical disorder.

For example, perhaps you are frustrated in your efforts to get a complete history in the time allotted. Is this because the patient is vague? Apathetic? Easily distracted? Exhibiting pressured speech and therefore difficult to interrupt? Tangential? Each of these is an important mental status finding. Perhaps you find yourself somewhat frightened. Is the patient belligerent, paranoid, agitated, impulsive? Again, these are important observations about the individual's mental state. The clues are in your feelings.

TRUSTING YOUR EXPERIENCES

Self-reflection in the interest of gathering data about the patient may be the toughest part of being a clinician. It is often quite difficult to hone in on exactly what you are responding to in a patient's presentation. It may be even more difficult to decipher how much of your reaction is a response to the patient and how much is based on meanings that you bring to the interaction. It is easy to second-guess your intuitions, and often important to get second opinions.

It is even easy to second-guess your perceptions. When it is just you and your patient sitting alone in an office and a momentary event occurs, it is easy to wonder whether what you saw had any significance, and it is easy to doubt whether you really saw anything at all. Was there really a micro-moment of slurred speech? Was that a tic or just a gesture? Did the patient fleetingly turn inward, or was that a brief alteration in consciousness? Was there alcohol on her breath? Is it significant or irrelevant that he seemed to lose his balance upon turning into your office doorway? When she smiled, was the asymmetry something of note? Did you imagine these things or interpret them as significant because of something coming from you? I am reminded of a story about how difficult it can be to trust one's perceptions.

My friend, Steven, had been swimming in shallow water along the coast of Costa Rica when he suddenly found himself caught in a powerful current. Apparently Steven had crossed an invisible, shifting line that divided the safe from the dangerous water. He was in a riptide. Steven swam as hard as he could, trying to get out of the current.

"I was just a few feet from a woman who grabbed my hand," he told me. "But she wasn't strong enough to pull me in. Eventually I let go, afraid she also would get pulled into the riptide." Steven was being drawn farther and farther away from the shore. As hard as he swam, he could make no headway. He was exhausted and utterly terrified, but he kept swimming toward shore, because "the alternative was the vast, empty sea." Luckily, within minutes, Steven was swept along to an area where his feet could touch bottom. It was far out but shallow. He caught his breath. Then help arrived.

What was remarkable about the incident was this: Steven told me that the moment he felt safe he began to doubt his experience. Had there really been any danger? Maybe he had just panicked. He was only a few feet from where he had been swimming all day. No one else had this experience. By dinnertime he had convinced himself that the dreadful sense that his life had been in jeopardy had been entirely a creation of his mind. This he found to be even more disturbing.

On the way out of the hotel restaurant that evening, Steven was rescued from this state of mind. A Costa Rican worker at the hotel passed my friend on the veranda and in a casual and warm voice said, "Hey, I saw what happened to you today. That's a mighty strong current. I was caught in it last week. Scared me to death."

Steven experienced this brief comment as empathic and generous. Ever since, he has been free of doubt about the veracity of his encounter with the riptide.

This story also illustrates the importance of validation in holding onto one's perceptions. When in doubt about a clinical situation or experience, it may be fruitful to talk with others who know the patient in order to ascertain whether your experience of the patient is unique or not.

UTILIZING YOUR REACTIONS TO MAKE A DIAGNOSIS

The following story illustrates how a therapist's emotional reactions to a patient were utilized to make a crucial, medical diagnosis.

I had already known Trisha for 8 years when she was fired by her employer and escorted from her office without warning or reasonable explanation. She had consulted me years before to help with her recovery from a string of abusive relationships, beginning with repeated sexual abuse by a neighbor. She also wanted support for her hard-won abstinence from alcohol.

Being summarily fired would surely reverberate with her early traumatic experiences; I knew it would revive memories of helplessness, bewilderment, a sense that she "must have done something wrong" and also intense shame. Predictably, Trisha became depressed.

In psychotherapy, Trisha expressed her anger about being treated unjustly and "like her feelings didn't matter." Despite my validation of her emotional reactions and despite my interpreting the link between her current loss, confusion, and humiliation with those same feelings in the past, Trisha's grim mood, lack of energy, and loss of motivation persisted. Given that Trisha and I had an established therapeutic relationship and that I had seen her through many other difficult life events, I expected that she would recover in a matter of months. But Trisha was not bouncing back from this startling and mortifying experience, even though, over time, it became apparent that her firing had been politically motivated and that she had done nothing that warranted her dismissal.

Trisha's mental state was going downhill, and I found myself unable to stop it. She complained of intense fatigue, slept for long stretches at night, and napped each day. She became accident-prone, smashing the car door into her leg, twisting her ankle on an uneven sidewalk, and so on. She had several emergency room visits for traumatic injuries, ragged lacerations that were difficult to suture. These accidents seemed to be a consequence of the patient's increased distractibility as well as her tendency to minimize pain and to experience actual numbing, typical with chronic posttraumatic stress disorder. I worried.

Then, in an unexpected way, a breakthrough occurred—I went on a 2-week vacation. Upon returning, when I saw Trisha in my waiting room, I was startled at my immediate, negative, gut-level reaction. I was seeing her with different eyes. In all likelihood, having been away for two weeks gave me a bit of distance on subtle changes that had been taking place in Trisha's body for some time, just as distant relatives are more able to see a child's growth than are the parents. Trisha suddenly looked to me like a chronic, end-stage alcoholic, just like the skid-row patients I remembered from my city hospital training. Her abdomen stuck out like a basketball and contrasted with her skinny legs and arms. Her face was round and red in the middle. But Trisha had stopped drinking more than 10 years before. Though it seemed unlikely, I wondered whether Trisha's current predicament had led this veteran AA member to surreptitiously reach for the bottle again.

I think that my sense of trust in Trisha, along with my empathy and fond feelings for her, led me to take a serious and considered look at the meaning of these vivid, negative thoughts and associations that I was having. These reactions were surprising to me, because they stood in stark contrast to my previous feelings toward Trisha. While reflecting on the situation, quite suddenly, I realized what was actually the matter with Trisha. It is difficult to reconstruct such an "a-ha!" experience, difficult to identify all the various factors that converge and, in a flash, lead to seeing things in an altogether new way. Such moments result from a process of unconscious synthesis. My interest in organic illnesses causing and complicating psychological disorders undoubtedly contributed to my unconscious problem solving.

I realized that the look of Trisha's body could have been produced by something other than chronic alcoholism. It could have developed as a result of chronic, excessive levels of cortisol, a hormone produced by the adrenal glands. Cortisol and various forms of this hormonal substance are familiar as "miracle" medications, used for a myriad of diseases, from asthma to poison ivy. I also realized that Trisha's unremitting depression could be a result of the same hormonal aberration.

If Trisha was suffering from excessive cortisol or related hormones, I figured that she would also have other signs and symptoms consistent with that diagnosis that could not be perceived from across the room. So, I asked Trisha. Did she have purple streaks, stretch marks, on her abdomen? Indeed she did. How tired had she really been? Bone tired, unlike anything she had ever experienced before with depression. Was her skin thinned? Yes, that's why the doctors had so much trouble suturing her lacerations; the stitches would "tear through." In fact, her skin had almost no resilience and would split open with a minor impact. This information put her accidents in a new perspective.

Trisha and I hatched a plan that seemed foolproof. First, she would share my diagnostic thoughts with her primary care physician, and then I would follow up with a phone call to him. We would rely on the PCP for a medical workup to see if my theory about Trisha's diagnosis would hold up to scientific scrutiny. We did not anticipate that Trisha's primary care physician would have the same gut-level reaction that I initially had. He simply said that, in his clinical opinion, Trisha's physical problems were a result of her alcoholism. Trisha felt deeply confused. Perhaps he was right. Perhaps she had done something wrong; perhaps her past drinking had ruined her long-term health. Whom should she trust?

I began to doubt myself as well. Perhaps the primary care physician was right. I had little experience with diseases of the endocrine system. In addition, I had to acknowledge that I was not a neutral observer. I cared about my patient and had been feeling badly about her not getting better. Perhaps I was engaged in wishful thinking. But Trisha had felt hurt by her PCP's sense of unwavering certainty and his dismissive tone. Trisha thought it was a good idea to take my suggestion and consult with an endocrine specialist. When Trisha saw the endocrinologist, she handed him a letter that I had written in which I carefully laid out the signs and symptoms in support of my diagnostic hypothesis. This physician confirmed that Trisha had excessive levels of cortisol-like hormones.

But the diagnostic investigation was not over yet. We still needed to uncover the source of the problem with Tisha's cortisol levels. Did Trisha have a pituitary tumor that was causing her adrenal gland to produce excess cortisol? Did she have a tumor of the adrenal gland? Or perhaps she was taking medications that contained cortisol or related hormones. In truth, it was difficult to track down the actual source of Trisha's problem. Only gradually did it emerge that a complex drug interaction played a role—the combination of an inhaler containing a form of cortisol plus nefazodone, an antidepressant that is no longer available in the United States. Trisha had been using inhalers for her chronic obstructive pulmonary disease for years; they had not caused her any trouble until she lost her job and began to take nefazodone as well. Over time this combination led to the physical and mental changes characteristic of Cushing's syndrome. Switching from nefazodone to a different antidepressant and temporarily stopping the inhalers led to a gradual improvement in Trisha's health and in her mood. Only then was she able to recover from the traumatic loss of her job.

When you get an inkling that your patient may have an organic condition, turn your thoughts inward. What were you responding to when you first thought, "organic"? Was there something about the patient's illness course that made you wonder about this possibility? Did you observe something important? Or, as you interacted with the patient, did you feel something that you now realize was a vital clue? Review the case. Make a list of your evidence.

Think Scientifically

Scientific thinking is different from diagnostic thinking, although both are utilized in clinical situations. Diagnostic thinking focuses on being able to categorize or name the problem: a mood disorder, a character disorder, an addiction, Cushing's syndrome, a pituitary tumor, sleep apnea, diabetes. In contrast, scientific thinking is the process of getting to that diagnostic solution.

Scientific thinking involves answering these three questions about the evidence: What do we know? How do we know it? And how certain is this knowledge? The clinician weighs the evidence and generates a list of possible diagnoses; this is called the differential diagnosis. Finally, the clinician comes up with a logical strategy for figuring out which of these diagnoses the patient actually has.

This may sound like a procedure one does with paper and pencil, deliberately in preparation for supervision or a case conference. Although it is useful to review one's thinking in such a conscious and reflective manner, scientific thinking also needs to be ever-present as an approach to the acquisition of information about a patient. In clinical work, scientific thinking is a continuous attitude of questioning the degree of certainty one has about those things one thinks one knows. It is also a continuous process of generating and testing hypotheses about what the patient's underlying diagnoses might be. This kind of thinking is actually quite natural. We do it all the time.

Here is an example of how a scientific approach to information occurs in the mind of a therapist during a therapy session.

> *One of my patients ran a small charitable organization. She was angry with Joe, the bookkeeper in her office. She told me that "this guy Joe" was "really problematic," and that he made "everyone in the office mad." I knew with reasonable certainty that my patient was a tolerant and flexible woman, so I thought it was quite likely (but not certain) that Joe was actually doing things that made her mad. My degree of certainty was enhanced by the patient's report that she was not the only one who found Joe problematic. I found myself wondering whether Joe might have a character disorder, but I knew that this was pure speculation.*
>
> *I asked my patient to tell me more about Joe and what made people so angry with him. "Well, on the one hand he's very reliable and precise in his work, but on the other, he's slow and really inflexible." I asked her for more details. "Okay, here's an example. He gets furious when staff members turn in their reimbursable receipts late . . . if they've traveled to a meeting or if they've taken a donor out for lunch. He really can't stand it. It throws off his books or something. And when contributors make out a check dated for the*

last day of the year but don't get it to him until mid-January . . . he simply doesn't know what to do with that. You know, donors want the donation to be recorded as an end-of-year donation, but Joe's already closed the books on that year. He's a rule-follower, and he's very into morality. He thinks the donors' behavior is wrong."

Now I was developing other ideas about Joe because I had new information. He was reliable and precise but slow. He was lacking in flexibility, a rule-follower. He had a strong sense of morality. Now I had a new idea. Perhaps Joe had an autism-spectrum disorder, but I knew that this was just a theory. "So, what's he like in other ways?" I asked. "Oh, his voice is too loud. Everyone can hear him on the phone from his cubicle. We've talked to him about it, but he doesn't listen. Really, I don't think he has any friends in the office. He's a bit odd. I don't stop by to say hello to him because he'll just bend my ear and go on and on. And, he never asks about me. He does have an amazing amount of information in that brain of his. He can be interesting, but I can never get away. I just don't have the time for it . . . even though I think he's really a sweet and lonely person inside." Now I'm starting to feel more certain about my autism-spectrum hypothesis.

She continued: "Oh, and let me tell you about how he is around office parties. First of all he just doesn't go to parties . . . well, unless we personally go and get him. Then he sits in a corner and doesn't participate. One time I felt really sorry for him, so I went over and we had a really nice talk. He told me about his license plate collection . . . . only plates from Missouri—where he's from. And you know what? He talked about that party for days after. He had a really good time."

Okay, now I had even more data. Joe seemed to shun group social interactions, although I didn't know exactly why. It would be premature to say he had social anxiety, especially as he seemed glad to talk to my patient whenever she did stop by his office. Also, it sounded as though Joe was verbose and perhaps encyclopedic in his knowledge, but only perhaps. Maybe he was pedantic, but I did not have any real evidence of that. I did know with certainty, however, that he had an odd hobby and one that was concrete. These bits of information were converging to form a clearer diagnostic picture.

I was feeling quite certain now that Joe had high-level autism, and I told this to my patient. She was startled. "That explains everything! Now I have a lot more empathy for the poor guy." Joe looked like he was "simply" an annoying, rigid, insensitive, inflexible, unsociable person, but probably he had a serious problem that had plagued him from childhood, namely an autism-spectrum disorder. Even though I felt quite comfortable about this diagnosis, I knew that I had never met Joe, so I would have to keep in mind that there was still some degree of uncertainty about this diagnostic impression.

The next story demonstrates the dangers of not utilizing scientific thinking. Several competent clinicians concluded that stress was the cause of this patient's symptoms, though it is not clear on what basis they made that diagnostic decision or how much private doubt each practitioner had. Wishful thinking may have trumped scientific thinking and led to a delay in identifying the true diagnosis.

Marilyn came to see me for therapy and told me this chilling story about her first husband, Jacob. Marilyn and Jacob had moved from the United States to Europe when Jacob got a new job working for a bank. It was a very stressful time, not only because of the move and the new job, but also because Jacob suspected that his new boss was involved in illegal activities.

Under these conditions, Jacob developed what he had called the worst headaches of his life; he had them virtually every day. He also had a peculiar symptom. He experienced "a sort of dizziness" on his way up to his office in the elevator each morning, but he did not experience this sensation on the way down in the elevator at the end of the day. Naturally, he came to believe that his symptoms were driven by his anxiety about the complex political situation he faced at work.

Jacob consulted a physician, who reassured him that his symptoms were caused by stress, but Marilyn was worried. She knew her husband, and she believed that this was not the way "my laid-back guy" would respond to such a circumstance. Jacob and Marilyn's close friends advised taking some time off. So happily, the couple set out for a week's vacation at a country inn. While driving there, Jacob developed another headache and vomited, but the couple felt reassured because acetaminophen seemed to relieve the headache.

After several months without symptomatic improvement, Jacob and Marilyn decided to return home to the United States and consult with their trusted family doctor. This physician also believed that Jacob's symptoms were stress-related, but now on home turf, Marilyn felt able to act on her determination "to get to the bottom of things." She consulted with a psychologist friend, whose concern led him to arrange for Jacob to be admitted to a psychiatric hospital for observation.

Initially, Jacob went along with this plan, partly believing that his symptoms were psychologically generated, partly confident that once he was in a hospital someone would figure out what was the matter. But after a short time at this psychiatric hospital he found it to be insufferable; he didn't feel that he belonged there. Now Jacob's vision became distorted and in a bizarre way; the upper and lower parts of his visual field were not aligned. It was easy for the staff at the hospital to believe this was a psychologically-generated symptom. Jacob was becoming more frightened. He checked himself out of the psychiatric unit against medical advice and went to see an optometrist.

The optometrist found evidence of bleeding into Jacob's retina, a clear sign that something was physically wrong. He advised that Jacob see an ophthalmologist. Immediately! The ophthalmologist's opinion was that Jacob's eye exam indicated a neurological problem. Despite having had to see a chain of consultants, at least now Marilyn and Jacob felt they were getting closer to "getting answers."

The neurologist they chose was a friend of a friend, because it was easy to get an appointment with him. He was quite reassuring. He explained that Jacob probably had a benign condition called pseudotumor cerebri. As the name implies, the presentation looks like a brain tumor but isn't one. He ordered some imaging studies. Imaging does not engage in wishful thinking. Jacob had a brain tumor. Even with the best of care, including surgical intervention and medical treatment, Jacob's tumor was lethal.

Looking backward, it isn't possible to know whether Jacob's life might have been saved with earlier medical intervention or what sorts of lingering mental disabilities he might have been left with had he been saved from dying. But we can say with some degree of certainty that it was possible to know early in the course of his illness that he had a brain tumor.

From the beginning, Jacob's situation had called for careful scientific thinking. It would have been possible to gather and weigh the significance of the historical and observational evidence and then go on to synthesize one's thinking and produce a list of possible diagnoses. Stress is not a diagnosis. Migraine was a possible diagnosis, but brain tumor also needed to be on that list. Moreover, a brain tumor is a diagnosis one cannot take the chance of missing. This possibility needed to be investigated with an early referral to a neurologist and imaging.

The scientific literature is clear that a chief complaint that includes "the worst headache of my life" requires a workup and an emergency workup at that (Morgenstern et al., 1998). This chief complaint is frequently associated with serious pathology. Upon reflection, it seems likely that the stressful circumstances of Jacob's life provided a diversionary story that influenced the clinicians who were involved. Jacob's vague dizziness may have reinforced the notion that his symptoms were purely psychologically motivated. How else could one explain why he had this symptom on the way up to work in the elevator and not on the way home? Unfortunately, "how else?" is not a convincing line of reasoning.

In hindsight, Jacob's symptoms could all have been attributable to an expanding mass within his skull. The symptoms he experienced going up in the elevator to work each morning were likely caused by the increase in atmospheric pressure that occurs upon going up in the elevator but not going down; ordinarily this change in pressure wouldn't be noticed, but the presence of a brain tumor within Jacob's skull shifted the baseline conditions such that even a slight change in pressure might be felt. That's how else.

Practicing Persistence and Patience

It may take quite a long time to make an accurate diagnosis when a patient has an underlying organic condition. As illustrated in many of the cases so far presented, it may also take a lot of active work to move the evaluation process along. Obstacles to progress in a diagnostic investigation may be generated by the patient, the patient's family, the illness, the medical care system, and/or by clinicians who are involved in the case, including one's self. Some of these impediments are passive, some active; some are conscious, some unconscious. Many are simply "in the nature of things."

The patient may be lacking in insight and not realize that anything is the matter; he or she might be disorganized and miss appointments or refuse to consider the idea that his or her troubles might be physical rather than psychological. The patient's family could actively or passively oppose the efforts of the clinician out of fear and denial, ignorance, or as a result of a long-standing alienation from the patient or hostility toward the patient. The illness might be indistinguishable from a psychological disorder for months before specific physical symptoms emerge, or the underlying disease might lead the patient to become apathetic and, consequently, the possibility of seeking help may never cross his or her mind. The patient's health plan might not cover important diagnostic procedures; preapproval for tests might take numerous phone calls, paperwork, and time; and this assumes that the patient actually has health insurance. Other clinicians involved with the patient might be uninformed about organic illnesses that could potentially look like functional disorders; medical specialists might be uncomfortable with a "mental" patient and readily dismiss the problem as entirely psychological.

In the face of such uphill battles, it is easy to give up. Persistence is indispensable. The diagnostic task requires both a steady foot on the accelerator as well as patience for a long journey and inevitable traffic jams along the way. Making a diagnosis also requires both focused conscious attention and unfocused subliminal thought over a span of time. The clinician may put in a great amount of deliberate hard work, but an inventive solution may emerge only after he or she has slept on it. Time is a necessary ingredient.

Listen to the unfolding of the following story about Dawn. Getting to the roots of this patient's problems required perseverance both inside the consulting room as well as outside, in the world of the health-care system. Patience was key to establishing deepening trust with the patient. Persistence was necessary to think through, evaluate, and treat the variety of disorders that successively came to light. And, in the end, absolute determination was required to get the patient to the correct specialist in order to document a crucial medical diagnosis. The long and winding quality of this story may give you a feeling for how much simultaneous push and patience were required to treat this patient successfully. In the end, significant questions about the patient's past remained unanswered, but an important diagnostic mystery was solved.

> *Dawn was a college-aged woman who was referred to me for treatment of depression. She had dropped out of school and was in a situation that is familiar to most therapists who treat individuals in this age group: She was bright but without direction, hungry for a relationship with a man but drawn to partners who treated her badly, hopeful for a happy future life but confused about how to create one.*
>
> *Dawn was depressed. She felt "down" most of the time, complained of early morning awakening, anxiety, and difficulty with concentrating. She spent much of her day in front of the television, as she had no real interest in or energy for other activities. After establishing the beginnings of a therapeutic relationship, I started Dawn on an antidepressant medication. Soon she began to feel less depressed. It was only then that I began to hear about other symptoms that Dawn had been experiencing all along. She had trouble getting out of the house because she had to check multiple times to be sure the door was locked. She especially had to check that the microwave oven was unplugged; she was terrified that the microwave might burst into flames. Now it was clear to me that Dawn had two diagnoses: major depression and obsessive-compulsive disorder.*
>
> *As Dawn's trust in the therapy deepened, I learned still more. Dawn revealed that she had been struggling with "drinking too much." Privately, she had believed that this was simply a way for her to deal with her depression. It was becoming clear that Dawn had a third diagnosis, substance abuse. Dawn drank socially, but she also felt compelled to "medicate herself" with large quantities of bourbon at certain times. Predictably, these times were when she had to deal with her father.*
>
> *This information opened a new doorway. Dawn's mother and father had been divorced when Dawn was about 10 years old. Her father gave her "the creeps," though she couldn't understand why she felt this way. Only rarely would he call and ask her to meet him for dinner; she detested these "command performances." There would be silence at the table, but sometimes he*

would help her out with some extra cash. Afterward, she would feel like a bad person, taking money from a man she disliked. Naturally, questions arose about why Dawn felt this way about her father. Was his behavior odd? Could he have an underlying psychosis? Did he perhaps have a disorder in the autism spectrum? Did she blame him for her parents' divorce? Had there been abusive or traumatic experiences associated with her father? These questions remained unanswered.

One evening I received a call from Dawn. She had just had dinner in a restaurant with her father. She felt suicidal. We talked. She told me that, during dinner, when she had looked across the table at her father, his face was "all distorted." She was utterly terrified and felt sure that she was going crazy. It was only then that she ordered a large glass of bourbon "to get through the rest of the meal."

This was the first time I had heard that Dawn had perceptual illusions. While hallucinations are created, so to speak, out of whole cloth, illusions are distortions of some actual sensory experience, such as the swish of running water that sounds like a voice, a shadow that is mistaken for a cat, or the sight of a face that might come to look monstrous or distorted. Dawn stated, "I remember the very first time it happened to me. Maybe I was 10 or 11. I was sitting on my bed. The whole room stretched out. It was weird, kind of like a bowling alley. It terrified me."

Now I felt quite certain that I had come upon a key piece of evidence. Perceptual illusions along with a sense of fear, intense emotional reactions without a clear historical genesis, anxiety, and drinking in an effort to calm her nervous system: These symptoms were all consistent with a partial seizure disorder. I believed that now I had identified an important, underlying medical disorder that could have been and might still be a crucial driving force in shaping Dawn's behavior. It had taken patience and perseverance to get this far, but my resolve was yet to be tested. There I was, on the phone with Dawn, trying to truly comprehend her subjective experience, trying to assess just how suicidal she was, and how drunk. I was also trying to see through to the underlying, driving forces behind her behavior. And all the while, Dawn had been downing a bottle of cough syrup. Finally she told me.

I was relieved once she was in the hospital, but the story does not end there. The hospital psychiatrist was focused on Dawn's alcohol abuse, which was a prominent feature in her presentation. He refused my entreaties to consider the possibility that a seizure disorder was driving her drinking, and he would not order an EEG. He was sure that alcohol abuse could explain all of her symptoms. Although that was possible, it was far from certain. An important possible diagnosis had not been ruled out, partial seizures.

I felt that it was important for Dawn to consult with a neurologist once she was discharged from the hospital. This was not easy to arrange. For one thing, in the hospital the patient had learned that she needed to "take full responsibility for her drinking as well as for her other self-defeating behaviors," such as choosing men who weren't kind to her. This was progress on one front, but what I faced on another front was the problem of convincing Dawn to see a neurologist when the very idea that she might have a seizure disorder that was beyond her control directly contradicted the whole thrust of her psychological treatment.

I was walking a tightrope. I tried to give Dawn enough information about seizures to convince her that she really might have this disorder, but I had to present it in such a way as to not undermine her sense of agency. And I had to give her enough information to motivate her to see a neurologist but not so much information that she would become overwhelmed or frightened into inaction. Eventually I succeeded.

Unfortunately, the story doesn't end here either. Dawn saw a neurologist through her health maintenance organization (HMO). She brought with her a letter from me in which I outlined my thinking, but this physician dismissed my diagnostic impression and the patient's symptoms and wrote in his note that he thought Dawn was psychotic. His diagnosis was based on her report of visual illusions and her history of a psychiatric hospitalization. He did not order any testing.

From my extensive experience with the patient, there was not a shred of evidence for a psychotic process. The patient did not have a thought disorder. She was well aware that her visual illusions were not real. That is precisely why she thought she was "crazy" and why she hadn't told anyone about them for so long. She knew that she these were distortions of reality. People who are truly psychotic believe that their experiences are real and, at least initially, they tell others about them because they have no reason to expect that they won't be believed.

At this point I began to lobby for the patient to see a seizure specialist outside her HMO, but privately I had begun to have doubts. Was I too invested in the seizure diagnosis? Perhaps the neurologist had been right; maybe there was something I wasn't seeing about the patient. Maybe she was psychologically sicker than I had thought. Dawn was someone who had kept secrets. Maybe there were other secrets she hadn't yet revealed to me. Maybe her visual illusions were hysterical. Perhaps posttraumatic stress disorder accounted for her intense fear. I did sense that the full story of what had transpired in her past was still a mystery. In truth, I did not yet understand what accounted for her intense negative feelings about her father.

At this point with Dawn's permission, I enlisted the help of the patient's mother, who was going to pay any bills for non-HMO doctors. I referred Dawn to a top-notch neurologist who specialized in epilepsy. He ordered an MRI and a sleep-deprived EEG, performed after the patient has been awake for the previous night. The honest-to-goodness truth *is that Dawn almost walked out of the EEG lab. She was frightened and became paranoid about the motives of the technician. But the printout of the electrical activity in Dawn's brain showed that this experience of paranoid fear was correlated with active spiking activity—certain evidence of a seizure. In addition, allaying all doubts about this medical diagnosis, the MRI showed a benign, congenital, structural abnormality in the brain region just where Dawn's seizures were originating.*

Antiseizure medications truly made a difference. Dawn reported that she no longer had visual illusions. She felt much calmer. In fact, until she had felt the quieting effects of the anticonvulsants, she hadn't been aware of the extent to which anxiety and fear had been her everyday companions. Dawn no longer felt an intense urge to drink. She returned to college and lived in an alcohol-free dorm. She was able to concentrate on her studies. She began to date. Sometime later, Dawn's mother filed an appeal with the HMO and was fully reimbursed for the costs of Dawn's definitive neurological consultation, workup, and treatment. And soon after Dawn completed her first successful semester at college, she stopped therapy.

Persistence and patience were needed to achieve a substantial improvement in Dawn's condition. This therapy was a roller-coaster ride. It was not only the therapist, namely me, who needed to have patience and persistence. It was important for me to work with Dawn to help her keep hope alive. Dawn also needed to have patience and persistence to stay the course.

Tolerate Uncertainty and Helplessness

One of the most difficult aspects of being a clinician is tolerating what seem to be nearly unbearable experiences. We sit with despair, terror, rage, bitterness, regret, grief, and horror. We witness extremes of psychic and physical pain. We are faced with the existential realities of life, aging, unfulfilled dreams, and lost capacities. These experiences threaten to shatter any complacency we might have had about our own vulnerability and mortality.

At the same time, we are aware that our patients and their loved ones want help with these painful realities and feelings. They want to know the causes of their pain and what will help, and we desperately want to be able to tell them. Our wish to help alleviate suffering is powerful. Not only do we believe that this is our job, but also this may have been an important part of the reason for having become a clinician in the first place.

All of these dynamics exert tremendous pressure on health-care practitioners to convey a sense of certainty to patients and families. "This is what is the matter. This is what we are going to do about it. You will feel better." It is extremely difficult to resist this drive toward providing reassurance by conveying a sense that you fully understand what is going on. It is extremely difficult to resist the drive to come to premature closure on clinical questions.

Yet premature closure to diagnostic questions is one of the largest sources of error in health care. Here's why: Tolerating uncertainty and helplessness is part of the infrastructure of clinical problem solving. The case must be kept open in order to solve it. This is a very difficult task to accomplish while providing emotional support for your patients and their families. It requires self-monitoring, insight, and maturity throughout your career.

In a clinical situation, what does premature closure look like? It looks like certainty. It can sometimes look like reassurance. Or it may look like arrogance. The clinician is sure that a particular diagnosis explains the patient's symptoms. That diagnosis might be depression, posttraumatic stress disorder, post-concussion syndrome, head trauma, alcoholism, Lyme disease, somatization disorder, or anything else. Once this kind of certainty emerges, the door is closed to further investigation or contemplation of the complexity that is inherent in any clinical situation, even if the patient is still suffering.

If a patient is continuing to have symptoms, it makes sense to resist premature closure of the case. In clinical care, of what use is absolute certainty other than to soothe the caregiver or the patient or both? It is possible to be both confident and decisive while maintaining clarity about the degree of uncertainty one has about a diagnosis or a treatment strategy. Certainty is not required. Clinical care involves taking action on the basis of believing that there is only a good chance that you are right. Perhaps it is difficult to face how often this is exactly what we do.

Many years ago, a wise patient asked me a question and then added this comment: "Remember, a completely legitimate answer to my question would be 'I don't know.'" In many cases "*we* don't know" is also true. Though the scope of our scientific understanding has expanded enormously, nonetheless we regularly encounter the limits of that body of knowledge. It cannot be stressed enough that one individual clinician cannot possibly know the limits of what is known. This is why utilizing consultants is crucial. Experts are individuals who know things that you and the patient don't know are known.

Here is an example from my outpatient practice in which part of the treatment involved managing the uncertainty about a diagnosis.

Early one evening, I walked into my office to turn on the lights before seeing Dr. and Mrs. Gleason for couples therapy. I could hear them arguing in the waiting room just down the hall. On the floor of my office was a note that had been slipped under my door. The note was from Mrs. Gleason. She wanted me to know that her husband had been having trouble with memory. She wrote that the secretary in the community college department where her husband worked had also noticed this and had complained to her—but not to him. Mrs. Gleason had spent much of her married adulthood trying to protect her husband's fragile self-esteem; now she couldn't figure out how to bring up this memory problem with him.

Dr. Gleason was in his early sixties but looked older. I knew that the emergence of memory problems in someone his age could have many possible causes. Dr. Gleason had had cardiac surgery a few months earlier, so it was possible that he had developed cognitive problems as a consequence of the surgery. I also knew that Dr. Gleason had a history of alcoholism, which could have affected his memory. He also had hypothyroidism, for which his replacement thyroid medication was currently being adjusted. The fact that he had needed heart bypass surgery also implied that he had disease of his cardiovascular system; therefore, the blood vessels of his brain might also be affected by arteriosclerosis.

In addition, I thought to myself that Dr. Gleason could have had a sleep disorder such as sleep apnea, which is a common cause of memory problems. Or perhaps he had an early frontal dementia or a garden-variety depression, affecting his ability to concentrate and, secondarily, impacting his memory. It was also likely that Dr. Gleason had always had a bit of attention deficit hyperactivity disorder and that when normal aging was added to the picture, difficulty with memory might be the symptom. I also had to consider the possibility that Mrs. Gleason and the departmental secretary were both angry at Dr. Gleason and that they were expressing their complex feelings by experiencing him as being impaired.

A clinical investigation always begins with uncertainty such as this. More often than we like to think, the uncertainty continues. In this case, I found a natural opening in the therapy conversation to ask Mrs. Gleason whether she had noticed any changes in her husband's "cognition, his attention, memory or ability to calculate, read, and so on." In my presence, Mrs. Gleason was able to tactfully make the case for some memory difficulties since the bypass surgery, including reporting on information the husband's secretary had shared with her. To Mrs. Gleason's surprise, her husband acknowledged noticing "that things do seem to slip by me." Privately, he had been "worried, but not a lot."

I referred Dr. Gleason to his primary care physician (PCP), who orchestrated what the patient called "the million-dollar workup." Dr. Gleason saw a neurologist and had an MRI plus extensive neuropsychological testing.

The testing revealed difficulties in the area of executive functioning, some impulsivity, and problems with attention. The cause of these difficulties wasn't clear, even after this extensive testing.

Meanwhile, the patient's internist told Dr. Gleason that all the tests showed him to be "fit as a fiddle." This struck Dr. Gleason as a bit dismissive, and the reassurance contradicted his own private experience of having to work harder to prepare his lectures and having to find new strategies to facilitate remembering things. It also contradicted his wife's experience of him and his secretary's experience as well. Dr. Gleason wondered whether his physician hadn't fully grasped what he was going through. Dr. Gleason acknowledged that initially he hadn't wanted to face what was happening to him and "hadn't wanted to worry my wife." Now he was glad that he no longer had to keep his concerns a secret. He was relieved to be able to be open with his wife and to problem-solve with me, but it remained difficult to talk with his PCP, even though he was "a nice guy."

There matters currently stand. The neuropsychological testing is going to be repeated in 18 months, after Dr. Gleason's thyroid medication has been adjusted. Then we will know more, but still not everything.

Clinicians often believe that certainty is reassuring to a patient. But when the patient believes that this certainty is false, as in the case with Dr. Gleason, it feels like the clinician is no longer available for a frank discussion. It feels as though the clinician may not be able to face the truth and like a door has been closed to further discussion. It feels like premature closure. It may feel like abandonment.

Here's a story from the perspective of another patient. It illustrates how important it is that, as clinicians, we keep the case open, tolerate our own uncertainty and helplessness, and avoid coming to premature closure.

My friend, Joan, had some unusual symptoms that she could not ignore. Periodically and for no apparent reason, her feet would become red, hot, and exquisitely painful. "It was like hot coals being applied to the soles of my feet. I couldn't stand it. Sometimes I would just have to sit with my feet up on the table, covered with ice."

These symptoms came and went, but when she had a doctor's appointment, they were usually not apparent. None of the many doctors she consulted were able to diagnose her problem. Worse still, she could sense that most of them thought her problem was all in her head. Her primary care doctor referred her for therapy.

After much searching, Joan found a social worker who believed her. That social worker referred Joan to Dr. Laguna, an excellent neurologist. Dr. Laguna ordered many medical tests. Some were painful, including a peripheral nerve biopsy. Dr. Laguna was persistent, and she was thoughtful.

One day, while Joan and the doctor were sitting together in the office, Dr. Laguna suddenly put her hand to her forehead. In that very moment, she had realized what was wrong with Joan, and she said that she was upset with herself for not having realized it sooner.

Dr. Laguna had seen one other case of erythromelalgia while she was in medical school many years earlier. Erythromelalgia is a rare disease that can affect the feet or the hands; Joan had every symptom. "Why didn't I think of it sooner?" Dr. Laguna asked. "You must be mad at me."

Joan wasn't the least bit mad; she was thrilled. Yes, she had been through painful tests that wouldn't have been necessary if Dr. Laguna had had this diagnostic insight earlier, but she felt grateful for the diagnosis, for her therapist's support, and for her neurologist's persistence.

In addition, Joan was deeply appreciative for another quality of these clinicians. "They never doubted me and never made me feel crazy. Dr. Laguna is the kind of doctor who doesn't close anything out," Joan told me. "When we talk about medicines, she says things like, 'Let's have a strategy,' or 'First we'll try this and then we'll try that.' Or she'll say, 'Well, you heard this and I heard that and let's find out what your husband thinks.' So, you never feel that this is your last chance. She keeps everything open. And I never once heard from her what I would hear from all my other doctors, 'Well, this could be psychosomatic.'"

Many books and articles have been written about situations that are the opposite of this one. The patient has numerous physical complaints that might shift from one body system to another: diarrhea, headaches, a lump in the throat, fatigue, back pain, and so on. Many of these patients are anxious and stressed; many have covert depression; many derive secondary gain from their symptoms and from their interactions with clinicians. These individuals are a significant challenge for every sector of the health-care community. They consume vast amounts of time and substantial resources. In these situations, the last thing that practitioners want to do is to keep the door open to more consultations and investigations. This may be entirely appropriate in many cases, but one needs to keep in mind that some of these patients may actually have undiagnosed organic disorders.

Simply because an individual presents with vague complaints that come and go over years or that shift from one part of the body to another does not mean that there isn't a clear physical cause. Numerous physical disorders can present in just this way. Here is one that is extremely common and underdiagnosed.

Migraines can take many forms, including what are called migraine variants in which the headache component is absent. A migraine may present with only one symptom or with a variety of symptoms: dizziness, abdominal pain, nausea, visual distortions and hallucinatory phenomena, light sensitivity, temporary loss of vision, and mood alterations, among others (Sacks, 1999). Patients who have migraines with only abdominal symptoms often will first consult a gastroenterologist; thorough and repeated gastrointestinal (GI) workups will show only that "everything is normal." Patients who only have dizziness may seek out opinions from neurologists or ear, nose, and throat (ENT) specialists. Again, these patients may not get a correct diagnosis, because dizziness is a relatively unusual presentation of migraines. Migraines are common. Migraines come and go, sometimes for reasons that are not apparent, sometimes in response to stress. Migraines are real and treatable and sometimes difficult to diagnose.

Dealing With Inevitable Blind Spots

Every clinician has blind spots, factors outside of awareness that limit the capacity to perceive important data. Some blind spots are quite personal. Examples abound: a negative, judgmental attitude toward patients with alcohol problems, a tendency to underestimate the seriousness of medical symptoms, the impulse to rescue emotionally fragile individuals or to routinely take the perspective of the teenager as opposed to the parent. Good individual supervision or a personal psychotherapy for the clinician may be helpful in identifying these kinds of behavioral patterns.

Some blind spots are universal, however. For instance, it is difficult for anyone to perceive very gradual change. A patient you see several times a week may develop a worsening medical condition right before your eyes. If the physical and psychological changes are gradual enough, you may not notice them: weight loss from an undiagnosed malignancy, a gradual decline in motivation from frontal lobe disease, bulging of the eyes from Graves' disease (an autoimmune hyperthyroidism), or the drying skin, coarsening of hair, and deepening voice that may be signs hypothyroidism (perhaps associated with taking lithium).

Looking at old photographs of the patient will sometimes reveal gradual, physical changes. You might ask whether friends or relatives who see the patient infrequently have remarked about any changes in them. Other ways to make gradual changes more perceptible are to obtain old medical records or to ask a patient to keep a chart of certain factors, such as weight, menstrual cycles, sleep and wake times, and so on.

Another universal blind spot is in the area of fully appreciating one's own influence in a clinical situation, even though you may know intellectually that the observer always influences the data. For example, if a therapist has even a subtle judgmental attitude about sexuality or religion or some other area, the patient may refrain from discussing these topics.

Sometimes simply the nature of a therapeutic interaction causes signs of a disorder to go underground. A good example of this phenomenon commonly occurs with patients who have attention deficit hyperactivity disorder (ADHD). A patient's husband may complain that he simply cannot get his wife's attention, that she is easily distracted and "gets nothing done all day." He is angry and believes that she "must have ADHD." Yet, in the consulting room, the wife is fully engaged and focused. In other words, what the therapist sees is a different behavior pattern than what the husband describes. The wife's ADHD symptoms are hidden. What explains this?

Individuals with ADHD are highly responsive to environmental circumstances. The individual therapy situation provides a peaceful surrounding with minimal distractions. In addition, the therapy is centered on the patient; the therapist is fully intent on listening without needing to be listened to; and the therapist is willing to shift topics at a pace set by the patient. This is an optimal focusing environment for many patients with ADHD. It is no wonder that the symptoms of this disorder may not be apparent to the individual therapist. The clinical situation has influenced the data.

Yet another factor that may create blind spots is the clinician's therapeutic distance from the patient. The concept of therapeutic distance attempts to capture something about how much the clinician identifies with or distances him or herself from the patient's experience. How much does the clinician see the situation through the patient's eyes? Being too close and sympathetic limits one's vision, as does being too distant and more purely clinical. Optimally, a clinician swings, like a pendulum, ceaselessly between the two positions, sometimes closer, sometimes more distant, with an ongoing, inner discourse utilizing information from the different perspectives.

Once again using the example of the wife with ADHD, too little therapeutic distance could lead the therapist to believe the wife's experience of the situation—hook, line, and sinker. Her view is that the husband simply doesn't comprehend how difficult it is to run a household with three children under the age of 10, let alone keep the place neat. Empathy for the wife's experience is crucial to fully understanding the dynamics of the family situation and to establishing a trusting relationship with the wife.

But it is possible for a clinician to lose one's way if he or she doesn't step back and wonder about why the husband is angry with his wife. Just how messy *is* the home? How *does* the patient use her time during the day? Does she employ "line-of-sight organization," an inefficient approach that is driven by the latest crisis or by whatever grabs the individual's attention? Maybe the husband's perspective has validity. Once that possibility enters the picture, the clinician may swing to a somewhat more cognitive mode and inquire about details of how the patient runs the household. It would also make sense to ask about the patient's behavior when she was a child since the diagnosis of ADHD requires evidence of the disorder from before the age of 7. Obtaining this information requires careful and methodical history-taking.

In order to contend with blind spots, it is important to push one's self to look at any clinical situation from a new perspective. This is extremely difficult. We each come to the relative equilibrium of our currently held notions as a result of many forces, some from within (our personal belief systems, memories of past experiences, and so on) and some from without (from our professional colleagues, our institutional associations, and the clinical and cultural environment in which we work). It often takes something fairly radical to shake up firmly held, relatively stable clinical and theoretical perspectives or formulations, especially in the context of an ongoing therapy.

How does one mentally step back to get a larger perspective? Try discussing your patient in a clinical case conference or with a respected peer group. Take advantage of the distance afforded by vacation breaks; look at the patient with fresh eyes when the vacation ends. Seek consultation on selected cases. Bring in another knowledgeable clinician whose opinion you respect and with whom you feel comfortable enough to freely share your actual experiences of the patient. Consider contacting a consultant from another field or someone who has a different theoretical perspective from your own.

One interesting way of thinking about blind spots in relation to the therapist's general attitude is in terms of signal theory. First developed in connection with radar operators, signal theory has many applications in diagnostics. Think of the metal detectors at the airport as diagnostic machines. If the detector is tuned to be very sensitive in picking up every bit of metal (e.g., bra hooks, belt buckles, eyeglass frames), then the lines through security checkpoints would be unnecessarily long; virtually everyone would require additional screening. But if the machine is tuned to a very low sensitivity, then even a weapon might elude detection.

In other words, either one picks up too many insignificant findings or one misses too many significant findings. When you minimize the chance

Convergent
Divergent

of missing an important metal item, you maximize the chance of picking up something that's not relevant. There is no way to avoid both kinds of errors at the same time. Take a field like radiology, in which it falls to the person reading the x-ray or the scan to decide if they are actually seeing something pathological or merely a variation of something normal, a shadow, or an artifact of the technology. Radiologists may cope with the inevitable error rates dictated by signal theory by having a second radiologist examine the data (Metz & Shen, 1992).

Similarly with a therapist, one can look too vigilantly for anomalous symptoms, just as one can be too lax. The therapist's ability to detect certain kinds of signals will be affected by being too distant on some occasions and too supportive on others, and in both kinds of situations, the therapist may not be fully conscious of how he or she is setting the viewing strategy. It is helpful for therapists to try to take different perspectives, to move back and forth along the spectrum of therapeutic distance, and also to seek second opinions or consultations.

Here is a story that illustrates how a biological disorder unfolded before the eyes of a group of sophisticated and experienced clinicians.

Some years ago, six therapists worked together on an inpatient psychiatric service in a financially troubled hospital. Because their jobs on the unit felt increasingly insecure, these clinicians decided to form an outpatient group practice. They included one social worker (Stuart), two psychiatrists (Susan and Evan), and three psychologists (Bob, Sylvia, and Carl). Though each had quirks, limitations, and blind spots, it was also clear that each had remarkable strengths to offer the group. They liked and respected one another, and they enjoyed working together.

Every Wednesday this group of close colleagues would meet over lunch in order to have an opportunity to discuss their most puzzling patients and to hash out difficult administrative issues. Mostly, they wanted to talk about doing psychotherapy for, as you know, being a therapist can be a lonely job. Over the years, they learned from one another, and this helped them to mature as individuals and as a group.

They prospered as clinicians, academic writers, and teachers. They explored and incorporated new theoretical ideas into their thinking. And remarkably, they were able to expose to one another more and more of the complex, inner experience of performing assessments and doing intensive psychotherapy.

But, of course, as with all groups, things weren't perfect. On numerous occasions, theoretical differences arose. Sylvia was remarkable in her ability to see the validity of the various points of view. Often she would also pass around academic papers on the theoretical topics in dispute in an effort to bring a more reasoned approach to the discussions. Over time the group members would gradually shift their views and resolve their conflicts, but some differences were never settled.

Bob's fundamental interest had always been in teaching, and, because his wife made a large income working for a financial services company, Bob was able to devote much of his professional time to what he pompously called "the academy." He spent less and less time in the group practice. Other members of the group were angry and secretly envious.

Stuart and Carl shared a passion for art and became "best" friends outside the group. They frequented local museums. They talked about writing a case report on their collaboration in treating a psychotic artist and his family. The special bond between Stuart and Carl created tension with the others who felt excluded.

There were also tensions between the two psychiatrists. They had conflicts about whether or not to accept drug samples from pharmaceutical salespeople. And they were competitive with one another. Who was getting more psychopharmacology consultation referrals from the other group members?

Gradually over many years, the group began to focus its discontents on Sylvia. Sylvia had always been obsessional in style. Now the group began to experience her as also being rigid.

The members now began to notice that, when Sylvia discussed her own work, her patients almost invariably described Dr. Sylvia as being distant. The patients often felt that she wasn't "connecting," and many seemed to be considering terminating treatment. Sylvia uniformly interpreted her patients' experiences as transference reactions, as the re-experiencing of early interactions with cold, unreachable mothers. Sylvia believed these were important, workable therapeutic impasses. The group, on the other hand, began to formulate that Sylvia's patients were, in fact, trying to tell her about their real experience of her as a therapist and as a person.

The group's view of Sylvia was reinforced in an unusual way. All had been invited to a reception to honor the retiring chief of the inpatient service where they had all originally worked. Sylvia had been invited to give one of the speeches. Her talk began well. She outlined the long history of the service and the retiring chief's commitment to multidisciplinary teamwork. But everyone expected Sylvia to end with something from the heart. She didn't. As Carl whispered to Stuart, "That was chillingly flat."

After the talk, other members of the group concurred. They knew that Sylvia had an obsessive nature, but this was extreme. Then more anecdotes were shared. Evan recalled how deeply injured and overtly angry Sylvia had been a few weeks earlier when he had needed to switch a meeting he had set up with her. Susan revealed that, just a day earlier, she had received an odd phone message from Sylvia. It simply said, "I need you to see one of my patients. Today." Not even "Hi, this is Sylvia."

The group consensus was that Sylvia was depressed and irritable. They decided to discuss their concerns with Sylvia directly. These were expert clinicians. They knew that talking to Sylvia would be difficult and emotionally complex. They expected her to be defensive. And they were aware of their own less than empathic feelings; for some time now the practice members had been finding Sylvia's rigidity and emotional limitations to be an impediment to their work as a group. They were angry. They were aware that they actually wished that Sylvia would leave the practice. In addition, they reasoned further and wondered whether, for some time, Sylvia had been reacting to this covert dynamic—their wish to exclude her. Of course, this made them feel guilty.

The talk with Sylvia went better than expected. It turned out that Sylvia had returned to psychotherapy with a senior clinician some months before and that she had recently begun taking an antidepressant. She even acknowledged feeling depressed and was optimistic that these treatments would help. This sounded good, but group members noted Sylvia's lack of complex self-reflection. They felt the absence of any real appreciation of how difficult it had been for them to discuss this with her or of how her depression had been affecting the group.

By now the feelings surrounding Sylvia had thoroughly contaminated the Wednesday lunchtime meetings. While in the past, members had treated this regular meeting schedule as nearly sacred, now somehow, one or another of them frequently found that other commitments conflicted. It was generally felt, but not openly acknowledged, that the group was in crisis. Time passed. Sylvia did not get better. Indeed, concerns about her continued.

Evan heard that Sylvia had become uncharacteristically angry with an administrator in the hospital garage. During a Super Bowl party, Sylvia approached Susan and began to scold her about how she had handled a patient Sylvia had referred to her for medications. Sylvia's voice was too loud and too angry. And the setting was inappropriate.

Then Bob was approached by some students who had taken a clinical workshop taught by Sylvia. Apparently Sylvia had been more than dull in her teaching role. In response to the cases they presented, she had said virtually nothing at all. Perhaps more than anything else, this input from students who were outside of the group seemed to galvanize the members to step back and look at the big picture.

What had happened to Sylvia? She had been a rising-star psychologist, a respected teacher and clinician, a peacemaker, a full member of this group practice. And right before their eyes, she had slipped. In full view of Susan, Evan, Bob, Stuart, and Carl, something had happened to Sylvia so that she was no longer the person she had once been. For the very first time they began to question their diagnostic formulation. Perhaps this was more than a depression in someone with an obsessional style. More? What exactly did that mean? What else could be wrong?

The group had been operating within its comfort zone, within the world of DSM and unconscious motivation, within the realm of psychological dynamics and talking therapies. But now the limitations of this world became startlingly clear. They got to work; they started by reconceptualizing Sylvia's behavior. Where they had seen depression, they now saw apathy. Where they had seen inappropriate aggression, they now saw impulsivity. Where they had seen a somewhat obsessive colleague becoming increasingly self-centered, rigid, and lacking in consideration for others, they now saw that Sylvia was losing executive functions involving social comportment, flexibility, and the capacity to monitor herself in relation to the social environment. To their horror they now saw clearly that Sylvia probably had an organic problem affecting the frontal lobes of her brain. They made a plan that included facilitating a consultation from Sylvia's primary care physician, a neuropsychologist, and a behavioral neurologist.

Stuart called Sylvia's husband and learned that he had been feeling helpless and confused about why "Sylvia's depression wasn't getting better." He said that he would support any of the group's efforts to get to the bottom of things, including talking with Sylvia's therapist and initiating the complete workup that the group had discussed.

The news was sad and disturbing. Sylvia's neurologic exam, neuropsychological testing, and MRI were consistent with a fronto-temporal dementia, a progressive degeneration of the brain that tends to affect individuals at a younger age than Alzheimer's disease. Early in its course, this kind of dementia often looks like depression. Lack of flexibility and inability to take initiative are often seen. Apathy is common as are disturbed social interactions, including disinhibited and inappropriate behavior. The mystery was solved; this diagnosis explained all of Sylvia's behavior.

Sylvia's slow downward slide had started years before, right before the eyes of five excellent clinicians. Given the personal nature of their relationship with Sylvia and the slow development of Sylvia's dementia, it is entirely understandable that initially they didn't detect a problem. This is the nature of blind spots.

Sylvia's decline would continue over a span of several tortuous years. Typical of frontal dementias is a craving for sweets and an expanding waistline, the development of language devoid of substantial content and eventually mutism—day care, nursing home care, and eventually and inevitably, death.

Cultivating Learning and a Spirit of Curiosity

Each habit of mind discussed in this chapter contributes in some measure to creating a more effective clinician. But perhaps the most fundamental of all is a habit of lifelong learning with a spirit of curiosity. This is not the commonplace curiosity of voyeurism, but a desire to understand deeply. This spirit of curiosity is the heart and soul of being a clinical caretaker, a diagnostician, a scientist, a detective, an empathic listener, and an engaged human being.

Curiosity motivated Richard Feynman, the physicist and daring, innovative thinker, who is best known for having diagnosed the cause of the *Challenger* space program disaster. What drove him was "the pleasure of finding the thing out, the kick in the discovery" (Feynman & Robbins, 2000, p. 12). Dr. Abraham Verghese, the acclaimed physician and author of *Cutting for Stone*, said that "infinite curiosity about other people" was both the joy and the prerequisite for both of his careers (Grady, 2010, p. D1).

Every patient story begins as a mystery. Making order out of mental chaos is what we try to do as therapists. Therapies of all sorts provide patients with what Daphne Merkin called "an opportunity unlike any other to sort through the contents of your own mind—an often painfully circuitous operation—in the presence of someone who is trained to make order out of mental chaos" (Merkin, 2010, p. 35). As therapists, we utilize our knowledge base and experience to try to make a diagnosis so as to provide the most effective treatment for our patients. Fueled by curiosity, we try to make order out of mental chaos, and sometimes this involves the elucidation of a covert physical disease.

References

American Psychiatric Association. (2000). *Diagnostic and statistical manual of mental disorders* (4th ed., text revision, DSM-IV-TR). Washington, DC: American Psychiatric Association.

Armstrong, K. (1993). *A history of God: The 4000-year quest of Judaism, Christianity, and Islam.* New York, NY: Knopf.

Armstrong, K. (2004). *The spiral staircase: My climb out of darkness.* New York, NY: Knopf.

Bauby, J. (1997). *The diving bell and the butterfly.* New York, NY: Knopf.

Bear, D. M., & Fedio, P. (1977). Quantitative analysis of interictal behavior in temporal lobe epilepsy. *Archives of Neurology, 34*(8), 454–467.

Bejjani, B. (1999). Transient acute depression induced by high-frequency deep-brain stimulation. *The New England Journal of Medicine, 340*(19), 1476–1480.

Bisiach, E., & Luzzatti, C. (1978). Unilateral neglect of representational space. *Cortex: A Journal Devoted to the Study of the Nervous System and Behavior, 14*(1), 129–133.

Blumstein, S. E., Alexander, M. P., Ryalls, J. H., Katz, W., & Dworetzky, B. (1987). On the nature of the foreign accent syndrome: A case study. *Brain and Language, 31*(2), 215–244.

Centers in Disease Control and Prevention. (1995). Lead poisoning among sandblasting workers—Galveston, Texas, March 1994. *MMWR: Morbidity and Mortality Weekly Report, 44*(3), 44–45.

Chuang, Y., Lin, T., Lui, C., Chen, S., & Chang, C. (2004). Tooth-brushing epilepsy with ictal orgasms. *Seizure, 13*(3), 179–182. doi:10.1016/S1059-1311(03)00109-2

Cohen, P. (2009). American roulette—Contaminated dietary supplements. *The New England Journal of Medicine, 361*(16), 1523.

Croskerry, P. (2003). The importance of cognitive errors in diagnosis and strategies to minimize them. *Academic Medicine: Journal of the Association of American Medical Colleges, 78*(8), 775–780.

Cummings, J. (1985). *Clinical neuropsychiatry.* Orlando, FL: Grune & Stratton.

Feinberg, T. E. (2002). *Altered egos: How the brain creates the self.* New York, NY: Oxford University Press.

Feynman, R. P., & Robbins, J. (2000). *The pleasure of finding things out: The best short works of Richard P. Feynman.* Cambridge, MA: Da Capo Press.

Foote-Smith, E. (1991). Joan of Arc. *Epilepsia, 32*(6), 810–815.

Goodwin, D. W. (1995). Alcohol amnesia. *Addiction (Abingdon, England)*, *90*(3), 315–317.

Grady, D. (2010, October 11). Restoring the lost art of the physical exam. *New York Times*.

Grill, J. D., & Cummings, J. L. (2008, March). A cry for help: Treating involuntary emotional expression disorder. *Current Psychiatry*, *7*(3), 101–111.

Gustavsson, P., & Gerhardsson, L. (2005). Intoxication from an accidentally ingested lead shot retained in the gastrointestinal tract. *Environmental Health Perspectives*, *113*(4), 491–493.

Hoenig, J. (1960). Epilepsy and sexual orgasm. *Acta psychiatrica Scandinavica*, *35*, 448–456.

Hoque, R., & Chesson, A. L. (2009). Zolpidem-induced sleepwalking, sleep-related eating disorder, and sleep-driving: Fluorine-18-flourodeoxyglucose positron emission tomography analysis, and a literature review of other unexpected clinical effects of zolpidem. *Journal of Clinical Sleep Medicine (JCSM): Official Publication of the American Academy of Sleep Medicine*, *5*(5), 471–476.

Hughes, J. R. (2005). The idiosyncratic aspects of the epilepsy of Fyodor Dostoevsky. *Epilepsy & Behavior*, *7*(3), 531–538.

Koranyi, E. (1979). Morbidity and rate of undiagnosed physical illnesses in a psychiatric clinic population. *Archives of general psychiatry*, *36*(4), 414–419.

Kuhn, G. (2002). Diagnostic errors. *Academic Emergency Medicine*, *9*(7), 740–750.

Kurtzman, N. (1967). President Kennedy and Addison's disease. *JAMA: The Journal of the American Medical Association*, *201*(13), 1052.

Lai, C. (2001). A forkhead-domain gene is mutated in a severe speech and language disorder. *Nature*, *413*(6855), 519–523.

Lishman, W. (1987). *Organic psychiatry: The psychological consequences of cerebral disorder* (2nd ed.). Boston, MA: Blackwell Scientific.

Liu, J., Zheng, B., Aposhian, H. V., Zhou, Y., Chen, M., Zhang, A., & Waalkes, M. P. (2002). Chronic arsenic poisoning from burning high-arsenic-containing coal in Guizhou, China. *Environmental Health Perspectives*, *110*(2), 119–122.

Lynch, E., & Braithwaite, R. (2005). A review of the clinical and toxicological aspects of 'traditional' (herbal) medicines adulterated with heavy metals. *Expert Opinion on Drug Safety*, *4*(4), 769–778.

Macknik, S. (2008). Attention and awareness in stage magic: Turning tricks into research. *Nature Reviews. Neuroscience*, *9*(11), 871–879.

Macmillan, M. (2000). Restoring Phineas Gage: A 150th retrospective. *Journal of the History of the Neurosciences*, *9*(1), 46–66.

Matte, T. D., Proops, D., Palazuelos, E., Graef, J., & Hernandez Avila, M. (1994). Acute high-dose lead exposure from beverage contaminated by traditional Mexican pottery. *Lancet, 344*(8929), 1064–1065.

Merkin, D. (2010, August 4). My life in therapy. *New York Times.*

Mesulam, M. (2000). *Principles of behavioral and cognitive neurology* (2nd ed.). New York, NY: Oxford University Press.

Metz, C. E., & Shen, J. H. (1992). Gains in accuracy from replicated readings of diagnostic images: prediction and assessment in terms of ROC analysis. *Medical Decision Making: An International Journal of the Society for Medical Decision Making, 12*(1), 60–75.

Morgenstern, L. B., Luna-Gonzales, H., Huber, J. C., Wong, S. S., Uthman, M. O., Gurian, J. H., Castillo, P. R., et al. (1998). Worst headache and subarachnoid hemorrhage: Prospective, modern computed tomography and spinal fluid analysis. *Annals of Emergency Medicine, 32* (3, Pt. 1), 297–304.

Ramani, V. (1991). Audiogenic epilepsy induced by a specific television performer. *The New England Journal of Medicine, 325*(2), 134–135.

Ross, E. D., & Mesulam, M. (1979). Dominant language functions of the right hemisphere? Prosody and emotional gesturing. *Archives of Neurology, 36*(3), 144–148.

Sacks, O. (1999). *Migraine.* New York, NY: Vintage Books.

Schachter, S. (2008). *Epilepsy in our words: personal accounts of living with seizures.* Oxford; New York, NY: Oxford University Press.

Senol, M., & Fireman, P. (1999). Body odor in dermatologic diagnosis. *Cutis: Cutaneous Medicine for the Practitioner, 63*(2), 107–111.

Shekhar, R. (2008). Transient global amnesia—A review. *International Journal of Clinical Practice, 62*(6), 939–942.

Sizer, T. R. (1997). *Horace's school: Redesigning the American high school.* New York, NY: Houghton Mifflin Harcourt.

Truss, L. (2004). *Eats, shoots & leaves: The zero tolerance approach to punctuation.* New York, NY: Gotham Books.

Winkelman, J. W. (2003). Treatment of nocturnal eating syndrome and sleep-related eating disorder with topiramate. *Sleep Medicine, 4*(3), 243–246.

Yates, B. L., & Koran, L. M. (1999). Epidemiology and recognition of neuropsychiatric disorders in mental health settings. In F. Ovsiew (Ed.), *Neuropsychiatry and mental health services.* Washington, DC: American Psychiatric Press.

Author Index

Subject Index

attention deficits, 189
CADASIL, 176
case studies, 47, 172, 210
consciousness, impaired, 183
eye movement abnormalities,
114
facial asymmetries, 113
focal signs and, 130–131, 133
foreign accent syndrome, 213
IEED and, 153
insight impairment, 181
judgment, impaired, 182
language impairment, 137,
168
memory loss, 200
motor abnormalities, 168
mutism and, 168
personality changes, 165
speech abnormalities, 34, 46,
213
TIAs as harbinger of, 209
unilateral neglect syndrome,
50
Subcortical dementia, 59, 137
Subdural hematomas, 187
Substance abuse. *See also*
Alcohol abuse
agitation caused by, 169
blackouts, 200–201, 203
brain pathology, 133
camouflaged, 29
delirium, 147, 169, 173
dementia, 133
emotional disturbances,
154–155
hallucinations and, 173, 176,
177
hypersomnia, 187
nutritional concerns, 236
patient history of, 100, 132,
233
psychosis with, 49
sexual dysfunction, 127
side effects, 54–57
signs of, 108
sleep problems, 121, 187, 236
slurred speech, 46, 213
unappealing traits of, 38
weight loss and, 125
Sundowning, defined, 147
Supplements. *See* Dietary
supplements
Symptoms and signs:
analyzing, 11–20
atypical, 57–58
camouflaged, 27–40
eliciting, 86–92, 97–102
emotional precipitants, 35–36
evolution of, 68–70, 97–102
gradual onset of, 22–27
inability to convey, 40–50
intermittent, 34–35
lack of physical, 50–57, 59–60
masking physical disorders,
1–10
mental status signs and
symptoms
affect-related, 150–153
agnosia, 218–220

altered sense of reality,
178–179
apathy, 166–167
apraxia, 217–218
attention-related, 189–190
automatic behaviors,
215–217
concentration-related,
189–190
confusion, 193–195
consciousness, impaired,
182–188
delirium, 143, 147
delusions, 179–181
in diagnostic process,
12–14
disorientation, 190–193
dissociation, 178–179
emotion-related, 150–163
executive functions decline,
221–222
hallucinations, 171–178
as harbingers of organic
illness, 51–53
illusions, 171–178
insight, impaired, 181
judgment, impaired,
181–182
language-related, 205–214
memory, impaired, 195–204
mind-body connection,
14–16, 78
misreading, 36–38
mood-related, 150–163
mutism, 167–168
overview, 149–151
perseveration, 214–215
personality changes,
163–166
reading/writing decline,
220–221
significance of, 11–14
vigilance-related,
189–190
physical signs and symptoms
assessing, 128, 223–240
asymmetry, 111–114
caveats, 105–110
energy-related, 121–123
eye-related, 114–115
versus mental, 14–16
motor abnormalities,
168–171
motor activity, 115–116
neurological, 110–111
sexuality-related, 125–127
signs versus symptoms,
103–105
sleep-related, 119–121
vegetative, 118–128
weight-related, 123–125
Synesthesia, 173
Synkinesia, defined, 110
Syphilis:
late-appearing, 60, 235
mania in, 162
personality changes, 165
psychosis with, 49
Wasserman test, 16

Tactile hallucinations, 177
Tandem walking, defined, 115
Tardive dyskinesia, 115,
170–171
Teamwork. *See* Consultations,
professional
Temporal lobe epilepsy. *See also*
Seizure disorders
camouflaged, 1
case studies, 79–81, 131,
158–159
déjà vu with, 131
hallucinations with, 3, 177
personality changes, 165
religious experiences and,
101, 227
Terminology:
patient's versus clinician's,
92–95
physical versus
psychological, 14–16
used in this book, 14–16
Thallium poisoning, 114
Therapists. *See* Clinicians
Thiamine deficiency, 108, 114,
204, 235–236
Thought disorders, 213–214
Thyroid disorders:
anxiety and, 160
camouflaged, 1, 25–26
case studies, 25–26, 32–33,
122–123
depression and, 12, 13
gradual onset of, 25–26
Graves' disease, 25, 107, 109,
268
hypersomnia and, 187
motor abnormalities, 168
myxedema madness, 49
postpartum, 12, 32–33
psychosis with, 49
signs and symptoms, 25, 101,
107, 110, 112, 114, 129,
268
speech quality and, 213
symptoms of, 25, 268
tremors with, 116
weight problems, 25, 125
TIAs. *See* Transient ischemic
attacks (TIAs)
Tics:
Tourette's, 36, 39, 116, 170,
212, 248
verbal, 212
Timeline, narrative. *See* History,
patient
Tinnitus, 175
Topiramate, 197–198
Tourette's syndrome:
case study, 248–249
clues to diagnosis, 115, 116,
170
motor behavior, 115, 170
sensory experience and, 36,
170
stress and, 36
tics, 36, 39, 116, 170, 212
unappealing traits of, 39
verbalizations, 212